# OPEN MANAGEMENT

## QUALITY CONTROL         VALUE ENGINEERING

### \\THE FEDS //

## STANDARD OPERATION PROCEDURE (SOP)
## FOR
## FUNCTIONAL EDUCATION DEPARTMENT SYSTEM

## QUALITY PLAN
## TO
## ENPOWER
## THE WORKFORCE

### TEACHING FUNDAMENTALS

### BY

John E. Soller
&
Harold G. Davies

Soller, John E. (John Edward), 1947-
    Functional education department system /
John E. Soller, Harold G. Davies.
ISBN 1-55369-289-6
    1. Research, Industrial--Employees--Training of.
I. Davies, Harold G II. Title.
HF5549.5.T7S64 2002 658.5'7'0715      C2002-901093-4

Order this book online at www.trafford.com
or email orders@trafford.com

Most Trafford titles are also available at major online book retailers.

Printed in the United States of America.

ISBN: 978-1-5536-9289-8 (sc)
ISBN: 978-1-4122-4635-4 (e)

Trafford rev. 01/10/2014

 www.trafford.com

North America & international
toll-free: 1 888 232 4444 (USA & Canada)
fax: 812 355 4082

# INNOVATIVE APPROACH TO MANAGEMENT: OVERVIEW

Functional Education Department System (FEDS) 22 6pp. @ $16,76 Retail
By John E. Soller and Harold G. Davies ISBN 1-553-69-289-6. To order:
Trafford Publishing @ 1-888-232-4444, Website: www.trafford.com
(Keyword: Education) or www.trafford.com/robots/02-102.html

### FORWORD:  TABLE OF CONTENTS: SUBJECT MATTER

Book excerpt articles and website information provides the reader with a baseline of subject matter (Table of Contents: pp. iii-Xiv) of ideas, principles, and functional concepts pertaining to quality control standards, value system engineering, teaching fundamental, and auxiliary material example. The subject matter material is basic information and advice the reader needs to establish (on-the-job) training program.

### FORWORD: BIG PICTURE  TABLE OF CONTENTS: REFERENCE GUIDE

FEDS functions as a training aid for business, manufacturing, and educational professionals. Every business should train their people with this management material to keep its competitive edge in the marketplace.

Using this book will put managers and employees, designer and engineers, teachers and students, on the same page within the organization or company. This will improve dialogue, which in turn will improve the skill of the work force. (pp.1)

### FEDS Brief  OPEN MANAGEMENT

The FEDS has the unique ability to be modified, when information either internal or external becomes available. The work force getting this information in a timely manner will improve their knowledge and skills, which will enable them to make a more intelligent decision about things that could affect their work and lives. In some circles this is called open management. For example: Directive A3 inst 29, Revision A3  pp. 27
COLLEGE APPLICATION / AID: The Complete Scholarship Book by Fastweb.com
Sourcebooks. 2000. ISBN 1570715300. www.FinancialAidSuperSite.com
www.FAFSA.ed.gov  www.fastweb.com

### FEDS REALITY CHECK  SYSTEM APPROACH TO TEACHING
### AUXILIARY MATERIAL

FEDS shows how a system approach to teaching, which is foreign to most readers, can help individuals improve their skills and performance in the workplace, if management uses FEDS subject matter as a training aid. (pp.38-42)

1. Time management-Define goals for improvement in academic standards.
2. Self-improvement- Library reference material. (pp. 20-27)
3. Increase parent involvement- Teaching fundamentals (pp. 44-51) (pp.61-69)
4. Cost benefit – Text can be used by teachers, parents and students.
5. Business practices –Quality Control standards (pp.52-60), and Value System Engineering. (pp. 70-96)
6. 3'R's basic information- Interface Auxiliary material. (pp. 97-165)

# FOREWORD

The information in this book tells how open-management (pp. 3), good reporting (pp. 20-27), training as a plan maintenance tool (pp. 28-96), and not re-inventing information (firstgov.gov) will help schools, businesses, and industries bottom line. "The bottom line is, improve performance, cut waste, and spend money wisely". (Synopsis)

The purpose of this book is to present a system designed to provide the reader with necessary fundamentals in area of quality control, value system engineering, and teaching fundamentals to understand, correctly analyze, and remedy work performance deficiency found at the workplace. (pp. 81-92)

## FUNCTIONAL EDUCATION DEPARTMENT SYSTEM (FEDS) DESIGN
## TABLE OF CONTENTS REFERENCE GUIDE

www.trafford.com/robots/02.102.html  or www.trafford.com (Keyword: Education)

FEDS text is arranged in a logical system sequence.
Part 1: A1 (pp. 1-14) furnish the hierarch charts and other information, etc. necessary to understand FED system parameters. Part 2 thru 4 Research & Development A2 thru A9 (pp. 15-96) table of content subject matter is also divided into logical divisional section that deal with quality control, value system engineering, teaching fundamentals, etc......
Part 5: Interface Auxiliary Material A10 (pp. 97-165) table of content subject matter, gives the reader example material necessary to develop plans (pp. 115-119) and instruction guidelines to follow, for teaching subject matter objectives. (pp. 120)

The goal of FEDS is to establish a training program, as plan maintenance tool for (on-the-job) training for company employees. The training is necessary at the workplace, because of the following reason:

1. Education community sometimes disregard Business community concerns and needs, which is, "Business need employees who are trainable and educated , not those who are uneducated and have not been trained to learn". (pp. 15-19)
2. Make workers conscious of management goals that can influence their life, work skills and performance with-in the system by keeping an up-to-date reference library and good reporting. (pp. 20-27)
3. Training as Plan Maintenance Tool-- Attention to detail and completing job assignment task correctly, depends to a great extent on a carefully planned and properly designed training program. (pp. 33-51)
4. Greater amount of knowledge and critical thinking skills are required of workers to properly and efficiently perform work assignments that deal with operation, service and repair of equipment, machinery, and software programs. (pp. 70-87)

Finally, taking a system approach to training puts everyone with-in the company or organization on the same page; also, lets everyone see the BIG PICTURE.

| Distribution List: | President-CEO | Quality Control / Mgr. |
| --- | --- | --- |
| | School Superintendent | Training Coordinator |
| | Human Resources Mgr. | Teachers / Students / Employees |
| | Curriculum Officer | Library |
| | Plant Supervisor / Mgr. | School Board |

# '' FEDS Brief ''

FUNCTIONAL EDUCATION DEPARTMENT SYSTEM ( FEDS ) is a new self management activity guide book providing creative approaches to open-management. FEDS function as a training aid for business, industry, and educational professionals.

FEDS system configuration has three departments: Research and Development ( R & D ), Quality Control ( QC ), and Value System Engineering ( VSE ) (pp. 13). Each department identify and compile a baseline function list of subject matter of interest pertaining to ideas, principles, and teaching fundamentals for On-The-Job training.

FEDS subject matter with FEDS # assigned (iii –Xiv) table of contents is your Cross-Functional Management List. (pp. 13). Having this management list of subject matter provides R & D Department the uniform plan to develop lesson plans (pp. 115-119), and instruction guide (pp. 120) for teaching subject matter objectives.

FEDS, R & D department communication center Interface Documentation (I&D) division, assign a control subject number, and issues directive for design changes or modification to this Management List and Table of Contents. (pp.20-21). In addition, all FEDS personnel have the ability to communicate with others by directives (pp. 14).

Each directive has established procedures to govern and guide its design, development, and execution. When I&D division issues a directive, the subject matter with assigned FEDS control subject number is placed at the top right corner of each page pertaining to that subject matter.

Another task, I&D division does is develop auxiliary material (Revision A10) Self Study & Home Schooling as input specific information used to support FEDS function number already assigned (pp.97-165). For example, if material or information needs to be added to a subject function number just place a decimal point and the number 1,2,3...etc. Ex:10-27.2 Radical, Exponents, and Logarithms (pp.160-162).

Beside conveying information, I&D division also establishes and maintains FEDS reference library. This library is necessary because in a lot of situation at work, people usually overlook how outside factors influence their life, work skills, and performance at the workplace. Ex: Directive: A3 inst 29    College Application / Aid   A3 (pp. -27)

In short, I&D division is FEDS command & control education center, that anticipates educational needs of the workforce; besides keeping everyone abreast about future direction of the organization (Dependability-Degree of Confidence).

In summary, open management and good reporting empowers the workforce, which translate into an enlighten workforce, that is educated and trainable to perform assign tasks significantly better. In turn, management will see less personnel turnover, and retain a skill workforce, this helps managers and supervisors bottom line...........

---------------------------------------------------------------------

IMPROVE PERFORMANCE, CUT WASTE, AND SPEND MONEY WISELY

---------------------------------------------------------------------

www.trafford.com/robots/02.102.html or www.trafford.com (Keyword: Education)

# "FEDS REALITY CHECK"

The "FEDS" aim is to have all business, manufacturing, and educational professionals re-focus their attention on society needs. Since having a knowledge base society requires that human capital be educated in today's workforce with skills needed to survive in a global economy. (pp. 3)

First, I purpose it's time to start running our schools like a business, since the fundamental problem of the current education system is the lack of understanding and emphasis on what the public schools curriculum objectives are and why teaching curriculum subject material is so important to students future. (pp.33-42)

Second, let's start with a system that everyone can comprehend, that is not complicated, that is politically correct with the goals of school districts. ( FEDS Brief)

Third, since consolidation at this time is politically incorrect, and quality of teachers usually reflex school districts tax base; politician are reluctant to increase taxes to shore up the education system. (pp. 99C )

Fourth, the most cost efficient way to improve the education is to have a system in place to address the goals and objectives of the "VISIBLE CURRICULUM". (pp 15-19). In addition, to putting in place a quality control process that reward teachers on how students meet "INVISIBLE CURRICULUM" standard objectives. (pp. 32)

Finally, the most important point is to reward teachers on how subject material objective are presented, along with standardized testing (pp. 28-31), grading of students knowledge, skills and attitudes in meeting subject material objectives goals. (pp.103-104) and (pp.109-112).

In short, there can be no improvement in academic standards, and accountability for these standards unless everyone knows the "BIG PICTURE".

( See: THE FEDS—Foreword: Author View)

( DISTRIBUTION OF "FEDS" DOES THIS )

www.trafford.com/robots/02-102.html or www.trafford.com (Keyword: Education).

Interface auxiliary material allows the user (parents, students and teachers) away to input specific information necessary for transferring subject matter (curriculum) in an orderly fashion into "FEDS".

Auxiliary material input data allows everyone to comprehend the basic concepts necessary to develop, and understand how to deliver the information needed for teaching subject matter objectives: using this "how-to" information will also take a lot of hassle and stress out of teaching.

For example: Design Parameters (D&P) curriculum training aid (A2-8F) "Instruction Sheets"- used to convey to students detailed information needed to understand the learning activity they must undertake. The six types are as follow:

1. Diagram Sheets (A10-10)        2. Information Sheets (A10-11)
3. Job Sheets (A10-12)            4. Problem Sheets (A10-13)
5. Assignment Sheets (A10-14)     6. Outline Sheets (A10-15)

## INTERFACE AUXILIARY MATERIAL PARAMETERS

1. Refresh parents, students, and teachers memory of subject matter and allow away to incorporate what they have learn into their daily routine: beside helping them reach the next level of learning. Ex: D&P; pp. 15-19.
2. Organize subject matter in such form that features clear instruction, and provide worked out examples to reinforce learning objectives. (pp. 97-165)
3. Explain useful methods of solving problems from the point of view that it is the individual best interest to learn, and remember the basics. Ex: A10-4; pp. 99-99C.
4. Provide supporting material that correspond, and aids "FEDS subject material in the area of fundamental of teaching, and home schooling. Ex: Standardized Testing & Reporting (T&R-A4) National Assessment of Educational Progress (NAEP). pp. 30.
5. List supporting material that correspond, and aids "FEDS" subject material in the area of quality control, and value engineering in sustainable development that relates to the understanding the full live cycle of products and services in the present and future. Ex: Life Cycle Concept Studies. (VSE-A9-15) pp. 85.
6. Make available material pertaining to math, and chemistry fundamentals because an individual who is going to furthering their education should know this material. Ex: Conversion problems A10-27; pp.132-165.

In addition, everyone should be familiar with "FEDS" material at the workplace. On the other hand, if the worker or student at this....time....doesn't understand 3R's basic, and llack a general understanding of science, math, and chemistry as it relates to the workplace, will find this information beneficial.

In summary, there are many books available as supplement to textbooks; however, these books usually are inadequate as a means of allowing parents, and students to "brush up" on what they forgot or would like to know. Besides, statistically it has been found that one of the indicators of a persons leadership potential is his or hers understanding of mathematics, and how to analyze a problem.

# TABLE OF CONTENTS REFERENCE GUIDE

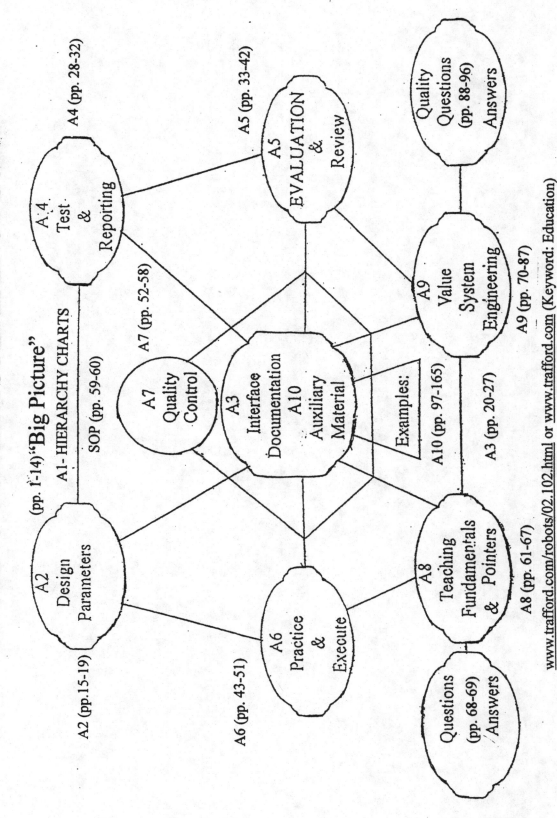

A1- HIERARCHY CHARTS (pp. 1-14) "Big Picture"

A.4 Test & Reporting — A4 (pp. 28-32)

A5 EVALUATION & Review — A5 (pp. 33-42)

Quality Questions (pp. 88-96) Answers

A7 Quality Control — A7 (pp. 52-58)

SOP (pp. 59-60)

A3 Interface Documentation

A10 Auxiliary Material

Examples: — A10 (pp. 97-165)

A9 Value System Engineering — A9 (pp. 70-87)

A3 (pp. 20-27)

A2 Design Parameters — A2 (pp. 15-19)

A6 Practice & Execute — A6 (pp. 43-51)

A8 Teaching Fundamentals & Pointers — A8 (pp. 61-67)

Questions (pp. 68-69) Answers

www.trafford.com/robots/02.102.html or www.trafford.com (Keyword: Education)

TABLE OF CONTENTS: THE REFERENCE GUIDE

PART 1                FEDS PARAMETERS

PART 5          FEDS SAMPLES

## FEDS TABLE NOTES

1. Trigonometric Equations & Identities
2. Trigonometric Functions & Signs of Function
3. Coordinate Systems : Polar & Rectangular
    Coordinate System Transformation
4. Trigonometric (Circular) Functions
5. Logarithms (Characteristic & Mantissa)

# TABLE OF CONTENTS

## APPENDIX & TABLES

## Table of Contents

Research and Development
Revision A2
Design Parameters (D&P) Description

Table of Contents

Research and Development
Revision A3
Interface Documentation (I&D) Description

Table of Contents

Research and Development
Revision A3 cont'd

Interface Documentation (I & D)     Description

## Table of Contents
### Research and Development
### Standardized Testing & Reporting (T&R) Description
### Revision A4

## Viii    Function Education Department System

Table of Contents
> Research and Development
> Evaluation And Review (E&R) Description
> Revision A5

<u>Subject Matter</u>        FEDS #

Table of Contents

### Research And Development
### Practice And Execute (P&E) Description
### Revision A6

## X      Function Education Department System

Table of Contents

### Research And Development
### Quality Control (QC) Description
### Revision A7

Table of Contents
Revision A7 Cont'd
Quality Control

## Xii    Function Education Department System

Table of Contents
### Research And Development
### Revision  A8
### Teaching Fundamentals And Techniques

Table of Contents
## Research And Development
## Revision A9
## Value System Engineering (VSE) Description

Table of Contents
## Auxiliary Subject Material
### Revision A10

# PREFACE

Functional Education Department System (FEDS) is a multiplex data network of functions to enlighten the workforce in Quality Control, Value Engineering and Teaching Fundamentals.

The Goal of FEDS are to secure for the workforce the following:

1. Workforce Empowerment... allow employees the means to use their knowledge of quality control standards and the manufacturing process to improve in- process control of a product.

2. Give the workforce a basic understanding of Quality Control, Value Engineering, and Teaching Fundamentals.

3. Allow the workforce the means to improve their own education with home-study.

4. Establishes a communication interface so information can be shared by all in the Workforce.

5. Give the workforce the flexibility to add to the baseline function list for their Special needs. For example:

    1. Metrology... : Revision A3 Hardware : <u>Pictorial Handbook of Technical Devices</u>.

    2. The Medicine Program: Revision A3: Quality of Life.

# FUNCTIONAL EDUCATION
## DEPARTMENT SYSTEM (FEDS)

## Introduction:

The purpose of any system approach is to provide a method by which an organization can analyze and apply all the elements that make up the system. "FEDS" is to ensure a systematic research and development (R&D) structure revision A1-A10 to follow as a way to improve the skills of the work force. To understand the "FEDS" revision A1-A10 research and development structure, visualize a system with three distinct but interrelated elements: principles of value system engineering, IS0 9000 quality control requirements, and teaching fundamentals and technique pointers.

The success of the "FEDS" depends upon the effectiveness of the individual elements. The user of this book must give equal attention and emphasis to each element of the system and to how each element relates to the others. Therefore, to be used as a training aid for business, manufacturing, and educational professionals you must address the importance of all three elements of the system.

## Value System Engineering (VSE).

Value system engineering as a function-oriented discipline will help to lower the cost by eliminating that which is unnecessary, and seek the most economical way to do that which is necessary.

## IS0 9000 Quality Control System.

IS0 9000 Quality Control System has 20 elements with emphasis on integration complementary capabilities of each element to meet specific situation through result oriented problem solving techniques by following Standard Operation Procedures (SOP).

FEDS (SOP) for a quality revolution "everyone plays", is the reason that VSE needs to be part of this quality plan to improve the skills of the workforce.

Function Education Department System (FEDS).cont'd.

Teaching Fundamentals and Technique Pointers.

Research and Development (R&D) structure of five divisional departments, has to follow the Installation Guidance Specifications (IGS) for quality training for this system to accomplish its goal. This guidance plan should make our schools improve by making educators re-focus their effort to better identify and meet the needs of students. In addition, this IGS for training provides the means to do the job right the first time. A quality control battle cry for "improvement".

Environmental Factors

In addition to these three integrating parts are the environmental factors seen in the business community although not part of FEDS, These factors increase cost and put competitive pressure on school resources, and need to be looked at also.

Summary

The subject matter in FEDS is general in nature and not therefore directed toward wordiness. The intent of FEDS is to improve the skills of the Workforce by making available idea, principles, and functional concepts pertaining to quality control, value engineering and teaching fundamentals thru open-management. Having a knowledge based society requires workers to know this management material in order to survive in today's economy.

FED System Parts

Functional Education Department System is made up of five parts they are as follow:

|  |  | Page |
|---|---|---|
| 1. Introduction...................Revision A1 | | 14 |
| 2. Research and Development..........Revision A2---A6 | | 37 |
| 3. Quality Control.....................Revision A7 | | 9 |
|    Teaching Fundamentals..............Revision A8 | | 9 |
| 4. Value System Engineering............Revision A9 | | 27 |
| 5. Interface Auxiliary Material..........Revision A10 | | 52 |
|    Home Schooling & Self Study | | 28 |

-------------------------------------------------------------------------------

Total = 17.6

## Functional Education
## Department System (FEDS)

Description:

The "FEDS" is a self-help book that can be used as a supplement text for training. The "Feds" aim is to have business, manufacturing, and educational professionals re-focus their attention on society needs. Since having a knowledge based society requires that human capital be educated in today's workforce with the skills needed to surive in a global economy.

The "FEDS" has the unique ability to be modified when information either internal or external becomes available. The workforce getting this information in a timely manner will improve their knowledge and skills, which will enable them to make a more intelligent decision about things that could effect their work and lives. In some circles this is called open management.

This book uses a system approach that establishes Revision A (first ) as the information guideline for a research and development team to follow. This is called Standard Operation Procedures (SOP) in most systems. Having an installation guideline of ideas, principles,and functional concepts in quality control and value engineering for sustainable development, and teaching fundamentals for home schooling will give the reader information not likely to find in one book anywhere else.

Using this book will put managers and employees, designers and engineers, teacher and students, on the same page with-in the organization or company. This will improve dialogue, which in turn will improve the skills of the workforce.

This book is recommended for anyone who would like to start a quality control program to improve our education system,  increase performance or efficiency, design a system, and develop or start a R & D team.

3

FEDS "Food for Thought"

The life blood of a knowledge base society are workers who have been taught to learn.

The heart and soul of a knowledge base is creativity and innovation.

To know your options requires a fundamental understanding of the problem.

*No student knows his subject: the most he knows is where and how to find Out the things he does not know. ~Woodrow Wilson

The man who can make hard things easy is the educator.
     ~Ralph Wallo Emerson

Learning without thought is labor lost. ~Confucious

## ABOUT THE AUTHOR

John Soller joined the Navy in Columbus, OH. In 1965. He went to Navy schools in Mare Island, CA. and Dam Neck, VA. for missile radar fire controlman.

Honorable discharge with rank of E-5 after making five West-Pac cruises on the guided missile destroyer USS. Robinson DDG-12 and one North Atlantic cruise on the guided missile cruiser USS. Albany CG-10.

Join the Navy Reserve in 1987, became "USNR-Retired" Sept. 1, 2002. Completed 24 years total service with 8 years active and 16 years reserves.

Spent nine years 1977-1985 at a research and development facility at Vitro Corp. Silver Spring, MD. Particular area of expertise was system hardware Integration. Developed system function diagrams on the Tartar Missile System. for display console, switchboard, power distribution, radar, director, and launcher.

Received 1 year certificate in Food Lab Technology @ Arkansas Vocational School, Ozark, Ar. Dec. 1989.

Received Associate in Quality Control @ WestArk. Community College, Fort Smith, AR. May 1992.

# QUALITY CONTROL HIERARCHY CHART

## STANDARD OPERATION PROCEDURE (SOP) FOR A QUALITY TRAINING PROGRAM

EDUCATION

SOCIETY NEED'S

SERVICE ECONOMY — INDUSTRY — INFORMED CONSUMER

KNOWLEDGE--BASED--SOCITY

PRIMARY AND SECONDARY EDUCATIONAL SCHOOLS

COMPANY

ELEMENTRY-- MIDDLE--HIGH SCHOOLS

STATE AND LOCAL SCHOOL BOARD

DIVISION

ENVIRONMENTAL FACTORS

BUSINESS / COMMUNITY / FINANCIAL RESOURCES

WORKFORCE

COLLABORATIVE LEARNING

SCHOOL FACULTY / ADMINSTORS

SERVICE

TEACHING STUDENTS

KNOWLEDGE

FUNCTION

TO LEARN

TRAINABLE EMPLOYEE

PRODUCT

DESIGN

CUSTOMER: HUMAN CAPITAL

5

EXPANDED: VALUE SYSTEM ENGINEERING APPROACH TO PRODUCT DESIGN    A1-2

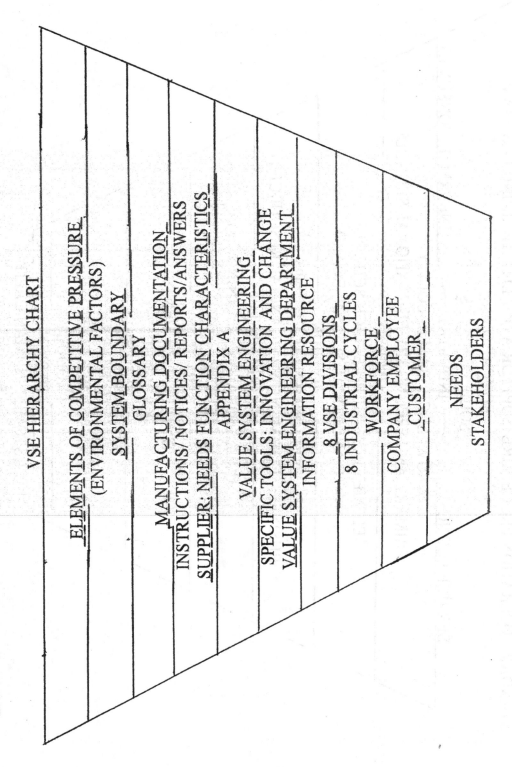

VSE HIERARCHY CHART

ELEMENTS OF COMPETITIVE PRESSURE
(ENVIRONMENTAL FACTORS)
SYSTEM BOUNDARY
GLOSSARY

MANUFACTURING DOCUMENTATION
INSTRUCTIONS / NOTICES / REPORTS / ANSWERS
SUPPLIER: NEEDS FUNCTION CHARACTERISTICS
APPENDIX A

VALUE SYSTEM ENGINEERING
SPECIFIC TOOLS: INNOVATION AND CHANGE
VALUE SYSTEM ENGINEERING DEPARTMENT
INFORMATION RESOURCE
8 VSE DIVISIONS
8 INDUSTRIAL CYCLES
WORKFORCE
COMPANY EMPLOYEE
CUSTOMER

NEEDS
STAKEHOLDERS

6

REVISION A1-A10 INSTALLATION GUIDANCE SPECIFICATION FOR QUALITY TRAINING A1-3

"VISIBLE CURRICULUM'
TESTBOOKS AND STUDY
READING MATERIAL
TRAINING AIDS

"INVISIBLE CURRICULM"
ATTITUDE AND EFFORT
WORK HABITS
HUMAN CONTACT

GOALS

ACADEMIC SKILLS

SOCIAL SKILLS

DESIGN PARAMETERS
(D&P)
CORE CURRICULUM

INTERFACE DOCUMENATION A3
QUALITY CONTROL ELEMENT 1-20
STANDARDIZED TESTING & REPORTING
(T&R)

OBJECTIVES LEARNED
PERFORMANCE SHEETS
(E&R)
EVALUATION & REVIEW
QUALITY TRAINED TEACHERS
(P&E)
PRACTICE & EXECUTE

MASTER SUBJECT MATERIAL

SELF-RESPECT
SELF- DISCIPLINE

COMPLETE HOME WORK

7

## VSE IMPORTANCE TO CONTRACTORS

The following is a list of why a company self interest is served by Value System Engineering:

1. Affect future profits: Past performance of vender is considered in the market place.

2. Reliable supplier: Assure a favorable rank with contractor.

3. Provides solid documentation: Enables a company to make contract changes to fit the contractors needs with reimbursement in accordance with the term of the contract.

4. Research and Development: Improvement of reliability, and maintainability.

5. Raise cost consciousness.

6. Improve quality, reduce cost, increase productivity, and competitiveness.

7. Shorten design time.

8. Flexible system configuration.

ISO 9000 SERIES QUALLITY CONRTOL IMPORTANCE--- Person responsible to operation of business that wish to:

1. Operate in or supply business competing in the European community.

2. Supply commercial industries that require suppliers to meet ISO requirements.

3. Be competitive in the 90s and beyond by providing a quality product and service to customers.

4. Perform a Department of Defense contract or supply a Dodd contractor.

# ENVIRONMENTAL FACTORS

Some efforts seen in the market place that increase the competitive pressure on manufacturing in producing a quality product at the lowest possible cost.

See figure 5 Environmental Factors; some other factors are listed below.

1. Technological Acceleration

2. Consumer Choice

3. World Wide Competition

4. Mergers

5. Plant and Equipment Improvements

6. Antitrust Laws

7. Lower Tariff Barriers

8. Less Patent Protection

9. Prefer Trade Status

10. Government Subsidies and Regulation

11. Federal Environmental Statutes (10-890)

# ENVIRONMENTAL FACTORS

This chart seeks to show only the more important agencies of the Government.

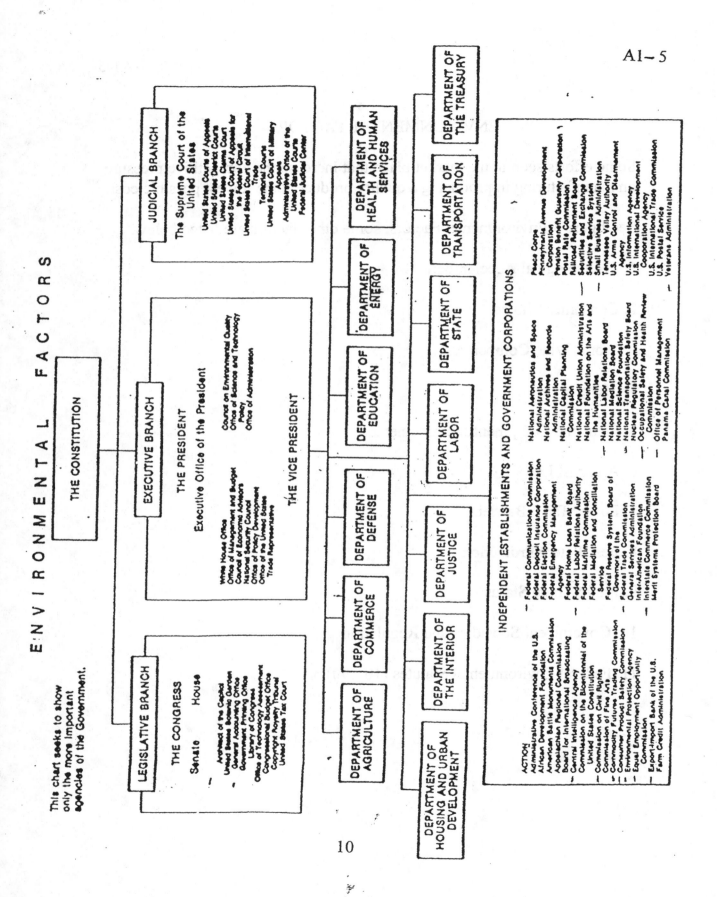

**THE CONSTITUTION**

**LEGISLATIVE BRANCH**

THE CONGRESS

Senate          House

Architect of the Capitol
United States Botanic Garden
General Accounting Office
Government Printing Office
Library of Congress
Office of Technology Assessment
Congressional Budget Office
Copyright Royalty Tribunal
United States Tax Court

**EXECUTIVE BRANCH**

THE PRESIDENT

Executive Office of the President

White House Office
Office of Management and Budget
Council of Economic Advisors
National Security Council
Office of Policy Development
Office of the United States Trade Representative

Council on Environmental Quality
Office of Science and Technology Policy
Office of Administration

THE VICE PRESIDENT

**JUDICIAL BRANCH**

The Supreme Court of the United States

United States Courts of Appeals
United States District Courts
United States Claims Court
United States Court of Appeals for the Federal Circuit
United States Court of International Trade
Territorial Courts
United States Court of Military Appeals
Administrative Office of the United States Courts
Federal Judicial Center

DEPARTMENT OF AGRICULTURE

DEPARTMENT OF COMMERCE

DEPARTMENT OF DEFENSE

DEPARTMENT OF EDUCATION

DEPARTMENT OF ENERGY

DEPARTMENT OF HEALTH AND HUMAN SERVICES

DEPARTMENT OF HOUSING AND URBAN DEVELOPMENT

DEPARTMENT OF THE INTERIOR

DEPARTMENT OF JUSTICE

DEPARTMENT OF LABOR

DEPARTMENT OF STATE

DEPARTMENT OF TRANSPORTATION

DEPARTMENT OF THE TREASURY

## INDEPENDENT ESTABLISHMENTS AND GOVERNMENT CORPORATIONS

ACTION
Administrative Conference of the U.S.
African Development Foundation
American Battle Monuments Commission
Appalachian Regional Commission
Board for International Broadcasting
Central Intelligence Agency
Commission on the Bicentennial of the United States Constitution
Commission on Civil Rights
Commission of Fine Arts
Commodity Futures Trading Commission
Consumer Product Safety Commission
Environmental Protection Agency
Equal Employment Opportunity Commission
Export-Import Bank of the U.S.
Farm Credit Administration

Federal Communications Commission
Federal Deposit Insurance Corporation
Federal Election Commission
Federal Emergency Management Agency
Federal Home Loan Bank Board
Federal Labor Relations Authority
Federal Maritime Commission
Federal Mediation and Conciliation Service
Federal Reserve System, Board of Governors of the
Federal Trade Commission
General Services Administration
Inter-American Foundation
Interstate Commerce Commission
Merit Systems Protection Board

National Aeronautics and Space Administration
National Archives and Records Administration
National Capital Planning Commission
National Credit Union Administration
National Foundation on the Arts and the Humanities
National Labor Relations Board
National Mediation Board
National Science Foundation
Nuclear Regulatory Commission
Occupational Safety and Health Review Commission
Office of Personnel Management
Panama Canal Commission

Peace Corps
Pennsylvania Avenue Development Corporation
Pension Benefit Guaranty Corporation
Postal Rate Commission
Railroad Retirement Board
Securities and Exchange Commission
Selective Service System
Small Business Administration
Tennessee Valley Authority
U.S. Arms Control and Disarmament Agency
U.S. Information Agency
U.S. International Development Cooperation Agency
U.S. International Trade Commission
U.S. Postal Service
Veterans Administration

In process control is a preventive technique used by quality control specialist that involve responding to problems when they first materialize, And establishing control charts to prevent problems from arising in the first Place.

(A)  Action is taken based on the signals from the control chart. If the Chart indicates that the process is in "in control" the process is left alone

(B)  If the process is "out of control" (changed), action is taken to get the Process back in control.

## STATISTICAL QUALITY CONTROL

SQC is the process of monitoring a process quantitatively and using statistical signals to determine whether to leave the process along or change it.

1.  SQC quickly identifies the impact of any change on the performance Of the entire process.

2.  SQC uses either variables or attributes data as a way to measure the Process, product or service.

(A)  Variables: characteristics which affect a product's performance.

(B)  Attribute: characteristics judge as either acceptable or

Unacceptable (go-no go).

11

# IN-PROCESS CONTROL (PREVENTIVE)
## MONITOR and ADJUST                A1-6

1. Feedback loop that envolves a sequence of step applying to the Control :

   (A) Inventory
   (B) Quality
   (C  Cost
   (D) Serviceability

## Process  SPC

1. Control Station or Sensing Points :  Variations  Inputs

   (A) Raw  Material- All Ingredients.
   (B)  Personal- Experience & Working Conditions
   (C   Machines- Produce the Product.

2.  Process:  Control Charts & Control Charting

   (A) Control Charts is the basic tool used to control the quality of a
       Manufacturing Process.
   (B) Control Charting determines how much the process can be expected,
       to  vary and if it is operating consistently.

## SERVICE Or PRODUCT

1.  Potential reduction or elimination by inspection.

2.  Customer needs or use- The finished product.

## 11A

PROBLEM SOLVING: The first step of problem solving is called <u>Problem Analysis</u>.

1. Problem solving begins with a cause and effect diagram as a means to identify the possible causes of a problem.

2. Cause and effect diagram shows a problem's possible causes, it allows you to trace a problem to its source.

CONTROL CHARTS: Before manufacturing can produce useable charts, the process must be capable of holding the tolerance.
    ( a ) The part of the chart which tells you the expected average value for the population is called the <u>central line</u>. This line is usually represented by a solid line.

    ( b ) The dashed lines above and below the solid lines on each chart represent the maximum allowable variation that product subgroups may have and still be acceptable. These lines are called the <u>upper and lower control limits</u>.

    ( c ) Control Limits are acceptable variations among groups of products which are determined by previous manufacturing data.

CONTROL: Measures current performance and guides the process towards some predetermined goal.

PROCESS CONTROL DOES THE FOLLOWING THINGS:
    ( a ) Documents work instructions.
    ( b ) Uses suitable production and installation equipment.
    ( c ) Establish criteria for workmanship.
    ( d ) Monitors product characteristic during production.
    ( e ) Maintain records of process, equipment, and personnel.
    ( f ) Abolition of full-time inspectors, with the work of inspection being taken up by production operators.
    ( g ) Quality staff specialist work on unsolved problems while delegating solved problems to the line organizations.
    ( h ) Looks for new ways of organizing the broad quality function to be responsive to modern needs.

In-Process Control (preventive measures) is compromised of the following basic elements:
    1. Customer (Finished Product)
    2. Product or Service
    3. Process (Statistical Quality Control)
    4. Input Variations (Machines, Materials, Workforce, Methods & Environment).

## FUNCTIONAL EDUCATION DEPARTMENT SYSTEM (FEDS)
### "CROSS -FUNCTIONAL MANAGEMENT LIST"          A1-7

| R&D DEPARMENT | QC 1-20 | QC DEPARMENT |
|---|---|---|
| 1. Design Parameters | RD-1 | 1. Management Responsibility |
| 2. Interface | RD-2 | 2. Quality System |
| 3. Test/Reporting | RD-3 | 3. Contract Review |
| 4. Evaluation& Review | RD-4 | 4. Design Control |
| 5. Practice&Execute | RD-5 | 5. Document Control |

**QC DEPARMENT**

1. Management Responsibility
2. Quality System
3. Contract Review
4. Design Control
5. Document Control
6. Purchasing
7. Purchaser Supplied Product for Customer
8. Product Identification & Traceability
9. Process Control
10. Inspection & Test Control 1
11. Inspection & Test Control 2
12. Inspection. Measuring&Test Equipment.
13. Control of Non-Conforming
14. Corrective Action
15. Handling. Cleaning, Storage, Packaging, & Delivery.
16. Quality Records
17. Quality Audits
18. Training
19. Service
20. Statistical Techniques

**Value System (VSE) Engineering Dept.**            QC 1-20

1. Marketing            VSE-1
2. Engineering            VSE-2
3. Purchasing            VSE-3
4. Manufacturing ENG            VSE-4
5. Manufacturing S & S            VSE-5

6. Mechanical I & T            VSE-6
7. Shipping            VSE-7
8. Installation            VSE-8

13

Function Education Department System
Research and Development

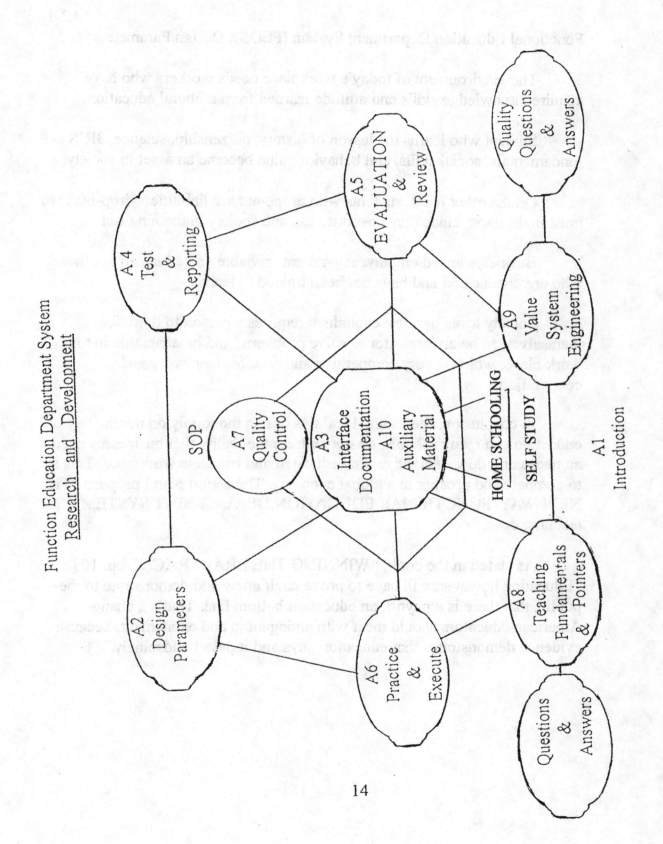

A5
EVALUATION
&
Review

Quality
Questions
&
Answers

A4
Test
&
Reporting

A9
Value
System
Engineering

SOP

A7
Quality
Control

A3
Interface
Documentation
A10
Auxiliary
Material

HOME SCHOOLING

SELF STUDY

A1
Introduction

A2
Design
Parameters

A6
Practice
&
Execute

A8
Teaching
Fundamentals
& Pointers

Questions
&
Answers

Functional Education Department System (FEDS): Design Parameters

The environment of today's workplace needs workers who have acquired knowledge skills and attitude learned from a liberal education.

Student who learns the lesson of history, citizenship, science, 3R'S fundamentals, social skills, and behavior value become an asset to society.

On the other hand, students who drops-out are liabilities- drop-outs we must understand, since they cost business and society in the long run.

Businesses need employees who are trainable and educated not those who are uneducated and have not been trained to learn.

Society loses because capitalism requires a person to think for themselves, to be an innovator to solve problems, and be adaptable in today's work place, which is very competitive and requires teamwork and cooperation.

In conclusion, States and localities has an monopoly on public education and many schools, do not address the reality that businesses need an unceasing flow of creative well educated and trainable workforce. This is to compete and prosper in a global economy. The action plan I propose "THE NEW WAY: FUNCTIONAL EDUCATION DEPARTMENT SYSTEM." To teaching does.

As stated in the book, "WINNING THE BRAIN RACE", pp. 103. "Educating however, will have to prove itself anew and demonstrate to the public, that there is a payoff, an education bottom line. That's a change American educators should meet with anticipation and excitement, because evidence demonstrates that education pays and it pays handsomely."

# FUNCTIONAL EDUCATION DEPARTMENT SYSTEM (FEDS)
## (D&P)
### D&P CURRICULM FOR: HEALTH IMPROVEMENT          A2-1

1A. HEALTH/ PHYSICAL EDUCATION
1B. SCIENCE/ TECHNOLOGY
1C. HEALTH/ FITNESS
1D. FOOD SCIENCE
1E. CHEMISTRY
1F. BIOLOGY
1G. PHYSICS

### 2. D&P CURRICULM FOR: LEADERSHIP SKILLS          A2-2

2A. ORAL COMMUNICATION
2B. COMPOSITION
2C. JOURNALISM
2D. WRITING
2E. ENGLISH
2F. BUSINESS MATH
2G. TRIGONOMETRY
2H. GEOMETRY
2I. ALGEBRA

### 3. D&P CURRICULM FOR: FAMILY LIFE ADJUSTMENT          A2-3

3A. CHILD DEVELOPMENT
3B. HOME ECONOMIC
3C. FOOD/ CLOTHING
3D. CHILD CARE
3E. PARENTING

### 4. <u>D&P CURRICULM FOR: VOCATION</u>                    A2-4
4A. GENERAL COOPERATIVE EDUCATION
4B. FOOD SERVICE MANAGEMENT
4C. AGRICULTURE SCIENCE/ TECHNOLOGY
4D. AGRICULTURE BUSINESS/ CONSERVATION
4E. SMALL ENGINES/ AUTOMOTIVE
4F. WORD PROCESSING/ COMPUTERS
4G. MULTI-MEDIA/ COMMUNICATIONS
4H. ELECTRICITY/ ELECTRONICS/ ROBOTICS
4I. MANUFACTURING PROCESS
4J. FOREST MANAGEMENT
4K. AQUATIC SCIENCE
4L. WELDING/ SHOP
4M. DRIVERS EDUCATION

### 5. <u>D&P CURRICULM FOR: CITIZENSHIP</u> <u>HISTORICAL DOCUMENT</u>    A2-5

| | |
|---|---|
| 5A. LAWS&ENFORCEMENT | 1. The Politics and Ethics of Aristotle |
| 5B. GEOGRAPHY WORLD | 2. The Republic of Plato |
| 5C. WORLD HISTORY | 3. The Declaration of Independence |
| 5D. AMERICAN HISTORY | 4. The Tenth Federalist Papers |
| 5E. AMERICAN AND STATE GOVERNMENT | 5. The United States Constitution |
| 5F. ECONOMIC AND FINANCE | 6. The Gettysburg Address |
| 5G. CIVICS | 7. Huckleberry Finn |

### 6. <u>D&P CURRICULM FOR: LEISURE TIME</u>                    A2-6
6A. SPORTS/ PEP RALLIES
6B. CLUBS/ ANNUAL STAFF
6C. STUDY HALL/ LIBRARY

### 7. D&P CURRICULM FOR: CHARACTER                                    A2-7
7A. SPANISH/ LANGUAGE
7B. STUDENT GOVERNMENT
7C. STUDENT COUNCIL
7D. SPECIAL EDUCATION
7E. COMMUNITY VOLUNTEERING
7F. TUTORING
7G. ART/ CRAFTS

### 8. D&P CURRICULM TRAINING AIDS                                     A2-8
8A. COURSE MATERIALS- Used in presenting instruction in a proper sequence, provides essential information you must understand to comply with the course developer's intent. Course materials include lesson plans, instruction sheets, and instructional media.

8B. LESSON PLAN- Use a blue print to complete the objectives. Parts of a lesson plan are: 1. Front Matter 2. Introduction 3. Presentation 4. Review and Summary 5. Application and assignment.

8C. LESSON PLAN PERSONALIZATION- Provides the information you want to add without deviating from approved course of instruction.

8D. TYPES OF PERSONALIZATION- Subject matter detail, teaching techniques, personal experiences, example and analogies.

8E. STEPS OF PERSONALIZATION:
   1. Understand what the objectives are trying to achieve.
   2. Understand the contents of a lesson plan.
   3. Research the reference materials.
   4. Understand the requirements of the objective and put into your own words.

8F. INSTRUCTION SHEETS- Use to convey to students detailed information needed to understand the learning activity they must undertake. The six types are:

FUNCTIONAL EDUCATION DEPARTMENT SYSTEM (FEDS)
D&P
DESIGN PARAMETERS CONT'D

## 8. D&P CURRICULM TRAINING AIDS (8F) CONT'D

ASSIGNMENT SHEET- Direct study of a student and contain the following:
1. Introduction  2. Topic Learning Objectives 3. Study Assignment
4. Study Question.

DIAGRAM SHEETS- Support instruction sheets. Eliminate the need for the student to
copy information during the lesson.

INFORMATION SHEET- Provide information matter required for course but not
readily available to students.

JOB SHEET  ( LABORATORY INSTRUCTION)- Direct the student in the step-by-
step performance of a practical task they will encounter in their job assignment.

Laboratory Handbook for General chemistry by Griswold, Neidig, Spencer,
Stanitski. Chemical Education Resources, INC. ISBN 0-87540-491-X.

Basic Mathematics for Beginning Chemistry by Dorothy M. Goldish, Macmillan
Publishing CO., INC. 866 Third Avenue, New York, New York 10022.
ISBN 0-02-344270-0

PROBLEM SHEETS- Effective way to help students learn to problem solve and to
help gain practice in applying what has been learned. Each sheet provides a clear
statement of the problem, the conditions and parameters affecting the problems,
and the direction and procedures for the solution to the  problems.

OUTLINE SHEETS-Provide an outline of discussion points of the topic, and allows
students to follow the progress of a topic.

EVALUATION- Use for the purpose of improving the course material provided.
Evaluators pay close attention to student safety and instructional practices in the
laboratory.

CLASSROOM TEACHER EVALUTION CHECKLIST: 1.Introduction 2.Presentation
3. Interaction 4. Summary.

LABORATORY EVALUATION CHECKLIST : 1.Teacher performance 2.Student
Performance 3. Facilities.

INSTUCTOR GUIDE: Allows FEDS the flexibility to expand the Cross- Functional
List Subject Matter.

## INTERFACE DOCUMENTATION
### (I&D)

The Revision <u>A1-A10</u> subject classification function number list is kept up-to-date by the Interface Documentation Department. Up-to-dating this is done when new information is found useful a Revision A function or by adding a new function to the list. This information either internal or external is forward to other departments by an instruction or notice.

Since most people overlook how outside factor can influence their life, work skills, and performance with-in the system. This problem is address by having a FEDS reference library of material to improve a person's knowledge, so that he may find the subject matter of interest. The information that was found during the research of this book is listed for this purpose. The FEDS ability to share information and flexibility, also will allow others to change this reference material to fit their own needs.

Auxiliary Subject Material, Revision A10 is use to support FEDS function numbers with-in the system. Usually by means of Instructor guide, are could be material be left out and needs to be added. If this is the case used the FEDS Function number followed by the decimal point and the number 1, 2, 3, ....etc.

<u>Interface documentation</u> cont'd;

Function characteristic is one of the most important concepts behind FEDS because every school core curriculum are different. The primary mission is to identify what the function characteristics of the core curriculum are and does. The list you compile of what the core curriculum does is your base line. This list is of great value when a function revision is being considered during the design stage of a curriculum.

This list or base line of the product also provides the uniform plan for assuring and maintaining directives. The three types of releases are used to provide information that is factual, on time, relevant, and easy to interpret are as follows;

instruction- directives that contain information or require action of a continuing nature. An instruction has permanent reference value and is effective until quality control department supercedes or cancels it.

notice- directives of a one-time nature and contain information or require action that can be completed immediately. A notice does not have permanent reference value and contains provisions for its own cancellation.

report- summarized instruction of information used in day-to-day regulation, factory, processes, and field performances.

You can better understand the numbering and identifying of directives by considering one following example;

|  | Revision A1--A10 | inst | FEDS# |  |
|--|------------------|------|-------|--|
|  | ( a ) | ( b ) | ( c ) | ( d ) |

a. The authorized abbreviation of the originator of the directive is placed here.
b. This part refers to the type of release in this case an instruction.
c. This is the control subject number, which is determined by the subject matter of the directive. It is obtained from the table of control subject classification numbers that should be set up by the school or organization.
d. Following the period is the consecutive number, which is found only on instructions. the originator assigns consecutive numbers to those consecutive instructions with the same classification number.

This type of information release allows each separate division a way to communicate change, which is necessary to improve education, and the work force. Once this communication base line has been established right decisions about cultural, social, economic, technological, political and legal elements can be documented.

Division (A3) is Functional Education Department System (FEDS) training program command & control education center. This center anticipate educational needs of the workforce, and communicate changes by sending- FEDS Directives. (FEDS Brief)

FEDS Directives (Note 1) allows other departments and divisions to input their ideas for solving a problem (A9-14). Each directive comes with easy to interpret instructions for quality control department to take corrective action and develop an action plan to deal with problems as they arise (A7-18).

FEDS Directive: A3 Inst. 001 change Cross Functional Management List (A1-7) subject matter functions: A2-3, A2-6, A3-26, A3-29, A5, A5-2, A7-1 to include website on line information. Note 1: Parentheses (FEDS#) denotes cross reference subject matter.

| LOCATION | SUBJECT MATTER | FEDS # |
|---|---|---|
| 3F | Home Education: On Line Resources | A2-3 |
| | Search Engines: www.google and Ask Jeeves Kids: www.ajkids.com | |
| 6D | Home Leisure Time | A2-6 |
| | Word game site: www.popo.com  Crossword puzzles: www.Puzzlemaker.com | |
| | Math site: www.aplusmath.com  Textbook Companion: www.harcourtschool.com | |

16                              Quality of Life                         A3-26
Health & Prescription Drug Information: On Line Resources
www.cdc.gov  www.hih.gov  www.ama.assn.org  www.cancer.org  www.amhrt.org
www.health.org  www.diabetes.org  www.aafa.org  www.hinem.org  www.web.com
www.advanceRx.com  www.themedicineprogram.com  www.medlineplus.com
Pain Management Service Information: On Line Resources
www.theacpa.org  www.ampainsoc.org  www.minds.nih.gov  www.assch.net
www.painfoundation.org

19                          College Application / Aid                   A3-29
www.scholarship.com  www.FinancialAidSuperSite.com  www.FAFSA.ed.gov
www.fastweb.com

Evaluation and Review                         A5
School Report Card: www.Homefair.com

Function of Guidance
4  Resource and referral persons of other agencies.                     A5-2
Softwarecashclass@aol.com  custssve@petersons.com  www.finaid.org/finaid
www.fast.web.com  www.finaid.org/finaid/vendors/software.html
www.finaid.org/finaid/documents.html.

Quality Control Department                     A7-1
www.firstgov.gov  "Laws & Reg" link "Fed Stats"

INTERFACE DOCUMENTATION
(I&D)
REVISION A3

<u>Library Reference Section</u>                    A3-1

1. <u>The Complete Guide to Public Employment</u> by Ron and Caryl Krannich, Impact
   Publications: Woodbridge, VA. ISBN 0-942710-23-1

Local Government-  1. The County Year Book              A3-2
pp.292             2. The Municipal Year Book

State Government-  1. Wants Federal-State Court Directory
pp.305             2. Directory of State Court Clerks and County Courthouse   A3-3
pp.311             3. The Book of the States             A3-4
                   4. State Elected Officials and the Legislatures

Federal Employment Information System--U.S. Office of Personnel Management
    Data Base:www.USAJOBS.OPM.gov
    Job application: OF-612

Federal Government-  1. Federal employees' Almanac
Pp.337, 338, & 343   2. Federal Personnel Guild          A3-5
                     3. The 171 Reference Book
                     4. How to be a Federal Intelligence Officer   A3-6
                     5. Writing an Effective SF-171

Non-Governmental-1. Encyclopedic of Associations         A3-7
Organization      2. The Consultants and Consulting Organization
pp.401               Directory
                  3. The Foundation Directory
                  4. Research Center Directory

Governmental- 1. Career Guide to Professional Associations    A3-8
Organization  2. Directory of National Trade and Professional
Pp. 401, 429,    Associations in the United States
   & 432      3. Directory of Professional and Trade Organization
             4. The Professional and Trade Association Job Finder
             5. Washington Representatives
             6. Washington Information Directory

22

Non-Profit      1. Terry W. McAdam's Careers in the non-profit Sector:      A3-9
Organization       Doing Well by Doing Good.

                2. IRS: Publication 72 Cumulative List of Organization
pp. 442, 446
                3. Society for Non-profit Organization The Non-profit World.

                4. Access; Networking in the Public Interest Opportunities in State
                   Government, Opportunities in Public Interest Law.

United Black Fund INC, Washington, DC. Directory of Community Service
Organizations.

Catalog On Career Resources: Impact Publications, Careers Dept. 4580 Sunshine Court
Woodbridge, VA 22192 Tel. 703/361-7300   FAX 703/335-9486.   pp. 505      A3-10

1. Winning the Brain Race by David T. Dearns and Denis P. Doyle, ICS PRESS:
   Institute of Contemporary Studies. San Francisco, California  P. 90-92.
   ISBN 1-55815-002-1

                     Historical Documents of Citizenship            A3-11
Politics and Ethics of Aristotle

The Prince

The Republic of Plato

The Essay Concerning Human Understanding

The Declaration of Independence

Tenth Federalist Paper

The United State Constitution

On Liberty

The Gettysburg Address

Letter from Birmingham Jail

23

Literature/Classic                                    A3-12

Iliad
Hamlet
Gulliver's Travels
Moby Dick
The Education of Henry Adams
The Sun also Rises
The Grapes of Wrath
Huckleberry Finn

2. <u>The Reader's Encyclopedia of American Literature</u> by Max J. Herzbert, Thomas Y.
   Crowell Company, New York, NY.

MATH                                    A3-13

3. <u>Mathematics of the Shop</u> 4<sup>th</sup> Edition by McMackin/Shaver/Weber/Smith, Delmar
   Publishers INC-Albany, New York, NY.
   <u>Computing With the Scientific Calculator</u> by Morton Rosenstein- CASIO Computer Co,
   LTD. Japan
   <u>Color Power Graphic CFX-9850 GB Plus-L</u>: CASIO Computer Co, LTD. Shibuya-Ku,
   Tokyo 151-8543, Japan

AGRICULTURE                                    A3-14

4. <u>Progressive Farmer</u> magazine, PO BOX 830069, Birmingham, AL. 35283-0069

EDUCATION AND TRAINING INFORMATION          A3-15

5. Peterson's Guides and Barron's Educational Series
   <u>The American Spelling Book</u> by Noah Webster, Applewood Books, 1999

   <u>McGuffey's First Electric Reader</u> by John Wiley & Son, 1997

   <u>World Almanac and Book of Facts</u>: World Almanac, 1999

   <u>Dr. Spock's Baby and Child Care</u> by Benjamin Spock, Steven Parker, Stephen
   Parker

   The Profession of Teaching by Harold W. Massey and Edwin E. Vineyard, 1961
   The Odyssey Press. INC. New York. pp. 89-115, 55-72

   American Guidance Service,Inc.  www.parentingeducation.com

   The Scholarship Book 2003 by Daniel J. Cansidy. Prentice Hall Press ISBN0735203679.

## DRIVERS EDUCATION                                     A3-16

6. State Farms Insurance Companies brochures:
   Designated Drivers programs complimentary kit, see your State Farm agent or write:
   Designated Driver, Agency Promotions C-1, One State Farm Plaza, Bloomington, Ill.
   61710-0001. "Final Choice....The brad Shipman Story." Video
   Application for international driving permit.
   Commercial driver license manual: see state revenue office for copy.

## VALUE ENGINEERING                                     A3-17

7. ASTM Publication Committee. Value Engineering in Manufacturing. New Jersey:
   Prentice-Hall, INC. P. 1967. 3, 40, 75-76 Library of Congress Catalog card number:
   67-12085

## QUALITY CONTROL                                       A3-18

8. The 90-Day ISO Manual by Stewart/ Mauch/ Strake. 1994. St. Lucie Press, INC.
   100 E. Linton Blvd. Suit 403B, Delray Beach, Florida 33483. Distr: CRC Press
   1-800-272-7738, ISBN: 1884015115
   Juran and Gyrna. Quality Planning and Analysis. New York: McGraw INC. 1980:
   12, 169, 520, and 4-575. ISBNO-07-33178-2
   Phillip B. Crosby. Quality Without Tears. New York. McGraw INC.1984.
   ISBN0-4522=25658-5

## ENVIRONMENTAL                                          3 -19

9. Miller, Willard E. and Ruby M. Miller. Environmental Hazards. Santa Barbara:
   ABC-CLIO, INC. 1991

   www.greenatworkmag.com

## BUSINESS LAW                                           A3-20

10. Clarkson W. Kenneth. West's Business Law Fifth ED. Minnesota: West's 1991:890

## GOVERNMENT STATISTICS                                  A3-21

11 . Hoel Airline A. Economic Sourcebook of Government Statistics. Massachusetts:
   D.C. Health and Company, 1983: 247

# APPLICATION
## for
## INTERNATIONAL DRIVING PERMIT
### or
## INTER-AMERICAN DRIVING PERMIT

A3-16

| FEE FOR |
| EACH PERMIT |
| $10.00 |

Issuance of Permit is restricted to persons EIGHTEEN YEARS or over who hold a valid U.S.A. or Territorial License. PERMIT VALID FOR ONE YEAR. Not renewable.

### CHECK DESIRED PERMIT

☐ International Driving Permit
(Fee $10.00 and 2 Passport Type Photos signed on back)

☐ Inter-American Driving Permit *** (see reverse side)
(Fee $10.00 and 2 Passport Type Photos signed on back)

### MANDATORY REQUIREMENTS

(1) Attach 2 recent signed Passport Type Photos (2" x 2")   (2) Enclose permit fee of $10.00 (NO CASH)
(3) If mailing application, a photocopy of U.S. Driver's License must accompany completed application.

NOTE: IT IS IMPORTANT THAT YOUR U.S.A. OR TERRITORIAL LICENSE BE CARRIED WITH THE PERMIT AT ALL TIMES. The International or Inter-American Permit is not valid for driving in the United States.

Mr. Mrs. Ms. (Circle One)

PRINT NAME IN FULL. No Initials

| FIRST | MIDDLE | LAST |
| --- | --- | --- |
| PHONE | HOME STREET ADDRESS | |
| CITY | STATE | ZIP CODE |
| U.S. DRIVER'S LICENSE NO. | STATE OF ISSUE | EXPIRATION DATE |
| BIRTHPLACE: CITY | STATE OR COUNTRY | BIRTH DATE (MO. DAY YEAR) |
| DATE PERMIT TO BE EFFECTIVE | DEPARTURE DATE FROM U.S. | |
| FOREIGN ADDRESS (If known) | | |

PLEASE CHECK THE APPROPRIATE BOX BELOW TO INDICATE THE TYPE OF VEHICLE FOR WHICH YOU NOW HOLD A VALID U.S.A. OR TERRITORIAL DRIVER'S LICENSE. AND FOR WHICH YOU DESIRE THIS PERMIT:

☐ MOTORCYCLE   ☐ PASSENGER CAR   ☐ VEHICLE OVER 7,700 LBS.   ☐ VEHICLE OVER 8 SEATS   ☐ VEHICLE WITH HEAVY TRAILER

I CERTIFY THAT THE ABOVE INFORMATION IS TRUE AND CORRECT. AND THAT THE LICENSE INDICATED HAS NOT BEEN SUSPENDED NOR REVOKED.

I FURTHER CERTIFY THAT I UNDERSTAND THAT A VALID STATE DRIVER'S LICENSE MUST ACCOMPANY THIS PERMIT. AND THAT THIS PERMIT IS VALID ONLY AS LONG AS THE STATE LICENSE IS VALID. BUT NOT TO EXCEED ONE YEAR FROM THE DATE THE PERMIT IS ISSUED.

| SIGNATURE (signature mandatory for issuance of Permit) | DATE |
| --- | --- |

25A

**Contracting States Which Honor International Driving Permits (Convention on Road Traffic, United Nations, Geneva 1949 as of March, 1995**

AFGHANISTAN*
ALBANIA
ALGERIA
ANDORRA
ANGOLA*
ANTIGUA*/**
ARMENIA*
ARGENTINA***
AUSTRALIA
AUSTRIA
AZERBAIJAN*
BAHAMAS
BAHRAIN*
BANGLADESH
BARBADOS**
BELARUS*
BELGIUM
BELIZE
BENIN
BHUTAN*
BOLIVIA*/***
BOTSWANA
BRUNEI*
BULGARIA
BURKINA FASO*
 (WAS UPPER VOLTA)
CAMBODIA
CAMEROON
CANADA
CAPE VERDE ISLANDS
CAYMAN ISLANDS*
CENTRAL AFRICAN REP.
CHAD*
CHILE***
COLOMBIA*/***
CONGO
COSTA RICA*/***
CROATIA*
CUBA
CURACAO
CYPRUS
CZECH REP.
DENMARK
DJIBOUTI*
DOMINICA*/**

DOMINICAN REP.***
EQUADOR***
EGYPT
EL SALVADOR*/***
ESTONIA*
ETHIOPIA*
FIJI
FINLAND
FRANCE (INCLUDING FRENCH
 OVERSEAS TERRITORIES)
FRENCH POLYNESIA
GABON*
GAMBIA
GEORGIA
GERMANY
GHANA
GIBRALTAR
GREECE
GRENADA
GUATEMALA***
GUERNSEY
GUINEA*
GUINEA-BISSAU*
GUYANA
HAITI
HONDURAS*/***
HONG KONG
HUNGARY
ICELAND
INDIA
INDONESIA*
IRAN*
IRELAND
ISRAEL
ITALY
IVORY COAST
JAMAICA
JAPAN
JORDAN
KAZAKHSTAN*
KENYA*
KOREA (REP.)
KUWAIT*
KYRGYSTAN
LAOS

LATVIA
LEBANON
LESOTHO
LIBERIA*
LIBYA*
LIECHTENSTEIN*
LITHUANIA
LUXEMBOURG
MACAO*
MADAGASCAR
MALAWI
MALAYSIA
MALI
MALTA
MAURITANIA*
MAURITIUS
MEXICO*/***
MOLDOVA
MONACO
MONTSERRAT*/**
MOROCCO
MOZAMBIQUE*
NAMIBIA
NEPAL*
NETHERLANDS
NEW CALEDONIA
NEW ZEALAND
NICARAGUA*/***
NIGER
NORWAY
OMAN*
PAKISTAN*
PANAMA*
PAPUA NEW GUINEA
PARAGUAY
PERU
PHILIPPINES
POLAND
PORTUGAL
QATAR*
ROMANIA
RUSSIA*
RWANDA
ST. CHRISTOPHER,
 NEVIS & ANGUILLA*/**

ST. LUCIA
ST. VINCENT & THE GRENDINES
SAN MARINO
SAO TOME & PRINCIPE*
SAUDI ARABIA*
SENEGAL
SEYCHELLES
SIERRA LEONE
SINGAPORE
SLOVAKIA
SLOVENIA*
SOUTH AFRICA
SPAIN
SRI LANKA
SUDAN*
SURINAME
SWAZILAND
SWEDEN
SWITZERLAND*
SYRIA
TAIWAN
TAJIKSTAN
TANZANIA
THAILAND
TOGO
TRINIDAD & TOBAGO***
TUNISIA
TURKEY
TURKMENISTAN*
UGANDA
UKRAINE*
UNITED ARAB EMIRATES
UNITED KINGDOM
UZEBEKIS
VATICAN CITY
VENEZUELA***
VIETNAM
WESTERN SAMOA
YEMEN*
YUGOSLAVIA
ZAIRE
ZAMBIA
ZIMBABWE

*Not party of 1949 Convention: International Driving Permit Honored.
**U.S. driver's license and International Driving Permit recognized on presentation to local police and payment of Special Registration Fee upon arrival.
***Contracting States Which Honor Inter-American Driving Permits (Convention on Regulation of Inter-American Motor Vehicle Traffic, Organization of American States, Washington, D.C. 1943) as of March, 1995. If you intend to drive in the following countries, be sure to check INTER-AMERICAN DRIVING PERMIT box page 1; Brazil and Uruguay.

**(FOR OFFICE USE ONLY)**

| AMOUNT | RECEIPT NO. | PERMIT NO. | DATE ISSUED |
|---|---|---|---|
| SENT TO: | | | |

MEDICAL          A3-22

12. <u>Basic Health Care and Emergency Aid</u> by Thomas Nelson. INC. Publishers 1990-3157.6 Varsity Company, Nashville, TN. 27214

    www.medlineplus.com          www.webmd.com

SELF HELP BOOKS          A3-23

13. <u>Getting your Book Published for Dummies.</u> By Sara Parsons Zackheim IDG BOOK WORLDWIDE,INC. 1-800-762-2974 An International Data Group Company 999 E. Hillsdale Blvd. Suite 400 Foster City, CA. 94404

<u>Prentice-Hall Handbook for Writers</u> by Geggett / Mead / Kramer 9th Ed. Prentice-Hall, INC. Englewood Cliffs, New Jersey. 07632, 1985 ISBN 0-13-695206-2

    www.lcweb.loc.gov

ELECTRONICS          A3-24

14. <u>Drafting for Electronics</u> by Gary Larmit and Sandra J. Lloyd. Prentice-Hall, INC. 3rd Ed. Simon & Schuster / A Viacom Company, Upper Saddle River, New Jersey.

<u>Allied Electronic Data Handbook</u> 5th Ed. October 1968. by Allied Radio Corp. 100 North Western Ave. Chicago, Ill. 60680, USA. Library of Congress Catalog Card No. 66-19667.

HARDWARE & ENGINEERING          A3-25

15. <u>Pictorial Handbook of Technical Devices</u> by Paul Graftsmen and Otto B. Schwarz. Chemical Publishing Co., INC. 1971 New York, N.Y.

<u>Audels Mathematics and Calculations for Mechanics,</u> by Frank D Graham, B.S., M.S., M.E., E.E., Theo Audel & Co., Publishers 65 West 23rd Street, New York, U.S.A

<u>Pocket Reference complied</u> by Thomas J. Glover 1st Ed. Sequoia Publishing, INC. Dept. 101 P.O. Box 620820 Littleton, CO. 80162-8020 Ph: (303) 972-4167 ISBN 0-9622359-0-3 Library of Congress Catalog Card No. 89-90848

16. The Medicine Program. PO. Box 520, Doniphan, Mo. 63935-0520

## TESTING                    A3-27

17. TEST: A Comprehensive reference for assessments in psychology, education, and business. By Sweetland and Keyser. Second Edition. 1986. Test Cooperative of America, 330 W. 47<sup>th</sup> St, Kansas City, MO.

Test CRITIQUES by Sweetland and Keyser. 1985. ISBN 0961128666.

## PUBLIC BROADCASTING                    A3-28

18. Public Television.  www.channel9store.com

www.aetn.org

## COLLEGE APPLICATION / AID                    A3-29

19. Dollars and Sense for College Students by Ellen Braitman.
Princeton Review. 1988. ISBN: 0375752064

The Complete Scholarship Book by Fastweb.com  3<sup>rd</sup> Ed.
Sourcebooks. 2000. ISBN: 1570715300

www.FinancialAidSuperSite.com

www.FAFSA.ed.gov  (Free Application for Federal Student Aid)

www.fastweb.com

Tendency of schools to offer courses that are considered "water down" and teaching a "bunch of facts" without placing emphasis on course subject matter fundamentals is why standardized test are given. As a result, State and National tests are given to determine if a student can demonstrate, in some measurable way, scholastic achievement of curriculum course objectives. The two types of testing are knowledge and performance.

Consequently, a distinction is needed between knowledge test and performance test. Knowledge test is concerned with measuring how familiar a person knows the course subject matter objective support material. Performance test, in contrast, is concerned with assessing person's self-management skills and transferable skills (A5-11) by demonstrating their ability to complete a procedure, produce a product or combination of both in a simulated work situation. For example, CPR (A10-9).

## TEST DESIGN

Knowledge test measure achievement of objectives through the use of test items written at the desired learning level of understanding as follow: 1. Recognition 2. Recall 3. Comprehension 4. Application 5. Analysis/Evaluation

1. Recognition—Students select from two or more alternatives to identify specific information taught during class.
2. Recall—Requires students to respond from memory instead of selecting the response from two or more alternatives.
3. Comprehension—Understanding what was taught by interpreting explaining, translating, and summarizing information.
4. Application—Require students to demonstrate knowledge through mental skill exercises such as problem solving in a real job-related situation.
5. Analysis/Evaluation—Analysis involves turning data to useful information. Evaluation determines what information is best with the option given.

In addition, test design questions can also be developed from other sources that complement guidance for learning (A6-1), and provide the information needed to achieve an understanding of course matter objective. Example, developmental activities (A6-3).

Consequently, knowledge test questions should be developed from curriculum course training aids (A2-8), from different instruction methods used (A8-10), and from the unit/lesson plan outline (A6-2).

More information on academic standards assessment is available @
Achieve Inc: www.achieve.org/ Council for Basic Education: www.c-b-e.org/
National Assessment of Education Progress: www.naep.ed.gov/nationsreportcard/

## TEST TYPES

Knowing the course objective support material and being made familiar of test item question design is the first step in preparing for any test and succeeding in it.(A10-13)

Since most test are timed and spending to much time on test questions that are difficult is not wise, often just reading test directions carefully and asking relevant questions (A10-5) about the information given is all you need to make an educated guess for the correct answer. Test question types commonly used are as follow:

## GENERAL TEST

A. Alternative Response   B. Multiple Choice   C. Matching   D. Completion
E. Short-Answer Essay    F. Discussion Item Essay

A. Alternative-Response—Generally of the true/false variety, or of yes/no variety.

B. Multiple-Choice—Usually in the form of question or incomplete statements.

C. Completion—Each blank is filled in with the response which correctly completes the statement. (Uses recall type of memory).

D. Matching—Match closely associated items.

E. Short-Answer Essay Exam—Features questions of the when, where, how many, define, identify, state and list varieties.

F. Discussion Item Essay Exam—Calls for contrast, comparison, outline, description, and explanation.

## OBJECTIVE SUPPORT MATERIAL (Math)                    A10

1. National Assessment of Educational Progress (NAEP). Solving math problems test your thinking power, recall memory, and ability to grasp mentally transposition of formulas terms for solving arithmetic, algebra, and geometry problems.

   Math comparison questions test your ability to simplify and recognize similar equations identities.

   Interpreting data questions test your ability to evaluate procedures or to draw a right conclusion with the data collected.

## OBJECTIVE SUPPORT MATERIAL (ENGLISH USAGE)     A10

2.   Written English usage questions test your ability to correct common errors in writing.

2.1   Basic Grammar--Recognize sentence structure and their parts use, for clarifying meaning by showing how to express relationship among different words, and how to change words to say what you mean to say.

2.2   Sentence Faults—Recognize faults on sentence construction like the use of improperly punctuated phases, clauses, common splices and awkward or confusion sentences. Correct faulty agreement, unnecessary shift in written style, misplaced parts of sentences, and dangling modifiers.

2.3   Effective Sentences—Show how using coordinating and subordinating conjunction clarify the meaning of a sentence.

## OBJECTIVE SUPPORT MATERIAL (PARAGRAPHS)     A10

3    Reading paragraphs test your understanding of the material presented on what is stated or implied, and what is the central thought? Example: Historical Documents of Citizenship (A3-11) and Literature Classic (A3-12).

3.1   Sentence Completion Questions-Test your ability to recognize logical organization of ideals to explain or decipher good English style.

3.2   Comparable Answer Question – Test your understanding of word relationship used to define a cause-effect relationship or concrete to abstract relationship.

3.3   Verbal Comparison Question—Test your vocabulary and familiarity with word meaning that are alike and unlike.

3.4   Analogy Questions—Require you to recognize how a logical relationship between words and ideas are used to convey a message or central thought.

## OBJECTIVE SUPPORT MATERIAL (ESSAY EXAM)     A10

4.   Short Answer Essay Exam—Feature questions of the when, where, how many, and ask to define, identify, state, and list varieties used and why.

Discussion Item Essay Exam—Calls for contrast, comparison, outline, use of description or an explanation of why the reasons, ideas, central thought is so.

1. National Assessment of Educational Progress (NAEP).
    The Math NAEP questions are based on five content areas as follow:
    1. Numbers and Numeral, Addition, Subtraction, Multiplication, Division,
       Positive Integers, and Signed Numbers.
    2. Fractions, Cancellation, Addition and Subtraction of Fraction, Multiplication
       and Division of Fraction, Decimal, Reducing Fraction to Decimals, Ratio,
       Proportion, and Variation.
    3. Direct and Indirect Measurement, Dependence, Function and Formulas.
    4. Percentage, Profit and Loss, Discounts, Simple Interest, Compound Interest.
    5. Data Analysis, Statistics and Probability; Algebra and Function.

2. General Achievement Test.- Measure Acquisition of knowledge in subject area of field
    study. For example: Reading, Spelling, Language, Arithmetic, Social Studies, Science,
    English, and Study Skills.

3. General Development Test- Measures the progress of growth on a persons ability to
    make functional applications of knowledge and understanding.
    Some area covered, as follow:  Understanding of Basic Social Concepts, Natural
    Sciences,  Correctness of Expression or View, Interpretation of Reading Material
    and General Vocabulary.

4. Aptitude Test- Valuable as a guidance tool for predicting a persons ability to learn in
    a specific subject or area as follow:
        Reasoning- Verbal, Abstract, and Mechanical
        Ability- Numerical, Clerical Speed and Accuracy, and Language usage.
5. Oral Testing- Use  to determine how well a person can organize his thoughts and
                express them verbally.
6. Essay Examination- Provide valuable experience in written expression.
                        Requires mental activity of a person  in organization of
                        material, critical thinking, value judgments, and interpretation.
7. Short-Answer Essay Exam- Features questions of the when, where, how many,
                        define, identify, state, and list varieties.
8. Discussion Item Essay Exam-Calls for contrast, comparison,  outline, discription,or
                        explanation.
9. Objective Test-Use for sampling of material covered, the provided little opportunity
                        for organization and expression of thought.

Quality control program procedures and guidance presented in elements 10 & 18 "Inspection and Test control (A7-14), and "Training" (A7-22) forms the foundation for curriculum maintenance updates.

After each test, Quality Control (QC) department professional development team (A7-3) list test results on student performance sheet (A10-8). This performance sheet provides each student with a track record that shows to what degree (prerequisite) subject matter objective goals have been reached.

In addition, the professional development team also completes the problem sheet (A10-13) by listing test design, type, and objective support material for each test item on the test. After which, this team then analysis test data and maintain the problem sheet as a record of test items missed by class number (A2-1 thru A2-7) problem / solutions corrected.

Any test item deficiency recorded on this problem sheet is forward to QC department for taking corrective action (A7-18). By QC department keeping this record, updates to curriculum are possible because these records will help to identify test item or subject areas that cause an individual or class the greatest difficulty.

Having this academic / social reporting program on scholastic achievement, attitude and effort, basic skills, and work habits will enable the instructor or teacher to give the student feedback for taking corrective action (A4-1 thru A4-4). Some key actions and planning questions for taking corrective action as stated by Zenger Miller Frontline Leadership is as follow:

## KEY ACTION

1. Point out the difference between present performance and agreed upon expectations.
2. Describe specifically the negative impact of the student performance.
3. Get the student view of the situation.
4. Ask for ideas on how the student can correct the situation and add your own.
5. Explain any steps you plan to take and why.
6. Agree on the action plan and a date for follow up.
7. Express confidence that the student can correct the situation.

## PLANNING QUESTIONS

1. What is the difference between present performances and agreed upon expectations?
2. What is the negative impact of the student performance? Does the negative impact really warrant corrective action?
3. Are there factors outside of the student's control that may be contributing to the student's performance problem?

## SCHOLASTIC ACHIEVEMENT
A4-1

1. Needs to prepare written assignments more carefully.
2. Needs to hand in assignment on time.
3. Needs to prepare oral assignments more carefully.
4. Needs to improve test scores.
5. Needs to contribute constructively to class activities.
6. Needs to show more improvement in specific class knowledge and skills.
7. Needs to attend class more regularly.

## ATTITUDE AND EFFORT
A4-2

1. Needs to make better use of leadership ability.
2. Needs to pay attention.
3. Needs to do work consistent with his ability.
4. Needs to corporate better with others.
5. Needs to respect the rights and feelings of others.
6. Needs to take better care of materials and equipment.
7. Needs to stop wasting time.
8. Needs to follow directions.
9. Needs to stop interfering with the learning of others.

## BASIC SKILLS
A4-3

1. Needs to speak more clearly and effectively.
2. Needs to improve in reading.
3. Needs to improve written expression.
4. Needs to improve spelling.
5. Needs to apply previous learning to new problems.
6. Needs to use mathematics correctly.

## WORK HABITS
A4-4

1. Needs to organize work more effectively.
2. Needs to have material ready for work.
3. Needs to use class notes more effectively.
4. Needs to use reference sources more effectively.
5. Needs to do work more neatly.

Quality control process of evaluation and review is a never-ending process that defines the term of the relationship between student and teachers. Academic standards and social behavior standards measures current performance of education design parameters.

The question of standards is a question of quality. Quality doesn't cost more it costs less. Quality teaching of students in social skills reduces money spent on drug enforcement, welfare, health care and the retraining by business their employee's. These programs cost the nations lost earnings and forgone taxes over time. Hence, schools accountability therefore can be measured in the students performance.

Schools and school districts should also evaluate themselves against private schools their toughest competitor. Having performance measurement allows the school, to see both how well they are doing and what their rate of improvement is.

In conclusion, innovating, flexibility, and the ability to change have become necessary teaching survival skills, but these skills mean little if a school does not have the leadership in management who can really help the school faculty to be creative, imaginative and devote to teaching and motivate students to learn. Teachers need to remember that in a quality control program the first measurement of performance is a student willingness to learn.

1. Evaluation- The appraisal of subject-matter achievement and skill development. That recognizes understanding, interests, appreciations, and attitudes.
2. Evaluation first aids then climaxes the teaching and learning process. Evaluation steps may be stated as follows:
    1. Determine the objective of the material course, unit or situation to be evaluated.
    2. Selection of test or other means of evaluating each objective.
    3. Application of test or evaluation procedure.
    4. Comparison of results by grade norm, age norm, percentile norm, or standard score.

## GUIDANCE PROGRAM A5-1

1. Adequate system of records.
2. Work toward the goal of self-study and self-direction of each individual.
3. An evaluation system, involving research and measurement.
4. Continuous process.

## FUNCTION OF GUIDANCE A5-2

1. Identify need, interests and abilities.
2. Make available information concerning requirements for arriving at solutions for their personnel, educational, and vocational problems. This is so an intelligent decision can be made.
3. Look for ways to help them to understand themselves-their strengths and weaknesses.
4. Resource and referral person of other agencies.
    1. Scholarship Search Services: Softwarecashclass@aol.com
       custsvc@petersons.com        mail@tpsoftware.com
    2. Department of Educations Books and Pamphlets Ph: 800-4-FED-AID
       The Student Guide, Looking for Student Aid
    3. Federal Student Aid Information Center, P.O. Box 84, Washington D.C.
    4. Web Sites- www.finaid.org/finaid   www.fast.web.com   20044
       www.finaid.org/finaid/vendors/software.html
       www.finaid.org/finaid/documents.html
5. Free Application for Federal Student Aid- Can be filed out any time between January 1 and June 30 ( www.FAFSA.ed.gov ).
6. Student Aid Report (SAR)- Details financial aid eligibility. Must be at your school of choice by August 31.

## PURPOSE OF FOLLOW-UP FUNCTION OF GUIDANCE A5-3

1. Identify training opportunities that are desirable.
2. To stay informed of difficulties encountered toward the goals of the individual.
3. Determine why a person is leaving
4. Locate persons who have not made a satisfactory adjustment, and to help them do so.
5. Evaluating the guidance program.

## HEALTH IMPROVEMENT                                    A5-4
1. Health Knowledge- Understand the basic facts concerning health and disease.
2. Health Habits- Learn how to protect his own health and that of his family and home.
3. Public Health- What can be done to improve the health of his community and environment.
4. Physical Fitness- Develop and maintain good health through planned exercise.
5. Social Science- Become aware how applications of scientific advances contribute to general welfare of the world and of man.

## LEADERSHIP SKILLS                                    A5-5
1. Effective Thinking- Ability to think and evaluate information such as: Analyzing a problem and/or a situation, and evaluate the results of the action.
2. Communication Skills- Develop skills in listening and observing. Be able to express their thoughts clearly, and read with understanding.
3. Ability to Make Relative Judgments- Recognize that education is important for the development of standards for work, personal economics, and safeguarding his interest.
4. Have a Sense of Valves- Learn respect and appreciation for human value and for beliefs of others.

## FAMILY LIFE ADJUSTMENT                                A5-6
1. Appreciates the family as a social institution.
2. How to become a contributing member of the family.
3. Know the likenesses and differences among peoples and the reason underlying them.
4. Be concerned with the present problems of youth as well as their future.
5. Give guidance and offer them learning experiences appropriate for improving family life at home.
6. Educate or teach homemaking skills. (Extension Homemaking Club).

## VOCATION                                          A5-7

1. Develop interest in activities as means to happiness, to social progress, and to continued growth. ( FFA, Homeroom, Assembly, Clubs, etc. ).
2. Give direction into avenues of study and work of specialized interests that may manifest, for work a person seems most fit.
3. Give supervised work experience as well as education in the skills and knowledge of their occupational choice.
4. Place a high premium upon learning to make wise choices, and the means of attaining a goal.
5. Seek career advancement through education.
    1. Students need to be aware that they are responsible for their own career.
    2. Let your school records be the testament of your career goals.
6. Maximize your opportunity your school record has earned you.
    1. What is the usefulness of this degree or training?
    2. How is this relevant in today's job market?
    3. Challenge the practicality of your career goals.
7. Seek excellence by setting educational or trade goals.
    1. What do you wont to learn more about?
    2. Ask questions, the knowledge you seek may not be part of the curriculum.
8. Value the education experience.
    1. Do more than ticket punching.
    2. Learn how to think for yourself.
    3. Learn something that you don't know. Learn a new concept, a new idea.

## CITIZENSHIP                                       A5-8

1. Understand the rights and duties of the citizen of a democratic society.
2. Show appreciation of our democratic heritage.
3. Become knowledgeable of civic rights and responsibilities and of American institutions.
4. Understand the meaning of citizenship and the responsibilities and privileges involved.
5. Understand the structure and function of government and the differences between democracy and other forms of government.
6. Learn the American economy and the individual's role in it.
7. Know valves essential to the development of active citizenship.
8. Develop skill for democratic citizenship such as: Being prompt, Co-operating, Leading, Following and Sharing.
9. Work with community organization as a volunteer.
10. Accept and discharge civic responsibilities.
11. Obey and show respect for the law.
12. Learn the civic duties of the community.

## LEISURE TIME          A5-9

1. Develop a mind set for quality time as a way to release your stress.
2. Be a participant and spectator in sports and other past times.
3. Enjoy a rich, sincere, and varied social life with friends.
4. Take a foreign language, study art, music or take part in some extra-class activities.

## CHARACTER          A5-10

1. Develop responsible direction to ones life by becoming your own person.
2. Develop critical judgment against propaganda.
3. Develop respect for your self and others, put human relationship first.
4. Develop appreciation for beauty, literature, art, music, and nature.
5. Develop behavior that reflexes a spiritual value and beliefs, for self-discipline and self-reliance.
6. Develop a sound philosophy for life.

SOURCE: The Profession of Teaching by Harold W. Massey and Edwin E. Vineyard, The Odyssey Press, INC. New York 1961: Ch-4, pp. 55-72. Objectives of American Education.

Evaluation and review of person skills can be used as a tool for measuring the effectiveness of a training program (A8-1), QC-in process control (A1-6), and workers job performance.(A9-14)  The two types of skills are self-management and transferable.

### Self-Management Skills (Adaptive Skills)

Self-management skills define "a good worker" and sets the criteria for evaluation and review of workers job performance.

Scholastic achievement, attitude and effort, basic skills, work habits, and other adaptive skills are important because employers hire people who they feel will fit academically and socially with the work group. These are the skills you use every day to survive and to get along with others. (A4-1 thru A4-4)

### Transferable Skills (General Skills)

Transferable skills define "a qualified worker" and sets the criteria for evaluation and review for hiring people management feel will fit into a company theme of things for improved output, quality, and cost control.

Critical thinking skills, thing or sense skills, people skills, leadership skills, dealing with data skills, and how you apply words or communicate ideas are general skills that can be useful on a variety of jobs. They are called transferable skills because they can be transferred from on job or even one career, to another.

In short, knowing your skills strength and weakness is key to maximizing job performance and job hunting. Since employers use a persons self-management skills and transferable skills as the criteria for interviewing a person for job opening (A10-23) and for assessing a person job performance on doing the job or task right the first time.

Keep in mind if you are doing an evaluation and review of a persons work performance, that there is no substitute though, for hand-on experience and dealing with real problems and situation. Consequently, making a person aware that their self-management skills and transferable skills should be a knowledge base to grow from, and by expanding that base, the faster they will become productive in the workplace.

A Final Thought. If you are starting a job search, first make a list of all the fields of work that interest you. For example, the computer field can be expanded to include job titles for technician, support repair, networking, and information specialist.

Second, use the resources at your local library to learn more about the jobs on your list. Two excellent sources organized specifically for job hunters are "THE WORLD ALMANAC NATIONAL JOB FINDER'S GUIDE" and "JOB BANK" series.

**Other Adaptive Skills:**

| | |
|---|---|
| Ambitious | Ask questions |
| Assertive | Assume responsibility |
| Competitive | Complete assignments |
| Creative | Decisive |
| Dependable | Detail - oriented |
| Diplomatic | Enthusiastic |
| Flexible | Friendly |
| Highly motivated | Ingenious |
| Integrity | Intelligent |
| Inventive | Kind |
| Learn quickly | Mature |
| Outgoing | Patient |
| Persistent | Tactful |
| Physically strong | Pleasant |
| Proud of doing a job | Results - oriented |
| Self - motivated | Sense of direction (purpose) |
| Sense of humor | Sensitive |
| Sincere | Sociable |
| Tolerant | Tough |
| Trusting | Understanding |
| Willing to learn new things | |

## Transferable Skills

These are general skills that can be useful on a variety of jobs. They are called transferable skills because they can be transferred from one job, or even one career, to another.

Critical Transferable Skills...... these tend to get you higher levels of responsibility and pay. Emphasize them in an interview as well as on your resume.

| | |
|---|---|
| Meet deadlines | Public Speaking |
| Supervise others | Accept responsibility |
| Solve problems | Project planning |
| Budgeting | Sales |
| Efficiency | |

Thing skills:

| | | |
|---|---|---|
| Sense of touch | Key boarding, typing | Manual Dexterity |
| Gathering    Separating    Sorting | | Assembling |
| Driving | Observing/Inspecting | Operating Machines |
| Balancing, juggling | Drawing, painting | Sewing |
| Weaving | Hammering | Hand Crafts |
| Precise tolerance or standards | | Physical agility |
| Strength | Endurance | |
| Finishing/refinishing | Restoring | Sandblasting |
| Grinding | Keypunching, drilling | modeling or remodeling |

"People" Skills:

| | | |
|---|---|---|
| Caring | Comforting | |
| Counseling | Consulting | |
| Diplomacy | Helping others | |
| Instructing | Interviewing | |
| Listening | Mentoring | |
| Negotiating | Outgoing | |
| Mediating | Group facilitating | |
| Communicating | Encouraging | Conflict |
| Management | Tolerance | |
| Diversity | Conflict resolution | |
| Respect | Empathy | |
| Sympathy | Sensitive | |
| Responsive | Problem solving | |
| Negotiating | Motivating | |
| Inspiring trust | Developing rapport | |
| Interviewing | Inquiry | |

Dealing with data:

| | |
|---|---|
| Analyzing | Auditing |
| Budgeting | Calculating/ computing |
| Checking for accuracy | Classifying |
| Comparing | Compiling |
| Counting | Detail - oriented |
| Evaluating | Investing |
| Financial records | Research |

40

| | | |
|---|---|---|
| Financial Management | Recording facts | |
| Synthesizing | Taking inventory | Detail |
| Surveying | Examining | |
| Oriented | Following instructions | |
| Financial or fiscal analysis | Cost analysis | |
| Organizing | Problem solving | |

**Using words, ideas:**

| | | |
|---|---|---|
| Articulate | Verbal communication | |
| Correspondence | Brainstorming | |
| Design | Edit | |
| Inventive | Logical | |
| Public speaking | Write clearly, concisely | Telephone |
| Skills | Imaginative | Quick thinking |
| Speech writing | | |
| Promotional writing | Advertising | |
| Publicity | Sign Language | |

**Leadership:**

| | |
|---|---|
| Competitive | Decisive |
| Delegate | Direct others |
| Influence others | Initiate new tasks |
| Decision making | Manage or direct others |
| Mediate problems | Motivate people |
| Negotiate agreements | Planning |
| Results oriented | Risk taker |
| Run meetings | Self - confident |
| Self - motivated | Solve problems |
| Judgment | Integrity |
| Coordinating | Work schedules |
| Results oriented | Self directed |
| Multi - tasking | Decisive |
| Goal setting | Strategic planning |

**Creative/Artistic**

| | |
|---|---|
| Artistic | Drawing |
| Expressive | Perform |
| Present artistic ideas | Dance, body movement |
| Visualize shapes | Designing |
| Model making | Handicrafts |

| Poetic images | Visualizing | | A5-11 |
| Illustrating, sketching | Photography | Mechanical drawing | |
| Researching a Company | | | |

## PRACTICE & EXECUTE A6
## (P&E)

Practice and Execute part of Installation Guidance Specification for a Quality Training provides the basic understanding on Guidance for Learning and Planning. Remember understanding without action is a waste of time. So is teaching for the sake of teaching without student's participating is a waste of time.

With the ever-increasing number of fairly complex core curriculum objectives both visible and invisible, a greater amount of knowledge is required to properly and efficiently teach today's students.

Practice and execute details for Guidance for Learning and Planning provide the teacher with the knowledge needed to accomplish these core curriculum objectives with a minimum of effort and without resorting to time-consuming guesswork and paperwork.

Two useful sources for information on education and training programs available to students and teacher are; Peterson's Guides and Barron's Educational Series.

Peterson's Guides, P.O. Box 2123, Princeton, NJ 08543-2123, Tel. 609/924/5338; and Barron's Educational Series, 250 Wireless Blvd, Hauppauge, NY 11788,
Tel. 516/434-3311.

SOURCE: Ronald L. Krannich, PH.D and Caryl Rae Krannich, PH.D. The Complete Guide to Public Employment. Impact Publications Woodbridge, VA. 1990: 106-107

<u>GUIDANCE FOR LEARNING</u>                         A6-1

1. Learned Experiences- Learning occurs as a result of experience with concepts, skills, that involve problem solving and decision making.

2. Maintenance of Attention and Motivation-
    (A) For learning a focus of attention is necessary.
    (B) Make assignment definite and clear and related to already existing interest, needs, and purpose.
    C) Use visual aids and reference materials.

3. Progressive Phase of Learning-
    (A) Practice and effort bring improvement of skills.
    (B) Each plateau is followed by another period of gain.
    C) Possible causes in performance lulls are:
        1. fatigue 2. low motivation 3. bad instructions 4. difficulty of task
        5. pacing of tasks 6. boredom
    (D) Use of the doctrine of gradualness in raising the level of complexity of concepts, processes and skills.
    (E) Diagnosis of errors and correct techniques are important.

4. Three Principles of Learning-
    (A) Principle of readiness
    (B) Principle of effect
    C) Principle of exercise

4A. Readiness- When readiness is not present it must be developed.
    (A) "Striking while the iron is hot"- be alert for opportunities to get your point across.
    (B) "Striking until the iron gets hot"- Arrange subject matter designed to develop readiness.
    C) Make present and future needs felt through exposure to challenge.
    (D) Develop curiosity with stimulation of thought and imagination.

4B. EFFECT- Reward and Punishment.

    (A) Manipulate rewards and incentives in such a fashion as to encourage the learning of desired behavior.

4C. EXERCISE- Skill and performance are improved through practice.

    (old idea of use and disuse).

    (A) That which is used to be retained and improved and that which is not used is forgotten.

    (B) Repetition merely provides more opportunity for the principle of effect to work.

    ( C) Motivated, purposeful practice is necessary In order for learning to take place.

    (D) Due to practice which involves contexts and application of technique and processes to different problems.

5. Evaluation of Learning- Evaluation is to be made in terms of the " GOALS " in mind.

    (A) Evaluate the class in terms of the objectives which are to be learned or accomplished.

    (B) Check accomplish task in terms of attitudes, understanding and demonstrated skills.

6. Retention of Learning- Items learned and retained longer area;

| More easily | Not as easy |
| --- | --- |
| Word lists | Nonsense lists |
| Prose | Word lists |
| Poetry | Prose |
| Principles | Facts |

6. Retention of Learning

(A) Learning of tasks are placed properly in relative time sequence with one another.

(B) Look and correct bad habits and preconceived notions before beginning tasks.

C) Remember fast learners retent more and retain the things learned longer than do slower learners.

(D) The more unity, coherence, pattern, integration, and proper sequence the material has, the easier to learn and retain.

(E) Remember that attitudes, Insights, and Understanding, once gained are practically never forgotten.

7. Transfer of Learning- Learning to non-school situations and problems need to be emphasis.

(A) Transfer takes place through the occurrence of the identical elements or component parts of two situation. Example: A word learned from a text is recognized in a newspaper at home.

(B) Transfer takes place in the use and application of principles. Example: A noun word that is singular becomes plural by adding the "s" sound.

C) Transfer takes place in problem-solving technique with some adaptation in the solution of different problems. Example: The general equation of interest- by the definition of interest we have: interest = principal (X) rate (X) time.

(D) Transfer of attitude learned may transfer to become attitude toward training training, authority figures, in the form of verbalism and symbolism, besides be directed at other people. Example: The use of bad languages.

## GUIDANCE FOR LEARNING: CONT'D          A6-1

7. Transfer of Learning-
    (E) Transfer takes place not by mental exercise, besides it is not entirely automatic; therefore, for transfer of learning to take place it must be planned, have a purpose and follow the above outline methods. 7A-7E.

## PLANNING          A6-2

8. Reasons for Planning-
    (A) Guides the process and prevent futile, wasteful rambling.
    (B) Gives assurance that the material will be covered skillfully.
    C) Makes it unnecessary to rely on memory or to concentrate on remembering all the material.
    (D) The process or material can be reviewed by others for change.
    (E) It wins the respect and confidence of the people involved that the lesson will succeed in its objectives.
    (F) Make for better control and moral.
    (G) It conserves time and energy.
9. Unit Plan- Means of developing and using subject matter, which has been organized around a central theme.
    (A) Structure of the unit plan
        1. Introduction
        2. Objectives
        3. Outline of the unit
        4. Activities and material
        5. Evaluation
        6. Reference and resources

# TEACHING FUNDAMENTALS AND TECHNIQUES.

## (FEDS): PRACTICE & EXECUTE

### PLANNING CONT'D

9. Unit Plan-                                                                A6-2

   (A) Introduction- Briefing that includes the title, time allotment, relation to other unit, and a brief overview.

   (A2) Objectives- Give direction and explain why. Unit purpose contribute to broader goal of the plan. Give both <u>General</u> and <u>Specific</u> objectives.

   (A3) Outline- Scope of the topic and the order of sub-topics and activities.

   (A4) Activities and Materials- Sequential place in the plan.
   1. Introductory- Orientation, pre-testing (oral and written), planning, and motivation.
   2. Developmental Activities- Panel discussion, reports, quest speakers, projects, problem solving, telling, listening, and audio-visual aids.
   3. Concluding Activities- Summaries, reviews, special points, or exhibits.

   (A5) Evaluation- Oral and written tests to determine if the objects were met.

   (A6) References and Resources- Books, pamphlets, charts, and other material.

### 9A4.2 DEVELOPMENTAL ACTIVITIES            A6-3

THE PROJECT- Practical application problem;

(1) Selection (life problems).

(2) Planning

(3) Execution

(4) Evaluation

(5) Projects- Are usually centered around the preparation, construction, or development of some material End-Product.

(FEDS): PRACTICE & EXECUTE

<u>PLANNING CONT'D</u>                           A6-3

## 9A4.2 DEVELOPMENTAL ACTIVITIES
PROBLEM-SOLVING PLAN- The problem is generally stated as a question.
    (1) Statement or Identification of the problem.
    (2) Collection or relevant data.
    (3) Determination or tentative solutions (Hypothesis).
    (4) Critical analysis of suggested solutions.
    (5) Testing hypothesis against agree-upon criteria.
    (6) Verification of apparent solution.

TELLING AND LISTENING- Characteristics of a good discussion are:
    (1) Has a purpose, direction, and meaning.
    (2) Information exchange.
    (3) Encourage participation.
    (4) Promotes respect of people rights or ideals.
    (5) Usually finishes with a summarization, conclusions or resolutions.
    (6) Helpful in improving attitude or behavior.
        1. Helpful to organize thought systematically.
        2. Helpful to improve communication skills of expression.
        3. Helpful to develop critical thinking.
        4. Helpful to make value judgment.
        5. Helpful to hear different views of thoughts.

GROUP DISCUSSION-Conducting a group discussion requires the following:
    (1) Leader to guide, but not to dominate.
    (2) Keep the group on the general subject.
    (3) Be prepared for the topic of discussion.
    (4) Face-to-Face seating arrangement.
    (5) Thoroughly explore all questions and views.

## 9A4.2 DEVELOPMENTAL ACTIVITIES CONT'D          A6-3

GROUP DISCUSSION CONT'D-
- (6)   Give everyone a chance to contribute in a manner that they are clearly understood.
- (7)   Correct statements or facts as need be.
- (8)   Raise question, which call for selection and organization of thought process.
- (9)   Encourage questions and challenges to different viewpoints.
- (10)  Follow one-at-a time procedure of speaking.
- (11)  Express approval for meritorious responses.
- (12)  Research question that are not answered.

UTILIZING AUDIO-VISUAL AIDS- Uses and why.
- (1)   Stimulate interest.
- (2)   Clears-up misunderstanding of purpose.
- (3)   Provide illustration and opportunities for application.
- (4)   Make things concrete, life-like and believable.
- (5)   Improve life experience through senses.
- (6)   Pictures and words are helpful in explaining something new.

AUDIO AND/OR VISUAL MATERIAL AVAILABLE ARE:
- (1)   Demonstration and lab experiments.
- (2)   Objects and specimens.
- (3)   Models, mock-ups, views of the interior.
- (4)   Globes, maps, planetaria, exhibits, charts,
- (5)   Graphs, diagrams, posters, blackboard, bulletin boards, cartoons.
- (6)   Books, magazines, bulletins, pamphlets, periodicals.
- (7)   Dramatization plays, pageants, dialogues.

# TEACHING FUNDAMENTALS AND TECHNIQUES.

## (FEDS) : PRACTICE AND EXECUTE

### 9A4.2 DEVELOPMENTAL ACTIVITIES CONT'D

**AUDIO AND/ OR VISUAL MATERIAL AVAILABLE ARE: CONT'D**
  (8) Field trips, exhibits, motion pictures.
  (9) Slides, projection, photographs, drawing.
  (10) Recordings, radio, television.
  (11) Computer software, Microsoft power point, internet, web-pages.

SOURCE: <u>THE PROFESSION OF TEACHING</u>.
 pp. 89-125,  by Harold W. Massey and Edwin E. Vineyard

## Quality Control Department

Quality Control Department main responsibility is to make executive reports and assist corporate staff personnel in keeping information resources running smoothly. The department does this by speeding the flow of information and ideas received by the consumers, suppliers, and engineers to the appropriate divisional workforce.

This information is then compared with statistics from the standard industrial classification, which is comparative data from the same industry. This is done to prevent time and resources from being wasted on re-inventing information. See: firstgov.gov "Laws & Reg" link "Fed Stats"

According to Juran/Gryna in Quality Planning and Analysis. New York: McGraw-Hill, Inc. 1980. Metrics for executive reports on quality and List of Corporate Quality Staff Activities are as follow:

A7-2

| Subject | Unit of Measurement | Department | Freq. |
|---|---|---|---|
| Negative Reactions | Number of Complaints | Field | M |
| Returns | Volume of Returns | Accounting | M |
| Service Calls | Number under Warranty | Field | Q |
| Guarantee Charges | Under Warranty | Accounting | Q |
| Product Reliability | Failure Rate | Field | M |
| Spare Parts Sales | Dollars of Sales | Accounting | A |
| Conformance | Average Defects | Inspection | M |
| Outgoing Quality | Demerits | QA | M |
| Vendor Performance | Purchase Cost | Accounting | Q |
| Quality Cost | Labor, Shop, Sales | QA | Q |
| Audits | Various | QA | S |
| Customary Relations | Various | Marketing | Q |
| Quality Improvements | Investment Returns | QA | Q |

- Frequency Control  M=monthly,  Q=quarterly,  A=annual,  S=special

* Material is reproduced with permission of the McGraw-Hill Companies.

According to Juran and Gryna in <u>Quality Planning and Analysis</u>, Quality Control Department other matter are listed below:

<u>List of Corporate Quality Planning Staff Activities</u>

Assistance to corporate management;

Develop corporate quality policies and objectives.

Prepare and publish corporate reports on quality performance.

Audit divisional quality performance.

Audit divisional compliance to government regulations.

Assistance to divisional management;

Provide consulting service to divisional general managers.

Provide assistance in start up of new divisions.

Appraise performance of divisional quality managers.

Participate in personal actions involving divisional quality manager.

*Material is reproduced with permission of the McGraw-Hill Companies.

### LIST OF CORPORATE QUALITY STAFF ACTIVITIES   cont:

Professional development:                                                                    A7-3

>    Keep informed on new developments which take place in the quality control field.
>    (see 20 elements of quality control listed below)
>    Disseminate this information to the divisions.
>    Collaborate with selected divisions in trying out promising new concepts and tools.
>    Prepare training programs, manuals, and courses. (see Appendix D class/lesson)
>    Conduct internal company conferences on matter of common interest.
>    Publish internal newsletters, case histories, and other forms of exchange of
>    experience.

Coordination of corporate quality matters                                    A7-4

>    Coordinate relations with standardization committees in government and industry
>    associations.
>    Coordinate relations with national standardization bodies.
>    Coordination relations with professional societies.
>    Provide interdivisional coordination within the company.

## 20 ELEMENTS OF A QUALITY CONTROL PROGRAM.   According to Foxboro
"Corporate Quality Assurance Plan "(2).

1. Management Responsibility:                                                     A7-5

>    (a) Quality Assurance Program.
>    (b) Quality Manager is responsible for establishing and implementing quality
>        program procedures
>    ( c) Quality standards is everyone's responsibility.
>    (d) Verification of quality standards is shared by the quality organization.

2. Quality System:                                                                      A7-6

>    (a) Operation procedures.
>    (b) Documentation of the quality control system.
>    (c ) Quality policy and procedures.
>    (d) Quality plan.

3. Contract Review:                                                                    A7-7

>    (a) Identify area responsible for contract review.
>    (b) Document requirements.
>    (c ) Resolve difference in contract requirements.
>    (d) Keep records of contract reviews.
>    (e) Translate requirement of customers to specifications.
>    (f) Establish acceptance criteria prior to release to manufacturing  facility.
>    (g) Document Engineering change proposals.

4. Design Control                                                                    A7-8
    (a) Develop design plan.
    (b) Develop change control procedures.
    (c ) Resolve technical issues.
    (d) Identify necessary resources.
    (e) Design suitable for production.
    (f) Identify characteristics that are crucial to the safe and proper function of the
       product.
    (g) Implement design control measures.
    (h) Maintain procedures for the identification, documentation and appropriate
       reviews and approvals of all changes and modifications.

5. Document Control:                                                             A7-9
    (a) A system shall be established which ensures appropriate control.
    (b) Identify those responsible for assurance of documents.
    (c ) Establishment and maintenance of current distribution list.
    (d) Review and approve all document changes.
    (e) Provide for the necessary records which permit the duplication of the product,
       system, or service sold.
    (f) Provide objective evidence that the "as built" product or system satisfies the
       specified quality criteria.

6. Purchasing:                                                                       A7-10
    (a) Selection of qualified suppliers.
    (b) Agreement of quality assurance.
    (c ) Agreement on verification methods.
    (d) Provisions for settlement of quality dispute.

7. Purchaser Supplied Product (Customer)                          A7-11
    (a) Establish and maintain procedures for verification , storage and maintenance
       of purchaser supplied product provided for incorporation into the company's
       system or product.

8. Product Identification and Trace Ability:                       A7-12
    (a) Shelf- life and deterioration control.
    (b) Establish and document for identification and control of materials, parts,
       components and products throughout the manufacturing process, delivery and
       installation.
    (c ) Provide trace ability of materials where required.

9. Process Control:                                                                    A7-13
      (a) Documented work instructions.
      (b) Use of suitable production and installation equipment.
      (c ) Suitable working environment.
      (d) Establish criteria for workmanship.
      (e) Monitor product characteristic during production.
      (f) Approve process and equipment, as appropriate.
      (g) Maintain records of process, equipment, and personnel as appropriate.

10. Inspection and Test Controls:                                                       A7-14
      (a) Identify and document all testing.
      (b) Provide written procedures for testing.
      (c ) Develop acceptance criteria for testing.
      (d) Maintain records of testing problem/solutions.
      (e) Provide necessary resources for adequate testing.

11. Inspection and Test Controls                                                        A7-15
      (a) Develop a program of inspections and tests to meet the specified technical and
          quality requirements.
      (b) Use only approved equipment.
      (c ) Records shall identify the authority responsible for the release of confirming
          product.
      (d) The appropriate markings, stamps, tags, labels for indicating conformance or
          Non-conformance of product with regard to QC inspection, production,
          inspection, and test performed.
      (e) Documents relating to inspection, audit inspection, and test must be generated,
          maintained, and retained.
      (f) Non-conforming items must be identified and segregated.

12. Inspection, Measuring, and Test Equipment:                                          A7-16
      (a) Be able to demonstrate the conformance of product to the specified
          requirements.
      (b) Establish, document and maintain calibration procedures.
      (c ) Maintain records to permit evaluation of calibration requirements.
      (d) Calibration of equipment must meet nationally recognized standards.
      (e) Ensure that the environmental conditions are suitable for the calibration of the
          equipment.

13. Control of Non-Conforming Items:                    A7-17
    (a) Establish a program for the identification, segregation, and disposition
       of items found to be non-co conforming.
    (b) Maintain a record on non-conforming item and their disposition.
    (c ) Identify those individuals or group having the authority to make
       disposition of non-conforming items.
    (d) Document with technical justification all non-conforming items
       labeled "use as is" where the item may effect product performance.
14. Corrective Action:                    A7-18
    (a) Report all corrective action to appropriate level of management if
       quality is adversely effected.
    (b) Find root cause to problems.
    ( c) Follow-up on corrective action plan to prevent reassurance.
    (d) Record all corrective action and action plan used.
15. Handling, Cleaning, Storage, Packaging, and Delivery:                    A7-19
    (a) Document the methods used as appropriate to the need in manufacturing
       and as required by contract or jurisdiction.
    (b) Develop method for authorizing receipt and the dispatch of material.
    (c ) Make finished material identifiable.
    (d) Provide adequate storage area to prevent damage.
16. Quality Records:                    A7-20
    (a) Provide retrievable records.
    (b) Maintain a system to identify, collect, index, and store quality records.
    ( c) Record data such as qualification of personnel, procedures and
       equipment and other documentation required for this program.
17. Quality Audits:                    A7-21
    (a) Qualified personnel who is independent from affected area should be
       used.
    (b) Audit team should review the results for corrective action.
    (c ) Audit process, product, and documentation.
    (d) Re-audit for follow-up on corrective action.
18. Training:                    A7-22
    (a ) Maintain training records to show education, and experience of
       up-to-date knowledge and techniques in the area of assigned
       responsibility.

19. Service:           A7-23

    ( a ) The service division shall establish and maintain procedures for checking performance and verify that services meets the specified requirements.

20. Statistical Techniques:           A724

    ( a ) Where appropriate, establish statistical procedure for identifying the acceptable techniques for verifying the process capability of upper and lower limits of the product characteristics.

    ( b ) Statistical information shall be collected and analyzed continually.

    ( c) Emphasis shall be placed on in-process controls utilizing statistical process control techniques. ( See: A1-6 ) In-Process Control.

## CERTIFICATION AND QUALIFICATIONS     A27-25

ISO 9000-2000 SERIES:

    International standards on quality management. The standards ( adopted as ANSI/SAQC Q90-2000 series in the United States ) are the basis for business which operate in the European community. Companies that sell products in Europe and suppliers of those companies will be expected to have a quality control system which meets ISO 9000-2000 standards

- Many commercial manufactures (refrigeration, pumps, electronics, valves automotive) now require their suppliers to meet their standards.
- The department of Defense has indicated that the ISO 9000-2000 series will replace Mil-Q-98580A and MIL-I-45208A standards.

Companies wishing to purse the Malcolm Baldrige National Quality Award or supply such companies will find the implementation of an ISO 9000-2000 QC system a valuable step.

PROFESSIONAL ASSOCIATION:

The Institute of Electrical and Electronics Engineers (IEEE) www.ieee.org

Internet Society- www.isoc.org/membership

ACCREDITING ASSOCIATION: NATIONAL

Accrediting Council for Independent Colleges and Schools (ACICS). 750 First St. NE, Suite 980 Washington DC 20002-4242

Accrediting Commission of Distance Education and Training Council. 1601 18th St., NW Washington, DC 20009-2529

National Home Study Council (NHSC) 1601 Eighteenth ST. NW. Washington,DC 20009

ACCREDITING ASSOCIATIONS: REGIONAL

Southern Association of Colleges and Schools (SACS) 1866 Southern Ln. Decatur, GA 30033-4097

North Central Association of Colleges and Schools (NCACS) 159 North Dearborn St. Chicago,IL.60601

Western Association of Schools and Colleges (WASC) 533 Airport Blvd. Suite 200 Burlingame, Ca. 94010

Quality Management-  Creating attitudes and control equals prevention of defects.
Everyone becomes obsessed with quality. Symbols help:
Paris High School Quality Motto could be-
"BIRDS FLY BUT EAGLES SOAR"

Become obsessed with quality-Do it right the first time.
Don't give upon quality- Quality is a never ending process.
In courage comment- Take action on suggestion. Have a suggestion box.
Have moral leadership- Don't let lousy service or poor quality destroy your credibility.
Attitude and emotional commitment to quality must translate to practical action every day.
Have a guiding system- Pick one system and implement it religiously.
Quality is measured- at the outset of the program, be visible and be done by the
participants.
Quality is rewarded- Have a quality-based incentive compensation.
Train everyone in problem cause-and effect analysis, statistical process control, and group-
problem-solving and group-problem-solving techniques.
Have a voluntary team to take on specific problems. Disband team when problem is
solved. You don't want a bureaucratic exercise.
Everyone plays- Look for quality improvement opportunities outside the natural work
group. Remember "CROSS-FUNCTIONAL MANAGEMENT"
is a major organizational tool in realizing (Total Quality Control )
improvement goals. Use QC Element as a guide.
Small is beautiful- Every improvement to qualify does make a difference.
Don't be afraid of change-Change is good, however; leave the structure alone.
Example of change: new goals, new themes, new rewards, new
team champions, new team configuration, new celebratory
events.

Create quality organization to encourage involvement.- Steering committee,
  a recognition committee, zero defect day celebration committee.
Have a quality team.- When quality goes up, cost go down. Reducing student
  dropout makes public schools more competitive. See "The five
  parts of installation guidance specification for quality training."

## CROSBY 4 ABSOLUTES TO QUALITY

1. Definition- Conformance to requirement.
2. System- Preventive (not appraisal).
3. Performance- Zero defects
4. Cost of non-conformance
    Cost of quality = Price of conformance + Price of non-conformance

## CROSBY 14 STEPS TO QUALITY

1. Management commitment
2. Team player system
3. Measurement
4. Education/ Training
5. Cost of quality
6. Quality awareness
7. Corrective action

8. Zero defect planning
9. Zero defect day
10. Goal setting
11. Error cause removal
12. Recognition
13. Quality council
14. Do it all over again

## QUALITY MANAGEMENT GRID OF MATURITY

1. Uncertainty- Today's problem ( present ).
2. Awakening- Not today (no comment to the future).
3. Enlightenment- Relaxation of tension of attitudes.
4. Wisdom- (hold what you got ) Everyone involve.
5. Certainty- Complete defect prevention.

## FIVE STEP OF PREVENTION OF NON-CONFORMANCE

1. Clear requirements.
2. Well define process.
3. Process proving of (process capability).
4. Controllable process (TQC problem solving ).
5. Policy and system of implementation.

# TEACHING FUNDAMENTALS AND TECHNIQUES.
## (FEDS): QC ELEMENT #18 TRAINING

1. Training System.                                                              A8-1
    (A) Preparation- Training requirements and establish the course material.
    (B) Delivery- Classroom management and course management.
    (C) Evaluation- Internal and External evaluation of course material.
    (D) Objective- Identify the purpose of a training program.

2. Development of Professional Qualities-                                        A8-2
    (A) Knowledge- keep-up with subject matter through practice, study, research and new developments.
    (B) Ability- Leadership and knowing the principles, methods, and techniques of teaching, also be able to apply them effectively.
    ( C) Personality- Character, behavior able, temperamental, emotional, and mental traits of an individual.
    (D) Objective- Determine traits for a basis for self evaluation and self-help.

3. Faculty Responsibilities- Notice changes in students' performance or behavior.   A8-3
    (A) Teach effectively.
    (B) Set a good example for them to follow.
    (C) Help them resolve conflicts that hinder training.
    (D) Safety in the classroom.

4. Motivation- Maslow's Theory                                                   A8-4
    (A) Individuals will seek higher growth needs only when lower order ( deficiency) needs have been satisfied. Physiology, social, ego, and Self actualization.
    (B) Principles-Needs and drives, interest, value, attitudes, incentives and achievement.

4. Motivation-Maslow's Theory cont'd:                                    A8-4
    (C ) Techniques- Make the subject matter interesting, establish goals, provide
        informative feedback, show interest in your students and encourage
        participation.
    (D) Application- Use techniques in each part of a lesson participation.

5. Principles of Learning-                                               A8-5
    (A) Ways of Learning- Imitation, trial and error, association, insight and transfer.
    (B) Motivation of Learning- Intrinsic, extrinsic, reward, punishment, competition,
        praise and reproof and knowledge of results.
    (C ) Laws of Learning- Readiness, effect, primacy, exercise and intensity.
    (D) Factor Affecting Learning-Motivation, 5 senses, retention, practice, and a
        person's ability to balance or move with coordination.
    (E) Objective- Identify the principles of learning, identify the factors that effect
        learning.

### 5B MOTIVATION OF LEARNING                                           A8-6
(1) Intrinsic Motivation- Personal satisfaction.
    Extrinsic Motivation- Prestige or salary increase, etc.
(2) Reward- Skill learned, accomplishment, understanding, school marks, prizes,
    certificates, award, honors. * IF SOCIETY VALUES LEARNING AND
    WISHES TO ENCOURAGE IT, THEN IT IS DESIRABLE TO REWARD
    IT.
(3) Punishment- Use to direct behavior into the proper channels, called "Testing
    the Limits". Set limit of behavior for operation of consistency.

## 5B MOTIVATION OF LEARNING CONT'D

(4) Competition- Competing with one's own previous records is desirable/group competition follows.

(5) Praise and Reproof- Use reproof and criticism sparingly; however; use praise to improve performance and group morale.

(6) Knowledge of Results- Update progress, make correction of errors and knowledge of progress is important to maintenance of a high degree of motivation.

6. Students Characteristics.                                                A8-7

    (A) What Common- Belief in their maturity, quick to form opinions, everyone makes mistakes, like to be treated like equals and like to be recognized for a job well done.

    (B) What Different- Physical and mental capabilities,

       1. Ability in processing information.

       2. Mental traits like ambition and reasoning ability.

       3. Students' experiences and background.

       4. Attitude and behavior.

       5. Gender Bias.

7. Effective Communication.                                                A8-8

    (A) Principles- Remove barriers like experience, confusion of concepts and ideas, fear of ignorance, disapproval, losing status and judgment; other barriers are environmental factors like noise, temperature, seating arrangement and location. In addition, a knowledge of the communication principles will assist you in communicating effectively.

    (B) Skills and Techniques- Listening, understandable speech, correct grammar, inflection, delivery, humor, and feedback makes the learning process an intercommunication between student and teacher.

8. ORAL Questioning-                                                      A8-9
    (A) Purpose- Arouses interest, stimulate thinking, and focuses attention on subject matter.
    (B) Characteristics- Ask questions using simple words, correct grammar, and complete sentences. Use the interrogatory word or phrase at the beginning of your question. Make question brief, and limit them to one thought.
    (C) Type- Factual, Thought- provoking, interest-arousing, multiple answer, yes/no, leading, and canvassing questions.
    (D) Techniques- Set the same standards for responding to questions and enforce them uniformly. Five step technique:
        1. State the Question       2. Pause          3. Call on Student
        4. Comment/Response       5. Repeat Answer


9. Instructional Methods- Educational approach for turning knowledge
    into learning.                                                       A8-10
    (A) Lecture Method- A presentation of information, concepts, or principles and depends primarily on student listening and note-taking skill for transfer of learning.
    (B) Lesson Method- Follow a lesson plan, checks for understanding thought out the lesson, uses training aids to support objectives.
    (C) Demonstration Method- Remember the law of primacy (STUDENTS RETAIN INFORMATION THEY LEARN FOR THE FIRST TIME LONGER THAN THEY RETAIN INFORMATION THEY MUST RELEARN). Show and explain the operation. Observe safety precaution. Give proper attention to terminology. Check student comprehension.

64

9. Instructional Methods cont'd                                      A8-10

  (D) Role-Playing-Requires the students to assume active roles in a simulated
      situation followed by a group discussion. Develops leadership and human
      relations skills. The steps are describe the situation. Then analyze and evaluate
      the enactment. Make correction.

  (E) Case Study- The main objective of a case study is for students to learn from
      experience and develop problem solving skills. Present the class with a case
      study in printed forms, pictures, role-playing, or oral presentations. Divide
      class into groups to analyze why or how the incident happened and how it can
      be prevented.

10. Discussion- Useful in teaching skills such as problem solving and          A8-11
      understanding cause-and-effect relationships. Involves an interchange of
      ideas, for the purpose of developing attitude toward a subject or situation.

11. Learning Objectives- Provide the foundation upon which course curriculum    A8-12
      is built.

  (A) Objectives- Identify the different types of learning objectives.

  (B) Objectives- Determine the various learning objective elements.

12. Learning Objectives Classification- Cognitive and affective plus psychomotor  A8-13
      domain is based on the assumption that learning outcomes can best be
      described as CHANGE IN STUDENT BEHAVIOR.

  (A) Cognitive Domain- Knowledge, comprehension, application, analysis,
      synthesis, and evaluation.

11. Learning Objectives Classification cont'd

    (B) Psychomotor Domain- Principles of learning closely associated with this
        domain include:  INITIATION, Trail and Error, Transfer, Association
        and Transfer.

    ( C) Categories of the psychomotor domain are as follow;

        1. Perception- Use of sensory organs to perform certain action.

        2. Set- Mental, physical, and emotional readiness to act.

        3. Guided Response- Learning through imitation and trial and error in the
           performance of defined criteria.

        4. Mechanism- Response learning were the students perform skills with
           confidence and proficiency.

        5. Complex Overt Response- Demonstrate proficiency in coordinated
           motor activities.

        6. Adaptation- transfer learning skills to perform new but related tasks.

        7. Origination- Emphasize creativity performance in using developed
           skill in responding to particular situation.

        8. Affective Domain- Measuring learning objectives associated with
           emotions and feelings toward the subject.                  A8-14

11. Learning Objectives Elements- Define what the student will be able to do,
        Under what conditions, and to what degree of proficiency.

    (A)  Behavior Element- Specifies student performance.

    (B)  Condition Element- Limiting Factor imposed upon the student.
               When combined with the behavior element, the
               condition element provides a clearer understanding
               of the learning outcome defined.

    ( C) Standard Element- Measure student accomplishment against some criteria,
               normally defined as time, accuracy, quantity, speed or
               other quantifiable measurement.

11. Types of Learning Objectives- Different approaches in measuring student     A8-15
Performance, behavior and skills.

   1. Course Learning Objectives- Guide for learning and as a guide for teaching.

   2. Topic Learning Objectives- Support course learning objectives in measuring
acquire knowledge and skills as a result of completing the topic.

   3. Terminal Objectives- Support the course mission statement and expect the
student to show a specific skill or performance as the result of training.

   4. Enabling Objectives- Supports a Terminal Objective and expects the student to
show a specific behavior as the result of training.

11. Construction of Learning Objectives- Learning objective is information that     A8-16
convey the message of desired learning outcome and the condition and standard
which the student must perform.

   1. What the student will be able to do; knowledge, mental skill and physical skill.

   2. Condition statement or limit and aiding factor to performance; State, solve, or
measure.

   3. Standard statement describing the criteria of acceptable performance.

SOURCE: NAVY INSTRUCTOR MANUAL. Pp. 1-71, by Navy Education and Training
    Command. NAVEDTRA 134. (NETPMSA), Pensacola, Florida.

## TEACHING FUNDAMENTALS AND TECHNIQUES.
## (FEDS): QC ELEMENT #18 TRAINING.

1. What is the goal of the system approach? To establish uniform training.

2. What are the three objectives of training? To develop knowledge, skills, and attitudes.

3. What is the greatest challenge for teachers in motivating students to learn? Getting students involved and interested in learning.

4. What are the key principles of the motivation theory? 1. Need & Drive 2. Interest 3. Values 4. Attitude 5. Incentives 6. Achievement

5. The lesson introduction is used to accomplish what action? To motivate students to learn.

6. What type of question do you direct to the students but don't expect them to answer. Rhetorical

7. The terms imitation, trial and error, association, insight, and transfer best describes What in regard to learning? Ways of learning

8. What law of learning is based on the maxim that practice makes perfect? Exercise

9. Training is aimed at what type of learner? Average

10. What barrier is one of the greatest obstacles to effective communication? Fear

11. What is the most powerful element of the teachers presence in front of a class? Direct eye contact

12. What is the primary purpose of oral questioning? Stimulate students to think

13. In teaching skills such as problem solving and understanding cause-and-effect relationships, what teaching method should you use? Directed discussion

68

QUESTION & ANSWER: A8-17

14. What learning objective element specifies student performance? Behavior

15. What learning objective element defines the degree of interaction within the classroom? Condition

16. What learning objective element specifies the criteria each student's performance must meet? Standard

17. What learning objective serves as a guide for the instructor to use in measuring student performance? Course

18. Teaches administer tests for what reason? To determine achievement of the objectives

19. What are the six types of instruction sheets? 1. Information 2. Assignment 3. Problem 4. Job 5. Diagram 6. Outline

20. Teachers effectiveness in keeping students involved in the learning process deals with what evaluation factor? Teacher-Student interaction

21. Who has responsibility of classroom management? Teacher

22. What is the most important document available to you as the teacher? Lesson plan

23. What is the primary purpose of media material? To increase student understanding

24. Using media material will help to do what? Expedite learning

25. What factor greatly improves the quality of teaching? Teachers evaluation

SOURCE: Navy instructional theory NAVEDTRA 834. NAVAL EDUCATION AND TRAING COMMAND. (NETPMSA) , Pensacola, Florida.

## GENERAL DESCRIPTION

Value System Engineering in manufacturing is an organized effort by management to draw together the skills, knowledge, goodwill of consumers, suppliers, engineers, designers, and employees to create a functional top-quality product at a reasonable competitive price.

The idea behind VSE is not merely try to make a product more efficiently, but to find out what the product must do, and what will make it sell, then find the most cost effective way of changing the products function characteristics for a customers line of business.

The New Way:  Value System Engineering in Manufacturing is a system concept for building an organization that shift away from individuals working alone to the individual as part of a group, a team approach with a specific set of shared responsibilities, goals, and values.

Making manufacturing companies organization competitive is what Value System Engineering does.  Value System Engineering is designed around the principles of value engineering, quality control, the eight stages of industrial cycle, and "Simultaneous Engineering".

Five main integrating parts make up this system for manufacturing they are as follow:

1. Quality Control Department
2. Value System Engineering Department
3. Value System Engineering Divisions
4. Function Characteristics
5. Function Analysis Decision Tables

In addition to these FIVE main integrating parts are the environmental factors seen in the market place.  Although not part of Value System Engineering these factors increase cost, and put competitive pressure on manufacturing.

Good management keeps one eye on the business and the other on the outward; the latter I call Value System Engineering.

According to American Society of Tool and Manufacturing Engineering, "Value engineering offers a planned, cooperative approach and broadened viewpoint in arriving at many of the basic decisions of an industrial enterprise. It is one of the tools which any rational management should deeply consider in manipulation of the resources under its control" (1-3).

For the purpose of this report; however, VSE is work that takes place entirely within the system boundary, a plan maintenance tool necessary for the survival of a company.

Using VSE as a plan maintenance tool allows a company to be flexible, fast, street smart, and charge oriented. A company does this by not re-inventing information, and by being conscious that the unknown and uncontrollable factor of the environment contain many elements that can effect the company cost and productivity.

Using accurate information enables plant managers to eliminate that which is unnecessary, and make the correct decision in what is necessary to keep cost down, and productivity up.

## VSE GOAL

Producing a product that is cost effective, efficient, and more reliable than the baseline design product is Value System Engineering Goal.

## VSE OBJECTIVE

VSE objective is to communicate progress and work areas; to stimulate all those associated in manufacturing a product, to make suggestions for improvement.

This objective is met by having eight separate division create higher-quality information out of lower-quality data for decision making. Divisional personnel meet the above objective by writing instructions and notices for management to plan and implement day-to-day changes in their organization.

Division personnel work as part of a group, a team approach with a specific set of share responsibility, goal, and value.

The reason for using a team approach is to mutually identify necessary skills, resources, and guidelines that are available. This helps to build realistic job expectation, and prevent misunderstanding later.

Using a team approach also improves individual performance by giving the employee the big picture in term of the job outcome, and how individual assign task fits into a company theme of things for improved output, quality, or cost control.

This is different than the old way in business where the vast majority of employees concentrate on two short-term goals; getting the job done and solving any problems that arise during the course of the job.

Informing divisional personnel of the task importance to the overall objective, available time and deadlines, and how much time they have for doing the task, and which task needs to be done first requires good reporting.

In addition, good reporting provides information that is factual, on time, relevant, and easy to interpret by upper management.

According to Juran and Gryna in "Quality Planning Analysis" there are four types of standard used for making a report(4-520). They are as follow:

1.  Engineering Standards is based on material usage, and labor hours. Managers use this type of report to show results which the engineering studies showed were attainable.

2.  Historical Standards is based on statistical computation of past performance. Managers use this type of report to see if things are getting better or worse in the company.

3.  Market Standards is based on competitors performance. Managers use this type of report to make a comparison of how we stand compared to our competitors.

4.  Planned Standards is base on company resources. Managers use this type of report to see if the overall planned goal is being obtained.

## VSE DIVISIONS

According to Dr. Juran, there are eight stages of the industrial cycle in manufacturing. In this book, "The Quality of product and Services" (5-12). However, for the purpose of this report, instead of being called cycles they are called divisions. Each separate industrial cycle is set-up as an integrating non-linear division.

The eight divisions and their guidelines for conduct, and what is expected from each division is as follows:

1. Marketing Division (VSE-1): Evaluates the level of quality which customers want and for which they are willing to pay.     A9-1

2. Engineering Division (VSE-2): Reduces marketing evaluation to exact specifications.     A9-2

3. Purchasing Division (VSE-3): Retains vendors for parts and material, and choose who will receive the contracts.     A9-3

4. Manufacturing Engineering Division (VSE-4): Selects the jigs, tools, and processes for production.     A9-4

5. Manufacturing Supervision and Shop Operation Division (VSE-5): Exert a major quality influence during parts making, subassembly, and final assembly.     A9-5

6. Mechanical Inspection and Function Test Division (VSE-6): Checks product conformance to specifications.     A9-6

7. Shipping Division (VSE-7): Influence the caliber of the packaging, transportation and trace ability of the product.     A9-7

8. Installation and Service Division (VSE-8): Help ensure proper operation by installing The product according to proper instructions and maintaining it through service.     A9-8

*Material is reproduced with permission of the McGraw-Hill Companies.

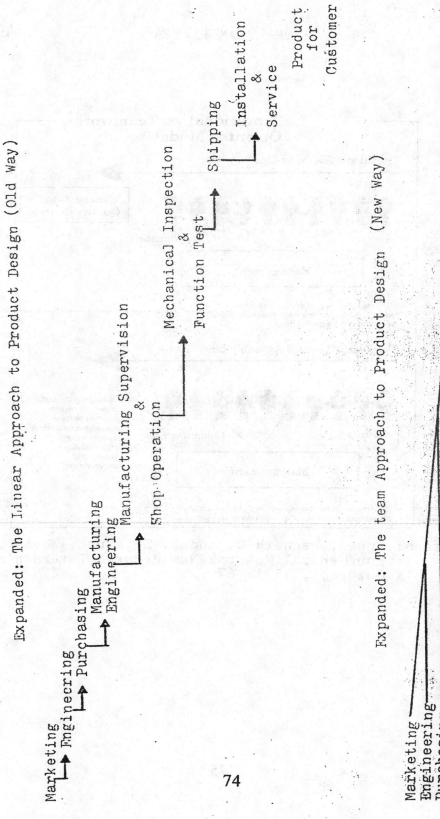

Expanded: The linear Approach to Product Design (Old Way)

Marketing
Engineering
Purchasing
Manufacturing
Engineering
Manufacturing Supervision
&
Shop Operation
Mechanical Inspection
&
Function Test
Shipping
Installation
&
Service
Product
for
Customer

Expanded: The team Approach to Product Design (New Way)

Marketing
Engineering
Purchasing
Manufacturing Engineering
Manufacturing Supervision & Shop Operation
Mechanical Inspection & Function Test
Shipping
Installation & Service
Product
Fit's Customer
Needs

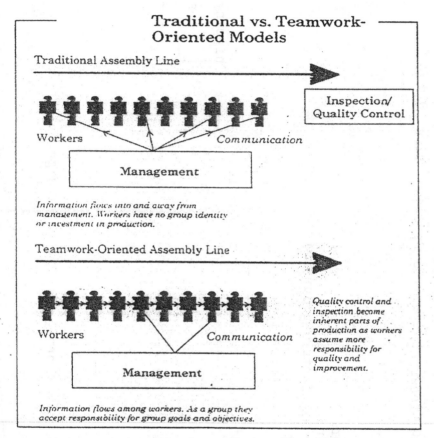

**Traditional vs. Teamwork-Oriented Models**

Traditional Assembly Line

Workers          Communication

Management

Inspection/
Quality Control

Information flows into and away from
management. Workers have no group identity
or investment in production.

Teamwork-Oriented Assembly Line

Workers          Communication

Management

Quality control and
inspection become
inherent parts of
production as workers
assume more
responsibility for
quality and
improvement.

Information flows among workers. As a group they
accept responsibility for group goals and objectives.

Sources: Green, Kenneth C. and D. Seymoure. Who's Going
         Run General Motors? New Jersey: Peterson's
         Guides P, 1991: 67 ·

## FUNCTION CHARACTERISTICS
### A9-10

Function is closely related to basic purpose of Value Engineering which is to identify and evaluate function, and provide this function at the lowest overall cost.

For example, a flashlight required function is to "provide light" and that, because of the particular design factor and environmental condition involved, a NO. 914 flashlight is developed. Note; appendix A. Only a part of the flashlight components are listed for the purpose of this example. The function of the components are described and compared to the function of the flashlight to determine if they are basic or secondary.

In evaluating an existing design (such as a NO. 914 flashlight), are to be studied. See visual description of NO. 914 flashlight. The design stage can begin after this evaluation of determining what a particular item's basic function is, and what approach will provide the overall function at the lowest cost.

Refer to NO. 914 it is interesting to note that only two components, the bulb and the battery, provide the basic function of the flashlight. Also, in reviewing the list of function which we feel are secondary, note that both the threads on the rear cap and body and the threads on the front cap and body provide an identical function-- "permit access."

Ask yourself must this function be provided twice? No. There are flashlights that provide access by only the front cap and body threads.

The function, "permit access," relates to either the front or the rear cap and body threads, is unnecessary and one of them can be eliminated.

APPENDIX A

No.914
HEAVY DUTY
FLASHLIGHT

VISUAL ILLUSTRATION DRAWING NO. 914 FLASHLIGHT

A9-11

PLASTIC LENS

INSIDE THREADS

#212 REPLACEMENT BULB

STEEL REINFORCED LIGHT REFLECTOR

BULB PROTECTOR

OUTSIDE THREADS

OCTAGON NO-ROLL HEAD

FRONT CAP ASSEMBLY
COLOR: YELLOW
WT: 3oz  LTH: 5cm

COLOR: YELLOW SWITCH

SWITCH GUARD

RIVETED POINTS

BATTERY HOUSING UNIT
COLOR: BLACK
WT: 1oz  LTH: 18cm

OUTSIDE THREADS

INSIDE THREADS

REAR CAP ASSEMBLY
COLOR: YELLOW
WT: 2oz  LTH: 4cm

RING HANGER

77

INTRODUCTION- General Description
The NO. 914 heavy duty flashlight is made of tough millimeter thick polyethylene construction that resists damage from oil, gas, grease, water, and most chemicals.

The flashlight is 25 centimeters or 8 inches in length, weighs 6 ounces without the batteries, takes a standard NO. 214 replacement light bulb, and uses (2) 1.5VDC class "D" cell battery for power.

The flashlight is American made, and comes in three main parts: Front cap assembly, rear cap assembly, and battery housing unit.

Description of Parts and Their Function
Front Cap Assembly:
The yellow front cap assembly features a non-roll octagon head. The threads inside the front cap assembly allows for easy access to reflector assembly.

The plastic lens inside the front cap is one millimeter thick, and has a diameter of five centimeters. The lens function is to protect the bulb, and keep water and dirt from entering the battery housing unit.

The steel reinforced light reflector contains the NO. 214 (incandescent) filament bulb. The bulb fits inside a polyethylene shell protector which is two centimeters deep. The base of the protector has a conductive copper strip that is one millimeter wide and long. The function of the copper strip is to maintain contact between batteries, bulb, and switch.

The front cap assembly screws onto the front of the battery housing unit. This assures a snug fit of the reflector assembly.

Total weight: 3 ounces;          Total length: 5 centimeters

Rear Cap Assembly:
The yellow rear cap assembly retains the tension spring. The tension spring is spiral in shape. The spring is made of metal that has conducting properties. The function of the tension spring is to maintain tension, and positive contact with other components.

## Rear Cap Assembly: cont'd

The threads inside the rear cap assembly allows for loading of the batteries. The rear cap assembly screws onto the back of the battery housing unit.

The ringer hanger attached to the base of rear cap assembly is made of metal and looks like a small horseshoe. The ringer allows the user to clip the flashlight on their person.

Total weight: 2 ounces        Total length: 4 centimeters

## Battery Housing Unit

The black battery housing unit holds (2) 1.5 VDC "D" class cell batteries. Inside the unit is conductive copper bar strip that is 15 centimeters long and 1 centimeter wide.

The on / off switch is located on the outside of the housing, when pushed forward, causes the contacts to make contact and slide along this bar. This action completes the circuit the circuit which is the function of the on / off switch.

The copper bar switch and the on / off switch are riveted to the housing. This keeps the bar and switch from being able to move; as a result the flashlight switch is more dependable, and is less likely to cause the flashlight to malfunction.

Total weight: 1 ounce        Total length: 18 centimeters

Note: Refer to Drawing for visual illustration of No. 914 Heavy Duty
       Flashlight.

| Item and Components | Function | Basic | Secondary |
|---|---|---|---|
| Flashlight | Provide Light | X | X |
| Lens | Protect bulb | | X |
| Rear Cap | Retain spring | | X |
| Thread on Rear Cap and Body | Permit access | | X |
| Bulb | Provide light | X | |
| Front Cap | Hold lens | | X |
| Threads on Front Cap and Body | Permit access | | X |
| Battery | Provide Energy | X | |

Basic Function: The specific purpose for which the item was designed.

Secondary Function: Action which supports their basic function, and results from a specific design approach.

Unnecessary Function: Those characteristics of an item which are not required either as a basic function or a secondary function.

According to Juran/Gryna in Quality Planning and Analysis.
New York: McGraw-Hill Inc. 1980

*Material is reproduced with permission of the McGraw- Hill Companies.

## FUNCTION ANALYSIS DECISION:

Function analysis decision tables are control guides to coordinate action of each division to achieve VSE goal of creating a top-quality, safe product at reasonable, and competitive price.

When doing a design analysis all VSE division personnel should remember that a function consists of more than just product performance.

The greatest benefit in doing a function characteristic analysis is recognized at the beginning of research and development. This is because a design engineer can analyze this design to determine an alternative design if necessary, however, this advantage decreases as the item is created.

The following list below should help a design engineer in determining an alternative design if necessary.

|  | VSE Parameter | A9-12 |

List of characteristics which is kept constant while other characteristics are being investigated.

|  | VSE Safety Precautions | A9-13 |

List of references that could have an impact on safety, they should be evaluated by the Safety Engineer prior to implementation. For example, Hydraulic Systems. A10-19

|  | VSE Cause and Effect | A9-14 |

Use problem solving techniques:  A10-4
1. Brainstorming- Quantity and diversity is your goal.
2. Gather Information- Making what is unknown is your goal.
3. Organize your Data- Find and trace your problem back through their symptoms for a solution.

|  | VSE Cost Effectiveness | A9-15 |

Design review by various specialists to provide early warning of potential trouble.

|  | VSE Questions for Developing Alternative Design | A9-16 |

A10-5

Starter questions for developing alternative designs. When asking these questions keep in mind that changes can effect degree of repeatability; also will this change make it easier to maintain or easier to use by the consumer.

1. What is the normal operating mode?
2. What is the moving capacity?
3. What is the physical location of the indicators?
4. What is the alarm set point?
5. What are the allowable operating limits?
6. How long will it last during continuous use?
7. Where are the parameters sensed or monitored?

VSE Safety Precautions & Compliance            A9-13

1. What are the safety devices and where are they located?
2. What are the handling precautions?
3. What are the specific markings noted: color mode?
4. What are the cleaning agents?
5. What are the lubricating aids?
6. What are the storage precaution/flash point?
7. What are the power sources?
8. What are the hydraulic safety precautions?
9. What are the pneumatic safety precautions?
10. What type of fluid is required?
11. What type of hoses are required?
12. Where are the gages located?
13. Where are the relief valves located?
14. Where are the automatic safety devices located?
15. Where are the interlocks located?
16. Where are the switches/circuit breakers located?
17. Where are the fuses located?
18. Where are the filters located?
19. Where are the guards/cover located?
20. Where is the alarm located?

Note: General Safety- Accountability/Training/Participation.
VSE Cause and Effect...............Fishbone Diagram.

Raw Materials                                                     A9-14

1. How are they produced?
2. How old are they?
3. How was their quality judged prior to your operation?
4. What was their level of quality?
5. How were they packaged?
6. How were they stored? For how long?
7. Does temperature, light or humidity affect their quality?
8. Who was the supplier? Has their been a change in supplier?

## Worker

1. Does he have adequate supervision and support?
2. Does he know what he is expected to do on his job?
3. How much experience does he have?
4. Does he have the proper motivation to do his work?
5. Is he satisfied or dissatisfied with his job?
6. Is he more or less productive at certain times of the day?
7. Does he have a physical condition that may affect his work?
8. Do physical conditions such as light or temperature in the place affect the work?
9. Does he have the tools he needs to do his job?
10. Whom does he contact when problems arise?
11. Is the work load reasonable?

## Inspection Methods

1. How frequently are products inspected?
2. How is the measuring equipment calibrated?
3. Are all products measured using the same tools or equipment?
4. How are inspection results recorded?
5. Do inspections follow the same procedures? (Is there set standards?)
6. Do inspectors know how to use the test equipment?

## Process

1. How old is the equipment or machinery?
2. Is it maintained regularly?
3. Is the process affected by heat or vibration or other physical features?
4. How does the operator know if the process is operating correctly?
5. What are the adjustments the operator must make during the process?
6. Have any changes recently been made in the process?

Note: see pp. 84     Fishbone Cause and Effect Diagram.

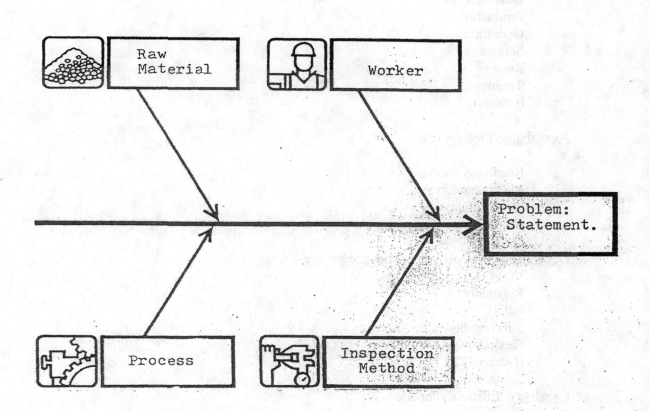

Total Costs (Life Cycle)

Concept Studies:
      Development
      Production
      Operation
      Service
      Repair
      Training
      (Others)

Availability: Free for use

      Readiness
      Maintainability
      Serviceability
      (Others)

Dependability: Degree of confidence for use

      Reliability
      Safety
      Survivability
      Flexibility
      (Others)

Capability: Efficiency for use

      Power
      Range
      Accuracy
      Speed
      Fidelity
      Number of channels
      (Others)

Source: Juran and Gryna. Quality Planning and Analysis.
      New York: McGraw, INC. 1980:169

*Material is reproduced with permission of the McGraw Companies.

General:

1. Can the design be changed to eliminate the part?
2. Can the present design be purchased at lower cost?
3. Can a standard part be used?
4. Would an altered standard part be more economical?
5. If the part is to be improved in appearance, is this justified?
6. Is there a less costly part that will perform the same function?
7. Can the design be changed to simplify the part?
8. Will the design permit standard inspection equipment to be used?
9. Can a part designed for other equipment be used?
10. Can a less expensive material be used?
11. Can the number of different materials be reduced?
12. Are there newly developed materials that can be used?

Machining:

1. Are all machined surfaces necessary?
2. Will a courser finish be adequate?
3. Does design permit the use of standard cutting tools?
4. Are tolerances closer than they need to be?
5. Can another material be used that would be easier to machine?
6. Can a fastener be used to eliminate tapping?
7. Can weld nuts be used instead of a tapped hole?

Assembly:

1. Can two or more parts be combined into one?
2. Can parts be made symmetrical?
3. Is there a newly developed fastener to speed assembly?
4. Are a minimum number of hardware sizes used?
5. Are stock components called for where possible?
6. Can roll pins be used to eliminate reaming?

## VSE Questions for Developing Alternative Design cont:

Specifications and Standards:

A9-16

1. Is there a standard part that can replace a manufactured item?

2. Can an altered standard part be used instead of a special part?

3. Can any specifications be changed to effect cost reduction?

4. Can standard actuating devices be used, such as cylinders or gear motors?

5. Is standard hardware used?

6. Are all threads standard?

7. Can standard cutting tools be used?

8. Can standard gages be used?

9. Is material available with tolerance and finish that will eliminate machining?

Source: ASTM Publications Committee. Value Engineering in Manufacturing. New Jersey: Prentice-Hall, INC. P, 1967:75

1. A quality program has the best foundation for success when it is initiated by: Chief executive of company.

2. The most important measure of outgoing quality needed by managers is product performance as viewed by: customer.

3. A fully developed position description for a quality engineer must contain clarification of: answers

4. When giving instructions to those who will perform a task, the communication process is completed: when the worker acknowledges these instructions by describing how he or she will perform the task.

5. From the definition of reliability, it follows that in any reliability program there must be:
   1. a quantification of reliability in terms of probability.
   2. a clear statement defining successful performance.
   3. a definition of the environment in which the equipment must operate.
   4. a statement of the required operating times between failures.

6. When the reliability people say they are breaking the monopoly of the designer, they mean: they intend to put the reliability engineer one level higher than the design engineer in the organization.

7. It is Reliability's job to see that all the tasks outlined in the reliability are: carried out by the department having the primary responsibility.

8. The process of dividing up or budgeting the final reliability goal among the subsystems is known as: reliability apportionment.

9. Reliability production is: a continuous process starting with paper predictions.

10. Reliability prediction and and measurement is primarily useful in:
    1. evaluating feasibility
    2. establishing reliability goals
    3. evaluating overall reliability
    4. defining problem areas

11. Preventive maintenance is defined as: action performed on a scheduled or routine basis to retain an item in a specified condition.

12. Reliability testing of parts is performed to yield which type of information?
    1. application suitability
    2. environmental capability
    3. measurement of life characteristics

13. Human factors inputs: should be incorporated during the detailed design phase.

14. Good housekeeping is an important quality factor in a supplier's plant because:
    1. it promotes good working conditions
    2. it minimizes fire hazards
    3. it enhances safer operations
    4. it reflects favorably on the efficiency and management of a company

15. A pre-award survey of a potential supplier is best described as an assessment audit.

16. The most desirable method of evaluating a supplier is: history evaluation.

17. The most important step in vendor certification is to: visit the vendor's plant.

18. During the pre-award survey at a potential key supplier, you discover the existence of a quality control manual. This means: that a quality system has been developed.

20. A vendor must perform tests on parts to determine functional capabilities under specified environmental conditions.

21. In recent months, several quality problems have resulted from apparent change in design specifications by engineering, including material substitutions. This has only come to light through Quality Engineering's failure-analysis system. You recommend which of the following quality system provisions as the best corrective action? establish formal procedures for specification change control.

22. When a quality engineer wants parts removed from a line which is operating for tolerance checking, he or she should: request the operator and/or supervisor to get them while being observed.

23. The quality engineer should be concerned with the human factors of a new piece of In-house manufacturing equipment as well as its operational effects because it:
    1. may speed the line to the point where a visual operator inspection is impossible.
    2. may require the operator's undivided attention at the control so the product cannot be fully seen.
    3. may remove an operator formerly devoting some portion of time to inspection.

24. The inspection plan for a new product line includes:
   1. detailing production schedule
   2. sampling procedures and techniques
   3. internal techniques for control and segregation of conforming or nonconforming products

25. Classification of defects is most essential as a prior step to a valid establishment of: economical sampling inspection.

26. When giving instructions to those who will perform a task, the communication process is completed: when the worker acknowledges these instructions by describing how he or she will perform the task.

27. The primary reason that nonconforming material should be identified and segregated is: so it cannot be used in production without proper authorization.

28. What type of sensory testing are used in a number of industries to evaluate their products?
   1. triangle test
   2. duo-trio test
   3. ranking test
   4. paired-comparison test

30. One of the major hazards in the material review board procedure is the tendency of the board to emphasize only the deposition function and to neglect the corrective action.

31. A technique whereby various product features are graded and varying degrees of quality control applied is called? Classification of characteristics.

32. One method to control inspection costs even without a budget is by comparing inspection hours as a ratio productive machine time to produce the product.

33. In a visual inspection situation, one of the best ways to minimize deterioration of the quality level is to: have a standard to compare against a part of the information.

34. A variable measurement of a dimension should include: a controlled measurement procedure.

35. If not specifically required by the product drawing (s) or specification, a nondestructive test (NDT) may be required during production and/or during acceptance at the discretion of the quality engineer responsible for the inspection planning: because NDT is a form of inspection (with enhanced senses) not a functional test.

36. When specifying the "10:1 calibration principle, "we are referring to what? The ratio of calibration standard accuracy to calibrated instrument accuracy.

37. A qualification test is used to determine that design and selected production methods will yield a product that conforms to specification. An acceptance that is used to determine that a completed product to conform to design. On this basis, a destructive test can be used for: qualification or acceptance.

38. Measuring and test equipment are calibrated to: determine and/or assure their accuracy.

39. A basic requirement for most gage calibration system specifications is: all equipment shall be labeled or coded to indicate date calibrated, by whom, and date due for next calibration.

40. What four functions are necessary to have an acceptable calibration system covering, measuring, and testing equipment?
    1. calibration sources
    2. calibration intervals
    3. humidity control
    4. utilization of published standards

41. Quality information equipment: makes measurements of either products or processes and feeds the resulting data back for decision making.

42. Calibration intervals should be adjusted when: a particular characteristic on a gage is consistently found out of tolerance.

43. A typical use for the optical comparator would be to measure: contours

44. The following is a legitimate audit function:
    1. identify function responsible for primary control and corrective action
    2. provide no surprises
    3. contribute to a reduction quality cost

45. In many programs, what is generally the weakest link in the quality auditing program? Follow-up of corrective action implementation.

46. The following items should be included by management when establishing a quality audit function within their organization?
    1. proper positioning of the audit function within the quality organization.
    2. a planned audit approach, efficient and timely audit reporting, and a method for obtaining effective corrective action.
    3. selection of capable audit personnel.
    4. management objectivity toward the quality program audit concept.

47. Assurance bears the same relation to the quality function that audit does to the accounting function.

48. The following technique should be used in a quality audit:
   1. select samples only from completed lots.
   2. examine samples from viewpoint of critical customer.
   3. use audit information in future design planning.
   4. frequency of audit to depend on economic and quality requirements.

49. The following quality provision is of concern when preparing an audit checklist for the upcoming branch operation quality system audit.
   1. drawing and print control
   2. engineering design change control
   3. control of special processes
   4. calibration of test equipment

50. The following schemes could be used in selecting the audit team to optimize continuity, direction, availability, and technology transfer required to establish an audit program of a quality system.
   1. a full time audit staff
   2. all-volunteer audit staff
   3. the boss's son and son-in-law
   4. by rid audit staff (a proportion of 1&2)

51. The following is the responsibility of the auditor:
   1. prepare a plan and checklist
   2. report results to those responsible
   3. follow up to see if the corrective action was taken

Source: Juran and Gryna. Quality Planning and Analysis.
(References: Quality Progress, February 1976, pp. 23-31; August 1978, p. 28.)

Answers to examples of examination questions used in former ASQC Quality Engineer And Reliability Engineer Certification Examinations.

Alternative: One of the two things which must be chosen.

Analytical Thinking: Mental activity leading from an unsatisfactory state to a more desired satisfactory state.

Certain Events: Events that already take place before the instance of observation.

Choice: Opportunity and privilege of choosing freely.

Choice & Selection: Conflict within the decision maker.

Components: Major units that make up a system when properly connected.

Component Part: Major part of a component.

Control: Process which measures current performance and guides it towards some predetermined goal.

Control Signal: Signal used to control electronic or mechanical devices.

Cost: Total of all payments made by a company for capital, physical facilities, material and manpower.

Cost Effective: Lowest overall costs considering all aspects of and effects on the business.

Cost of Services: Placing a dollar equivalent value on the function usages.

Creativity: The ability to think about alternatives.

Decision: Settles external conflict of one sort or another.

Decision Process: Option, Choice, Selection, and Decision.

Defect: Critical- Affects Life and Safety.
    Major- Affects Product Function.
    Minor- Affects Product Appearance.

Environment: Relates to the system's goal, needs, activities and individuals interacting with the system.

Esteen Value: Characteristic which makes the user want to own the item.

**Esthetic Value:** Characteristic which makes an item appealing or a thing of beauty.

**Evaluate by Comparison:** Placing a dollar equivalent value of something readily known.

**Exchange Value:** Properties or qualities of an item which enables it to be traded for something else. Use Value + Esteen Value = Exchange Value.

**Factors of the Environment:** Not part of a system. The distinction between "in-the system" and environment" is drawn along a system boundary.

**Function:** Purpose or objective of the product or operation under consideration on those explicit performance characteristics that must be possessed by the hardware if it is to sell.

**Fundamentals:** Basic facts, theories, law or principles.

**Growth:** Progressive development of a company.

**In-Process Control:** Preventive technique used by Quality Control Specialist that involves responding to problems when they first materialize and establish control charts to prevent problems from arising in the first place.

**Innovation:** Search for Change.

**Interlock:** Protective device to prevent the unsafe operation of equipment or to sequence the action of systems, components, or component parts.

**Leadership:** Lead you into your job; entails providing an environment that will inspire and motivate people to overcome obstacles.

**Maintenance:** System work that takes place entirely within the system boundary; concerned with ensuring components to perform their proper function in a proper way.

**Non-Value Adding Operation:** Those operations that take time, resources or space, but do not add to the value of the product itself.

Normal Operating Value: Point at which satisfactory performance may be expected.

Operating Limits: Maximum and minimum allowable value.

Operator Action: Optimum for normal operation or proper operation to stop before damage may occur, operation require to open or shut a device.

Option: Right to exercise the power of choice.

Parameters: Variable (Temperature, pressure, flow rate, voltage, current, frequency etc.) That must be indicated, monitored, checked or sense during operation or testing.

Problem Solving: Recognition, Definition, and Solution.

Selection: Picking out one or more items from a larger number or similar items.

Sensing Point: Point in a system at which a signal may be detected.

Set Point: Value of a parameter at which (a) an alarm is set off. (b) operator action is required (c ) value open or shut. (d) proper operation required to stop something before damage may occur, or (e) optimum value for normal operation.

Sources of Power: Circuits or devices that supply power energy or charge to a component/compo net parts; includes: electrical, mechanical, hydrulicand pneumatic.

System: Groups of components that operate together to perform specific function, also, composed of functions that are related to each other to achieve a goal.

System Boundary: Set of system functions whose behavior is not solely determined by the behavior of other system functions.

Teamwork: Emphasizes on individual and group responsibility for completing the assigned task.

Policy: Guidelines for conduct and what to expect from the organization.

Uncertain Events: Events expected to take place after the instance of observation, and may not happen at all.

Value: Purchasing power.

Value Engineering: Functionally oriented efforts to remove production cost prior to the release of design to production.

Value System Engineering: Technique of evaluating the function of the product or service rather than the item.

Simultaneous Engineering: A system of organization that begins solving manufacturing problems at the same time as the design process is under way.

Reverse Engineering: Technique used by the competitor to alter or make a product that is similar without paying for patent rights from the original designer.

Interface auxiliary material allows the user (parents, students and teachers) away to input specific information necessary for transferring subject matter (curriculum) in an orderly fashion into "FEDS".

Auxiliary material input data allows everyone to comprehend the basic concepts necessary to develop, and understand how to deliver the information needed for teaching subject matter objectives: using this "how-to" information will also take a lot of hassle and stress out of teaching.

For example: Design Parameters (D&P) curriculum training aid (A2-8F) "Instruction Sheets"- used to convey to students detailed information needed to understand the learning activity they must undertake. The six types are as follow:

1. Diagram Sheets (A10-10)          2. Information Sheets (A10-11)
3. Job Sheets (A10-12)              4. Problem Sheets (A10-13)
5. Assignment Sheets (A10-14)       6. Outline Sheets (A10-15)

## INTERFACE AUXILIARY MATERIAL PARAMETERS

1. Refresh parents, students, and teachers memory of subject matter and allow away to incorporate what they have learn into their daily routine: beside helping them reach the next level of learning. Ex: D&P; pp. 15-19.
2. Organize subject matter in such form that features clear instruction, and provide worked out examples to reinforce learning objectives. (pp. 97-165)
3. Explain useful methods of solving problems from the point of view that it is the individual best interest to learn, and remember the basics. Ex: A10-4; pp. 99-99C.
4. Provide supporting material that correspond, and aids "FEDS subject material in the area of fundamental of teaching, and home schooling. Ex: Standardized Testing & Reporting (T&R-A4) National Assessment of Educational Progress (NAEP). pp. 30.
5. List supporting material that correspond, and aids "FEDS" subject material in the area of quality control, and value engineering in sustainable development that relates to the understanding the full live cycle of products and services in the present and future. Ex: Life Cycle Concept Studies. (VSE-A9-15) pp. 85.
6. Make available material pertaining to math, and chemistry fundamentals because an individual who is going to furthering their education should know this material. Ex: Conversion problems A10-27; pp.132-165.

In addition, everyone should be familiar with "FEDS" material at the workplace. On the other hand, if the worker or student at this....time....doesn't understand 3R's basic, and llack a general understanding of science, math, and chemistry as it relates to the workplace, will find this information beneficial.

In summary, there are many books available as supplement to textbooks; however, these books usually are inadequate as a means of allowing parents, and students to "brush up" on what they forgot or would like to know. Besides, statistically it has been found that one of the indicators of a persons leadership potential is his or hers understanding of mathematics, and how to analyze a problem.

SUBJECT:_____

INTRO = Introduce self & your subject-history.


OBJECTIVE (S):  Reason for this class.


MAIN SUBJECT BODY:


CONCLUSION:  Review high points.


CLOSE - QUESTION & ANSWER:  Ask questions for review or ask for questions from class.


_____

_____          _____          _____
Class Instructor                                                       Date of Class

_____          _____ YES - NO
Class Location                         Class Roster

Material, tool, equipment and/or authorization for same needed for class:

_____

_____

_____

Classification: Classified, Unclassified, Secret, etc.
Allotted class time: 60 minutes/120 minutes
References:

Instructional Aides:
      i.e. Materials, tools, handouts, equipment, projectors or authorization for same.

I    Intro:
        A. Establish contact - introduce self and lesson
            1. Instructors name and rate - write on chalkboard if available.
            2. Instructors background - qualifications to give class.
            3. Lesson topic - write on chalkboard.

        B. Lesson Objectives - after this class you will be able to.......
            1. Explain the function of......
            2. Recognize the components on......
            3. Etc. - list as many as you have for subject.

        C. Motivation or Reason for Lesson:
            1. This lesson relates to - career benefits, civilian benefits, personal benefits, personal experiences

II Presentation:
        A. Lesson Subject - refer students to handout, etc.

        B. Components, Parts, Principles, etc.
            1. Major components

        C. Additional pertinent or related materials

        D. Safety
            1. Operator, handler or personnel in immediate area

III Summary
        A. Restate Objectives

        B. Review - major lesson & high points
            1. Ask if there are any questions.

IV Practice Exercise - Instruct the class to complete the practice exercise. Handout or orally given.

V Review
        A.  Answers to Practice Exercise

        B.  Remediation - Review correct answers to exercise.

1. List Deviation Statement (consequence)
2. Specify the Problem (what, where, when, and how much)

|  | IS | IS Not |
|---|---|---|
| What | ? | ? |
| Where | ? | ? |
| When | ? | ? |
| How much | ? | ? |

3. Develop Possible Causes. ? ?
4. Distinguish the Difference between is and is not.
5. Test for most probable cause.
6. Verify

## EXAMPLE PROBLEM

1. A TRAIN IS OPERATED BY THREE MEN, SMITH, JONES, AND ROBINSON, BUT NOT RESPECTIVELY.

2. ON THE TRAIN ARE THREE PASSENGERS, MR. SMITH, MR. JONES, AND MR. ROBINSON.

3. MR. ROBINSON LIVES IN DETROIT.

4. THE BRAKEMAN LIVES HALF WAY BETWEEN DETROIT AND CHICAGO.

5. MR. JONES EARNS $20,000.00 PER YEAR.

6. SMITH BEATS THE FIREMAN AT BILLIARDS.

7. THE BRAKEMAN'S NEAREST NEIGHBOR, WHO IS ONE OF THE PASSENGERS, EARNS THREE TIMES AS MUCH AS THE BRAKEMAN WHO EARNS $10,000.00 PER YAER.

8. THE PASSENGER, WHOSE NAME IS THE SAME AS THE BRAKEMAN, LIVES IN CHICAGO.

## ANSWER

7. The Brakeman makes $10,000.00 His nearest neighbor makes $30,000.00 Since we know Mr. Robinson lives in Detroit this means that __Mr. Jones__ lives in Chicago, Leaving __Mr. Smith__ as the Brakeman nearest neighbor.
8. Since __Mr. Jones__ lives in Chicago this means that __Jones__ is the Brakeman.
6. Means Smith is either the Engineer or the Brakeman. Since we already know that __Jones__ is the Brakeman this leaves __Smith__ as the Engineer.

1. List deviation statement (consequences).
2. Specify the problem (what, when, where, and how much), (is/is not).
3. Develop possible causes.
4. Distinguish the difference between is and is not.
5. Test for most probable cause,        (6). Verify.

## MATH EQUATION

1. Assign a math symbol to each quantity defined in the relationship.
   Relationships: Physical Constants, Conversion Factors (Metric/Standard),
   Variable (Independent/Dependent), Proportionality (Direct/Inversely), and
   Ratio.
2. Use these Math symbols to show relationship between symbols.
3. Use equal sign to show what is equivalent to what.

## GRAPHS

1. Graphs show relationships between two or more quantities.
2. Independent variable (one that is changed) is plotted usually on the x-axis.
3. Dependent variable (one that shows results of change) is plotted on the
   y-axis.

## SOLVING A PROBLEM

1. Write the unit of the answer needed.
2. Set this equal to the quantity given with its units times some conversion
   factor (s)- Length/Area/Weight/Volume/Temperature/Time.
3. Multiply the original quantity by whatever factors are needed to convert its
   units to the unit needed.

## 1ST STEP

1. First decide from the mature of the problem what kind of thing is represented by the result. Ex: if you know that the length and width of a rectangle are given in feet, the product of the number representing these dimensions gives the area in square feet.

## 2nd STEP

2. If the problem has fractions clear them. That is, remove all fractions from the equation. remember that the denominator of a fraction shows is division. To remove the denominator, perform the inverse operation, multiplication. That is, multiply both sides of the equation by the denominator of all fractions present.

## 3rd STEP

3. Second, group all terms that are added or subtracted. Then, do such other operations as are necessary.

   Note: True algebraic logic applies to mathematical problems whether or not a calculator is used.

   Note: Parentheses are used as part of the technique when the solution to the problem requires that the calculator's built-in priorities be disregarded.

   Note: Multiplication and division take precedence over addition and subtraction.

   Note: A group of calculations are clustered together by using the open parentheses key. The functions within that pair of parentheses are completed by pressing the close parentheses key.

   Note: Parentheses are used to separate the numerator portion from the denominator.

   Note: Parenthesis that occur at the beginning or end of a calculation need not be entered on the calculator.

## 4th STEP

4. Cancel terms that both appear in the numerator and denominator.

Property tax problems- Given the cities budget and population determine how much tax each person shall pay ( fair rate of taxation ). Show how the assed value of taxation rate and assessed valuation ( scale ) is used to find the tax to be paid for distribution on actual property value of $24,665.

### Distribution of Taxes Paid ( Milliage 42.6)

| FUND | MILLIAGE | VALUATION | AMOUNT |
|---|---|---|---|
| School District | 30 | 1,850 | 55.50 |
| City General | 4 | 1,850 | 7.40 |
| City Firemen | .4 | 1,850 | .74 |
| County General | 4 | 1,850 | 7.40 |
| County Road | 4 | 1,850 | 7.40 |
| County Library | .2 | 1,850 | .37 |
| Total Tax | | | 78.81 |

Relationship: Property taxes is expressed as so many mills per dollar, cent per hundred dollars, or as a rate per cent of the assessed valuation. Example:

$$1 \text{ mill} = .1 \text{ cent per dollar} = 10 \text{ cents per hundred dollars} = .1\%$$
$$5 \text{ mills} = .5 \text{ cent per dollar} = 50 \text{ cents per hundred dollars} = .5\%$$
$$10 \text{ mills} = 1 \text{ cent per dollar} = 100 \text{ cents per hundred dollars} = 1\%$$

Thus:  42.6 mills, 426 cents, or 4.26%, all express the same rate

Problem:

$$\text{Fair rate of Taxation} = \frac{\text{Town Population}(37,240)}{\text{Town Budget } \$2,800,000} = \text{rate } (.0133)$$

Assed Value of Taxation Scale = 0-100 = 75% of Actual Value
Assed Value of Taxation = .0133 x 10 = .133
1 divided by .133 = 7.5% of Actual Value

The assed value of taxation scale decides what taxation of the actual value is appropriate for the condition of the property. In this case the scale of 10 is used. This tax unit (10) shows a property in a low income neighbor with actual Property Value of $24,665 . This $24,665 is than multiplied by .075 the assed value of taxation to give the property owner the assed valuation of $1,850 .

## Taxes Due: $1,850  X  .0426 (Milliage 42.6)  =  $78.81

Define (What is _____) ?

How does _____ work?

What was the effect or cause of _____?

What is the function of _____?

What is the relationship between _____?

Compare& contrast _____?

What if _____?

Of course, if you don't ask good questions-those similar to your instructors' exam questions-this method won't help you very much. Here are some ways to improve the quality of your questions:

How do I learn to ask myself the kinds of questions which my instructor thinks are important? Some questions are better than others. Won't I just ask unimportant questions, since I'm only a student?

It's true that asking good questions is a process-it doesn't just happen automatically. Here are some things you can do to improve the quality of your questions-so that you really will be predicting exam questions:

### Write full questions, not just phrases.

We have found that something about asking real questions helps improve learning-helping students sort out information in relation to their questions. Also, we have found that writing out full questions helps students generate more complex questions.

### Show your lecture-note questions to your instructor.

Most instructors will be very pleased to see that you are actively working with your notes by writing questions. They will often tell you if you are on the right track and point out those questions you have written which are better than others.

### Compare your questions to those on quizzes and exams.

If you analyze your quizzes early in the semester, you will have a better chance of predicting questions similar to those you will get on later exams. (This also applies to objective tests-we will talk about this in the Information Mapping and Exam Analysis sections of this book.)

## Don't write too many "What is...?" questions.

Questions which ask "What is...?" ask you to define terms. They are good for sections of your notes where new terms are introduced. However, most important questions ask more than the "What?" of an event or concept. "Why...?" "How...?" "What is the relationship between...?" are better question forms. They are more likely to reflect important issues.

## Compare your questions to those of a friend taking the same class.

Going over your lecture note questions with a friend may help both of you see the most important points being raised in class.

## Combine small questions into major, essay-type questions.

For example, imagine you wrote these questions from lectures about 19th century American history:

> "What was the effect of industrialization on city life?"

> "How did improvements in transportation affect city life?"

> "How did improvements in communication affect city life?"

You might make up one large essay question covering all these points:

> "How did innovation in industry, transportation and communication affect city life?"

Note: when you finish writing your lecture note questions each day, write a summary question for the lecture as a whole. This will help you understand and recall the parts of what you have learned in class, and it will help you see the relationships among several lectures in a row.

**EXAMPLE**

TIME: 45 min.  FUNCTION # ( )  1 2 3 4

TEST  SCORING VALUES FOR TEST – 20 MAX  SEMESTER

TEST ITEM

| EXERCISE PROBLEMS | 1 | 2 | 3 | 4 | 5 | 6 | 7 | 8 | 9 | 10 | 11 | 12 | 13 | |
|---|---|---|---|---|---|---|---|---|---|---|---|---|---|---|
| 1 | 1 | 1 | 1 | 2 | 1 | 1 | 1 | 1 | 2 | 4 | 1 | 1 | 1 | |
| 2 | 1 | 1 | 1 | 2 | 1 | 1 | 1 | 1 | 2 | 3 | 2 | 1 | 1 | |
| 3 | 1 | 1 | 1 | 2 | 3 | 2 | 1 | 1 | 3 | 2 | 3 | 2 | 1 | |
| 4 | 1 | 2 | 2 | 2 | 3 | 2 | 2 | 3 | 3 | 1 | 4 | 2 | 2 | |
| 5 | 1 | 1 | 3 | 2 | 2 | 2 | 1 | 1 | 2 | 4 | 4 | 3 | 2 | |
| 6 | 1 | 1 | 1 | 2 | 2 | 2 | 1 | 1 | 2 | 3 | 3 | 3 | 2 | |
| 7 | 1 | 1 | 1 | 3 | 1 | 3 | 1 | 1 | 4 | 2 | 2 | 4 | 3 | |
| 8 | 1 | 2 | 1 | 1 | 1 | 3 | 3 | 2 | 2 | 1 | 1 | 4 | 4 | |
| 9 | 1 | 1 | 2 | 1 | 3 | 3 | 1 | 4 | | | | | 4 | |
| 10 | 1 | 1 | 3 | 1 | 2 | 1 | 1 | 3 | | | | | | |
| 11 | 1 | 1 | 1 | 1 | 1 | | 1 | | | | | | | |
| 12 | 1 | 2 | 1 | 1 | | | 2 | | | | | | | |
| 13 | 1 | 1 | 1 | | | | 1 | | | | | | | |
| 14 | 1 | 1 | 1 | | | | 2 | | | | | | | |
| 15 | 1 | 1 | | | | | | | | | | | | |
| 16 | 1 | 2 | | | | | | | | | | | | |
| 17 | 1 | | | | | | | | | | | | | |
| 18 | 1 | | | | | | | | | | | | | |
| 19 | 1 | | | | | | | | | | | | | |
| 20 | 1 | | | | | | | | | | | | | |

**1 PT** – NUMBER AND NUMERAL, ADDITION, SUBTRACTION, MULTIPLICATION, DIVISION, POSITIVE INTERGERS AND SIGNED NUMBERS.

**2 PT** - FRACTION, CANCELLATION; ADDITION AND SUBTRACTION OF FRACTIONS, MULTIPLICATION AND DIVISION OF FRACTIONS, DECIMAL, REDUCING FRACTIONS TO DECIMALS, RATIO, PROPORTION, AND VARIATION.

**3 PT** – DIRECT AND INDIRECT MEASUREMENTS, DEPENDENCE, FUNCTIONS, AND FORMULAS. (WORD PROBLEM)

**4 PT** – PERCENTAGE, PROFIT AND LOSS, DISCOUNTS, SAMPLE INTEREST, COMPOUND INTEREST, COMPOUND INTEREST. (WORD PROBLEM)

EXAMPLE

TIME: 45 min.

TEST

FUNCTION # (   )

SCORING VALUES FOR TEST – 20 MAX

1 2 3 4

SEMESTER

TEST ITEM

| EXERCISE PROBLEMS | 1 | 2 | 3 | 4 | 5 | 6 | 7 | 8 | 9 | 10 | 11 | 12 | 13 | |
|---|---|---|---|---|---|---|---|---|---|---|---|---|---|---|
| 1 | | | | | | | | | | | | | | |
| 2 | | | | | | | | | | | | | | |
| 3 | | | | | | | | | | | | | | |
| 4 | | | | | | | | | | | | | | |
| 5 | | | | | | | | | | | | | | |
| 6 | | | | | | | | | | | | | | |
| 7 | | | | | | | | | | | | | | |
| 8 | | | | | | | | | | | | | | |
| 9 | | | | | | | | | | | | | | |
| 10 | | | | | | | | | | | | | | |
| 11 | | | | | | | | | | | | | | |
| 12 | | | | | | | | | | | | | | |
| 13 | | | | | | | | | | | | | | |
| 14 | | | | | | | | | | | | | | |
| 15 | | | | | | | | | | | | | | |
| 16 | | | | | | | | | | | | | | |
| 17 | | | | | | | | | | | | | | |
| 18 | | | | | | | | | | | | | | |
| 19 | | | | | | | | | | | | | | |
| 20 | | | | | | | | | | | | | | |

**1 PT** – NUMBER AND NUMERAL, ADDITION, SUBTRACTION, MULTIPLICATION, DIVISION, POSITIVE INTERGERS AND SIGNED NUMBERS.

**2 PT** - FRACTION, CANCELLATION; ADDITION AND SUBTRACTION OF FRACTIONS, MULTIPLICATION AND DIVISION OF FRACTIONS, DECIMAL, REDUCING FRACTIONS TO DECIMALS, RATIO, PROPORTION, AND VARIATION.

**3 PT** – DIRECT AND INDIRECT MEASUREMENTS, DEPENDENCE, FUNCTIONS, AND FORMULAS.

**4 PT** – PERCENTAGE, PROFIT AND LOSS, DISCOUNTS, SAMPLE INTEREST, COMPOUND INTEREST, COMPOUND INTEREST. (WORD PROBLEM)

NAME: A10-8

# STUDENT PERFORMANCE SHEET

PERIOD:

1 2 3 4
SEMESTER

| TEST | 1 | 2 | 3 | 4 | 5 | 6 | 7 | 8 | 9 | 10 | 11 | 12 | 13 | 14 | 15 |
|------|---|---|---|---|---|---|---|---|---|----|----|----|----|----|----|

ANSWERS
20
19
18
17
16
15
14
13
12
11

RIGHT
10
9
8
7
6
5
4
3
2
1

↑ ID #                    " FUNCTION #

(D) GRADE – 10 RIGHT
(C) GRADE – 13 RIGHT
(B) GRADE – 16 RIGHT
(A) GRADE – 19 RIGHT

CLASS STANDING
1. TOP 10%      4. BOTTOM 25%
2. TOP 25%      5. LOWEST 10%
3. AVERAGE

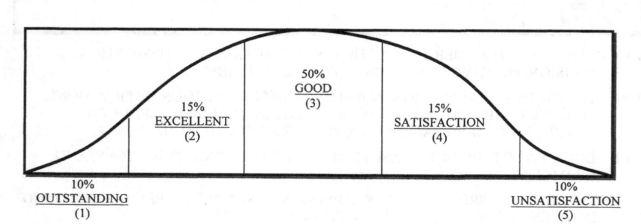

50%
GOOD
(3)

15%
EXCELLENT
(2)

15%
SATISFACTION
(4)

10%
OUTSTANDING
(1)

10%
UNSATISFACTION
(5)

# Adult One-Rescuer CPR

Name _____ Date _____

| Step | Objective | Critical Performance | S | U |
|---|---|---|---|---|
| 1. AIRWAY | Assessment: Determine unresponsiveness. | Tap or gently shake shoulder. | | |
| | | Shout "Are you OK?" | | |
| | Call for help. | Call out "Help!" | | |
| | Position the victim. | Turn on back as unit, if necessary, supporting head and neck (4–10 sec). | | |
| | Open the airway. | Use head-tilt/chin-lift maneuver. | | |
| 2. BREATHING | Assessment: Determine breathlessness. | Maintain open airway. | | |
| | | Ear over mouth, observe chest: look, listen, feel for breathing (3–5 sec). | | |
| | Ventilate twice. | Maintain open airway. | | |
| | | Seal mouth and nose properly. | | |
| | | Ventilate 2 times at 1–1.5 sec/inflation. | | |
| | | Observe chest rise (adequate ventilation volume.) | | |
| | | Allow deflation between breaths. | | |
| 3. CIRCULATION | Assessment: Determine pulselessness. | Feel for carotid pulse on near side of victim (5–10 sec). | | |
| | | Maintain head-tilt with other hand. | | |
| | Activate EMS system. | If someone responded to call for help, send him/her to activate EMS system. | | |
| | | Total time, Step 1—Activate EMS system: 15–35 sec. | | |
| | Begin chest compressions. | Rescuer kneels by victim's shoulders. | | |
| | | Landmark check prior to hand placement. | | |
| | | Proper hand position throughout. | | |
| | | Rescuer's shoulders over victim's sternum. | | |
| | | Equal compression–relaxation. | | |
| | | Compress 1½ to 2 inches. | | |
| | | Keep hands on sternum during upstroke. | | |
| | | Complete chest relaxation on upstroke. | | |
| | | Say any helpful mnemonic. | | |
| | | Compression rate: 80–100/min (15 per 9–11 sec). | | |
| 4. Compression/Ventilation Cycles | Do 4 cycles of 15 compressions and 2 ventilations. | Proper compression/ventilation ratio: 15 compressions to 2 ventilations per cycle. | | |
| | | Observe chest rise: 1–1.5 sec/inflation; 4 cycles/52–73 sec. | | |
| 5. Reassessment* | Determine pulselessness. | Feel for carotid pulse (5 sec).† If there is no pulse, go to Step 6. | | |
| 6. Continue CPR | Ventilate twice. | Ventilate 2 times. | | |
| | | Observe chest rise: 1–1.5 sec/inflation. | | |
| | Resume compression/ ventilation cycles. | Feel for carotid pulse every few minutes. | | |

* If 2nd rescuer arrives to replace 1st rescuer: (a) 2nd rescuer identifies self by saying "I know CPR. Can I help?" (b) 2nd rescuer then does pulse check in Step 5 and continues with Step 6. (During practice and testing only one rescuer actually ventilates the manikin. The 2nd rescuer simulates ventilation.) (c) 1st rescuer assesses the adequacy of 2nd rescuer's CPR by observing chest rise during ventilations and by checking the pulse during chest compressions.

† If pulse is present, open airway and check for spontaneous breathing: (a) If breathing is present, maintain open airway and monitor pulse and breathing. (b) If breathing is absent, perform rescue breathing at 12 times/min and monitor pulse.

Instructor _____ Check: Satisfactory _____ Unsatisfactory _____

## A—CLEAR AIRWAY   B-RECUE BREATHING   B—CIRCUATION

At least one adult in every household should know first aid basic and how to do CPR. It can mean the difference between rapid recovery and long hospitalization, or even between life and death. Check with American Heart Association, American Red Cross and National Safety Council for instruction in CPR and first-aid classes. Addition information @ www.cpr-ecc.americanheart.org www.redcross.org www.nec.org

### A. CLEAR AIRWAY

Somebody drops to the ground, without any sign of life. First thing you do is make sure the area is clear of any danger, then proceed to determine unresponsiveness of the person. Turn the person on his back and make sure the airway is open. To determine unresponsiveness scream in the person's ear and give him a study nudge. A hard rub of the knuckles against the breastbone will usually determine whether he is really out. If the person is really out, stay with victim and feel for carotid pulse on near side of the victim neck (5-10 sec). If no pulse send someone to call 911 for help, make sure that person knows to give victim location.

### B. RESCUE BREATHING

Make sure the persons head is on the floor, with no pillows or folded underneath. To determine breathlessness put one hand on his forehead, another under his neck and tilt. Knell and put your face down next to the victim's nose and mouth to listen for moving air and feel for the warmth of breath. If no sign of breathing, begin mouth to mouth rescue breathing. Ventilate twice. If however, you do not feel comfortable about doing this step, or not qualified to do CPR ---doing the next step ---start circulation ---is better then doing nothing at all.

### C. START CIRCULATION

Start the persons blood circulation by doing compressions on the chest. You do this by placing the heel of your hand on the breastbone in the center of the chest. Push down firmly 2 inches with only the heel of your hand touching the chest, then release. Keep elbows locked and arms straight.

Began compression/ventilation cycles--- Do (4 cycles) of 15 compressions and 2 ventilation per cycle.

Do reassessment--- If no pulse continue CPR until help arrives.

# BLADED PROPELLERS
### (Looking from Stern toward Bow)

A10-10

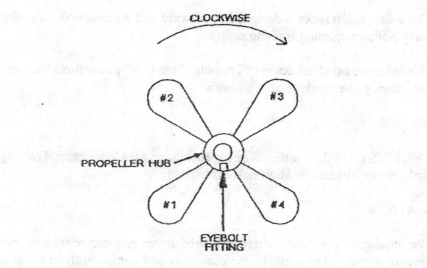

4 - BLADED PROPELLER (TYPICAL)

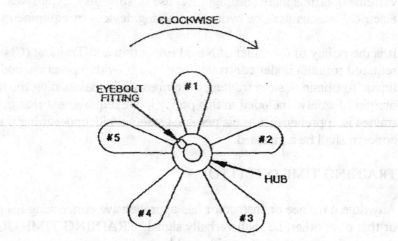

5 - BLADED PROPELLER (TYPICAL)

# INFORMATION SHEET

## SAFETY POLICY FOR CONDUCTING TRAINING    A10-11

### A. INTRODUCTION

1. This information sheet is designed to provide you with an understanding of Navy policy regarding training safety.

2. This information sheet covers "Training Time Out" procedures that are to be used during the conduct of this course.

### B. REFERENCES

1. CNETINST 1500.20 series, Safety procedures for Conducting Training in Arduous or Potentially High risk Activities.

### C. INFORMATION

1. The mission of the Navy dictates the need for an aggressive training program to prepare personnel to perform professionally and competently in many high risk activities under diverse and possible adverse conditions. Potentially high risk training includes, but is not limited to, training requiring exposure to potentially hazardous conditions involving the environment (water entry, temperature extreme-), atmosphere (fire fighting, use of solvents), explosives (weapons), electrical, mechanical, or hydraulic training devices or equipments.

2. It is the policy of the Chief of Naval Education and Training (CNET) to provide required training under controlled conditions, within practical and realistic limits, to obtain desired training outcomes while maintaining the maximum margin of safety. Included in this policy is the requirement that in the event a trainee is apprehensive of his personal safety while undergoing training, that concern shall be addressed.

3. TRAINING TIME OUT (TTO)

Any time a trainee or Instructor has apprehensive concerning his personal safety or that of another, he shall verbally signal "TRAINING TIME OUT" to stop the exercise and receive provided additional instruction as appropriate in accordance with CNEINST 1500.0 series.

Example Information Sheet

A. Introduction

Underwater hull inspection requires a thorough knowledge of the components and conditions peculiar to underwater operations. This Job Sheet will allow you to practice the step-by-step procedures required to conduct underwater hull inspections. A major benefit of this exercise is that you will have the opportunity to make the same decisions that will be required to perform this task in your duty assignment.

B. Equipment The following equipment is required:
1. Open circuit SCUBA outfit.
2. 12" rule.
3. Tending lines.
4. Hull inspection report.
5. Underwater lights (night dives)
6. Chem-lite; one per buddy team (night dives)

C. References
1. NAVSHIPS Technical Manual, and Underwater Work Techniques Manual, Volume 2
2. Underwater Ship Husbandry Manuals, S0600-AA-010 series
3. U.S. Navy Diving Manual, Volume 1

D. Safety Precautions: Review TTO procedures in the Safety/Hazard Awareness Notice.

E. Job Steps. The following job steps apply:
1. At Diving supervisor's direction, dress in open circuit SCUBA following safety checklist in the Underwater Work Techniques Manual Vol. 2, page 3-2.
2. At Diving supervisor's direction, make proper water entry. Review safety checklist in the Underwater Work Techniques Manual, Vol. 2, page 3-3, before entering water.
3. At Diving supervisor's direction, descend on craft and make an underwater inspection of the craft's hull. Review safety checklist in the Underwater Work Techniques Manual, Vol. 2, page 4-5 before entering water.
4. Upon surfacing, sound off, "Maximum Depth_____, Bottom Time_____."
Failure to report this information will result in a failing grade for this Job Sheet.
5. At Diving supervisor's direction, make proper water exit.
6. Await further instructions from Diving supervisor.
7. Complete an underwater hull inspection report (one per buddy team).
8. Two percent will be deducted for each line pull signal not given or given incorrectly.

F. Self Test Questions:
Note: To be developed.

**Example Job Sheet.**

## PROBLEM SHEET
## DIAGNOSING GROUP PERFORMANCE

A10-13

### A. INTRODUCTION

The ability to evaluate student and group performance is developed by practice. The purpose of a Problem Sheet is to provide data for your consideration and allow you to determine why performance was poor. Using the data provided below, diagnose the probable cause (s) of poor group performance.

### B. PROBLEM

1. Class No:
2. Test
   a. New: #
   b. Existing:
3. Practice Time:
   a. Scheduled: N/A
   b. Received: N/A
4. Testing Schedule
   a. Day of the week: Wednesday
   b. Amount of time since last test: One week.
5. Prerequisite Skills: a check of the training background of the class revealed that the students came to class having mastered supporting objectives in previous lessons.
6. Test Item: Passing test score is 60. Test questions and objectives will not be available to you for analysis to determine test item quality, you will only have the data in Items 1-5 and the information in the chart below to determine test item quality.

Example: Problem Sheet. (Sheet 1 of 3)

# TEST ITEM MISSED BY CLASS NO.

|  | 1 | 2 | 3 | 4 | 5 | 6 | 7 | 8 | 9 | 10 |
|---|---|---|---|---|---|---|---|---|---|---|
| STUDENT 1 | X |  | X |  |  | X |  |  | X |  |
| STUDENT 2 |  |  |  |  | X | X |  | X |  | X |
| STUDENT 3 |  | X |  |  |  | X |  |  | X |  |
| STUDENT 4 |  |  |  | X | X | X |  |  |  |  |
| STUDENT 5 |  |  | X |  |  |  | X | X |  | X |
| STUDENT 6 |  |  |  |  |  | X |  |  |  |  |
| STUDENT 7 | X | X |  | X |  | X |  |  |  |  |
| STUDENT 8 |  | X |  |  | X |  | ' | X | X |  |
| STUDENT 9 |  |  | X |  |  | X | X |  |  | X |
| STUDENT 10 | X |  | X |  |  | X | X |  |  |  |

| TEST ITEM(S) | OBJECTIVE SUPPORT |
|---|---|
| 1, 2, 3 | 1.1 |
| 4, 5 | 1.2 |
| 6, 7, 8 | 1.3 |
| 9 | 1.4 |
| 10 | 1.5 |

Example Problem    Sheet.   (2 of 3)

110

From this instructors previous class on same test as class No.___

| | 1 | 2 | 3 | 4 | 5 | 6 | 7 | 8 | 9 | 10 |
|---|---|---|---|---|---|---|---|---|---|---|
| **STUDENT 1** | | | | | | | | | | |
| **STUDENT 2** | | | | | | | | | | |
| **STUDENT 3** | | | | | | | | | | |
| **STUDENT 4** | | | | | | | | | | |
| **STUDENT 5** | | | | | | | | | | |
| **STUDENT 6** | | | | | | | | | | |
| **STUDENT 7** | | | | | | | | | | |
| **STUDENT 8** | | | | | | | | | | |
| **STUDENT 9** | | | | | | | | | | |
| **STUDENT 10** | | | | | | | | | | |

From another instructors class on same test.

| | 1 | 2 | 3 | 4 | 5 | 6 | 7 | 8 | 9 | 10 |
|---|---|---|---|---|---|---|---|---|---|---|
| **STUDENT 1** | | | | | | | | | | |
| **STUDENT 2** | | | | | | | | | | |
| **STUDENT 3** | | | | | | | | | | |
| **STUDENT 4** | | | | | | | | | | |
| **STUDENT 5** | | | | | | | | | | |
| **STUDENT 6** | | | | | | | | | | |
| **STUDENT 7** | | | | | | | | | | |
| **STUDENT 8** | | | | | | | | | | |
| **STUDENT 9** | | | | | | | | | | |
| **STUDENT 10** | | | | | | | | | | |

Example problem        Sheet.    (3 of 3)

C.  Problem Causes ( ) Group Performance Data       Class  No.  A2-2 #21 Algebra

1. Incorrect Answer Key ( )  2.  Insufficient Practice ( )   3.  Poor Test Scheduling ( )

4. Lack of Prerequisite (A10-28).

5. Poor Test Item ( )

6. Poor Instruction ( )

## TEST ITEM REVIEW

Use the following guidelines as a checklist to effectively review test items. The five types of test item are: (General Test A4).

1.  Use true-false items to test recognition, comprehension, application, or evaluation.
2.  Construct multiple-choice item either as a question or incomplete statement.
3.  Use matching test items for testing recognition, comprehension and application.
4.  Use completion test item for testing memory of subject matter without the possibility of guessing.
    A.  Ask direct question to test for comprehension of technical terms or knowledge of definition.
    B.  Write a computational equation, define terms, list part names and function.
5.  Use essay test item for testing a person ability to organize data and write correctly their thoughts when they write.

## TEST ITEM CRITERIA

1.  Focus attention on subject matter that must be recalled precisely, such as usage in correct terminology, function of parts, and safety precautions.
2.  Plan questions that require thinking before answering. Make questions brief state the sentence by inverting the subject and verb.
3.  Use the auxiliary verb (do) to form questions and to give emphasis. (Tense & Voice)
4.  Create direct open questions by using interrogative pronoun or adverb (who, when, what, which, etc.)
5.  Ask factual, though-provoking, and interest-arousing question, use the topic sentence to open a paragraph. State clearly and precisely what type of response is required.

STUDY ASSIGNMENT                                                                      A10-14

1. Study EE125-FA-MMF-010/E110-BRR-6, FOMM Technical Manual Support Volume for
   Radio Receiving Set AN/BRR-6, Volume 1, glossary; tables 1-1 and 2-1 through 2-7;
   paragraphs 1-1, 1-2, 1-2.1 through 1-2.12, and 1-3 through 1-6; and figures 2-1 through 2-8,
   5-1, and 5-3.
2. Study NAVSEA S9SSB-X9-SSM-900/(U) 726V6P3B13 (SSM V76P3B13), Habitability, Ship
   Handling, and Emergency Systems Operating Instructions, 01637-11, paragraph 1-1

STUDY QUESTIONS

1. How many units comprise the BRR-6?
2. What is the frequency range of the BRR-6?
3. What is the maximum speed allowable for towing the buoys?
4. What is the maximum speed for launching a buoy?
5. Is it good practice to stream the buoyant cable and fly a buoy at the same time?
6. How many buoys are associated with each BRR-6?
7. What is the minimum depth for launching a buoy?
8. How much cable does each cable have?
9. What does FOMM mean?
10. Which units of the BRR-6 are located in the IRR?
11. Which units of the BRR-6 are located in the Command and Control Center?
12. How many antennas are associated with the Towed Buoy?
13. What is the purpose of the Depth and Destruct Canister? Where is it located?
14. Which unit controls all the buoy electronics?
15. How close to the surface must the buoy be before Unit 10 can take over depth control?
16. How does Unit 9 (Towed Buoy Antenna Control Unit) communicate with the buoy
    electronics?
17. Where are the tow cable cutters located?
18. Where does the BRR-6 receive its 115 vac 60 Hz power?
19. Do the navigation center signals go through the AIS cabinet in the IRR?

Example Assignment Sheet. (Sheet 3 of 3)

# UNDERWATER HULL INSPECTION

## A. Introduction

Underwater hull inspection involves the examination of the exterior underwater hull and components to determine the condition and needs for maintenance and repair. In this topic, you will be taught the components to be inspected and the procedures for inspection.

## B. Enabling Objectives:

7.1      IDENTIFY the components of the ship's hull in accordance with the Underwater work Technique Manual, Volume 2.

7.2      DESCRIBE the stages of growth commonly found on underwater hulls in accordance with the NAVSHIPS Technical Manual, Waterborne Underwater Hull Cleaning of Surface Ships, Chapter 081, and the Underwater Work Techniques Manual, Volume 2.

7.3      STATE the general contents of the Fouling Rating Scale, and the Paint Deterioration Rating Scale, in accordance with NAVSHIPS Technical Manual and Waterborne Underwater Hull Cleaning of Surface Ships, Chapter 081.

7.4      DESCRIBE the fouling areas of hulls in accordance with the NAVSHIPS Technical Manual, Waterborne Underwater Hull Cleaning of Surface Ships, Chapter 081, and the Underwater Work Techniques Manual, Volume 2.

7.5      APPLY the safety precautions associated with underwater hull inspections in accordance with the U.S. Navy Diving Manual, Volume 1; the Underwater Work Techniques Manual, Volume 2; and the NAVSHIPS Technical Manual, Waterborne Underwater Hull Cleaning of Surface Ships, Chapter 081.

7.6      PERFORM underwater hull inspections by day in accordance with the NAVSHIPS Technical Manual and Underwater Work Techniques Manual, Volume 2.

7.7      PREPARE the ship's hull inspection report in accordance with the Diving Training Standards.

## C. Topic Outline
1. Introduction
2. Ship Hull Components
3. Stages of Sea Growth
4. Fouling Rating Scales
5. Critical Fouling Areas
6. Planning for a Dive
7. Use Repair Safety Checklist
8. Perform Underwater Hull Inspection
9. Hull Inspection Report
10. Summary and Review
11. Assignment

**Example outline sheet**

GENERAL BIOLOGY-1254
WESTARK COMMUNITY COLLEGE
SPRING SEMESTER-1990

I.   CATALOG DESCRIPTION
1254 General Biology (4)
   (Three hours of lecture and two hours of laboratory per week)
1254 Fall, Spring, and Summer

This study of the general concepts and principles that underline biology includes
the principles related to molecular and cellular biology, heredity, development
biology, anatomy, and physiology.

II.  COURSE DESCRIPTION
Freshmen course for non-science majors and for science majors. A strong
background in biology, chemistry, and physics is not necessary, but basic concepts
in these fields, which are related to biological principles, are presented.

III. COURSE OBJECTIVES
To develop in the student insight into some of the fundamental characteristics of
the living world. To conduct a study leading to a discovery of basic biological
principles, their foundations, and consequences.

It is hoped that this will instill in the student an appreciation for the unity
underlying the diversity of life, an appreciation for the living world in general, and
that the course will impart to the student the implications of biology upon his life
and the society in which he lives. It is further hoped that the student will become
aware of the vast practical application of the study of biology in understanding
one's body and persona health, in grappling with the epical questions that face us
as citizens, and in sensing both our place in the web of interdependent living things
that our need to help protect the delicate ecological balance that sustains us all. In
order to accomplish these goals, both well established and new concepts and
principles will be presented.

IV.  TEXTBOOKS AND MATERIALS
Lecture: (1) Biology - 1st edition, by Wessels and Hopson
        (2) Study Guide to accompany Biology by Wessels and Hopson

Laboratory:   (1) Life in the Laboratory by Humphrey/ Van Dyke/ Willis
             (2) A dissecting kit containing an assortment of instruments
             (3) A Guide to Biology Lab, by Thomas Rust

A. Exams- There will be three major 100-point exams during the semester. All exams will mainly be some form of objective test. Also short tests may be given throughout the semester at the discretion of the instructor. Two lab exams worth 50 points each will be given during the lab portion of the course. Weekly lab reports will be worth 10 points each.

Exam Schedule:

Chapters 1, 2, 3, 4, 5, 6 ………………………………….. EXAM I - 100 Points

Chapters 7, 8, 9, 16 (in part), 10,
    11, 12, 13, 15 (in part)…………………….. EXAM II - 100 Points

Chapters 23 (in part), 24 (in part),
    16, 34, 31, 32, 33, 35, 37,
    and 18 …………………………………............ EXAM III - 100 Points

Short Tests…………………………………........................................100 Points

Lab Exam I……………………………………….......................................50 Points

Lab Exam II……………………………………........................................50 Points

B. Grades

One final course grade for biology 1254 will be received at the end of the semester. The lecture portion of the course will comprise 75 percent of the final grade, while the lab will count 25 percent.

The final course grade will be computed by dividing the total number of points accumulated by the total points possible and then determining the percentage.

Final grades will be assigned according to the following scale:
    90 - 100 = A
    80 -  89 = B
    70 -  79 = C
    60 -  69 = D
  Less than 60 = F

C. Absence Policy

Regular attendance in <u>both</u> lecture and lab is required. Students may be dropped from the course for excessive absences. A pattern of excessive absences in either <u>lecture</u> or <u>lab</u> will have a definite negative impact on the final course grade received!

116

## BIOLOGY 1254

| TOPICS | CHAPTERS |
|---|---|
| Organization of the Study of Biology: The Scientific Method | Chapter 1 |
| Atoms, Molecules, and Simple Chemistry: Enzymes | Chapter 2 |
| | Chapter 3 |
| | Chapter 4 |
| Cell Structure and Function | Chapter 5 |
| | Chapter 6 |

End of Material for Test #1

---

| | |
|---|---|
| Cell Metabolism: Obtaining and Utilizing Energy (Photosynthesis and Respiration) | Chapter 7 |
| | Chapter 8 |
| Cell Reproduction: Mitosis and Meiosis | Chapter 9 |
| | Chapter 16 |
| | (Pages 360-369) |
| Heredity | Chapter 10 |
| | Chapter 11 |
| | Chapter 12 |
| | Chapter 13 |
| | Chapter 15 |
| | (Pages 341-345) |

End of Material for Test #2

---

| | |
|---|---|
| Tissues | Various Chapters |
| Life Cycles | |
| Moss | Chapter 23 |
| | (Pages 529-531) |
| Fern | Chapter 23 |
| | (Pages 544-546) |
| Flowering Plant | Chapter 24 |
| | (Page 559) |
| Animal Development | Chapter 16 |

Organs and systems:

_____

End of material for Test #3

_____

SPRING SEMESTER 1990
LAB SCHEDULE

| LAB NUMBER | WEEK | EXERCISE |
|---|---|---|
| | January 8-12 | Introduction to Lab Work: Lab Seating Charts |
| 1 | January 15-19 | Looking at Life: Observational Tools (Ex. 1) |
| 2 | January 22-26 | Enzymes (Handout) |
| 3 | Jan 29-Feb 2 | Cells: Structure & Function (Handout Sheets) |
| 4 | February 5-9 | Animal Cell Specialization (Ex. 4) |
| 5 | February 12-16 | Plant Cell Specialization (Ex. 4) |
| 6 | February 19-23 | Mitosis (Exercise 6) |
| 7 | Feb 26-Mar 2 | Lab Exam I |
| 8 | March 5-9 | Drosophila Genetics (Ex. 7) |
| 9 | March 12-16 | Human Heredity (Handout Sheets) |
| 10 | March 19-23 | Mammalian Digestive Systems (Exercise 12) |
| | March 26-30 | SPRING BREAK |
| 11 | April 2-6 | Mammalian Respiratory & Circulatory Systems (Exercise 13) |
| 12 | April 9-13 | Mammalian Urogenital Systems (Exercise 14) |
| 13 | April 16-20 | Mammalian Control Systems (Handout Sheets) |
| 14 | April 23-27 | Lab Exam II |
| | April 30-May 4 | NO LAB-FINAL EXAM WEEK |

COURSE TITLE: ENVIRONMENTAL HAZARDS

TOPIC: HAZARD COMMUNICATION PLAN

TIME: 1 HOUR

INSTRUCTIONAL REFERENCES:
1. Occupational Safety and Health ADM. (OSHA) Hazard
   Communication Standard, 29     CFR-1910, 1200

INSTRUCTIONAL AIDES:
1. Miller, Willard E. and Ruby M. Miller Environmental Hazards. (7)

2. Chalkboard and Chalk

3. Videotape/Film

4. Hazard Communication Plan

MAJOR TEACHING POINTS:

A. List of hazardous chemicals which may be found in the workplace.

B. Material Safety Data Sheets (MSDS).

C. Method of informing employees.

D. Method of informing outside persons.

E. Description of the system used to label hazardous chemicals.

F. Personnel responsible for administering the plan.

G. Personnel capable of evaluating hazards.

H. Procurement procedure for MSDS.

I. Emergency procedures.

J. Special tasks.

1. Communicate your skills on how safety you can work to others.

2. Put your skills to work safely.

3. Anyone can do it poorly...show you know how to do it right safely.

4. Show you know how to use the right tool for the job.

5. Show you know how to measure your material accurately.

6. Show you know how to finish a job.

7. Learn safe working habits...take wearing your safety glasses, hard hat, ear protection, and other personal protective gear as second nature...a given.

8. Become aware of safety hazards and how to guard against them, follow the rules...pay attention to danger and caution sign, and be aware of walk-ways danger around machinery...keep safety rails, chains and guards in place.

9. Be conscious that getting hurt and not working safely has consequences.

10. Some consequences from not working safely are;
    1. physical toll
    2. lost productivity
    3. workers compensation
    4. insurance cost
    5. OSHA reports
    6. medical expenses
    7. material damages
    8. affect bottom line
    9. turn-over of employee
    10. death

# HYDRAULIC SYSTEMS

## General Precautions.

Personnel operating pressurized hydraulic systems must recognize the hazardous character of the systems and perform all procedures in a careful and alert manner. Personnel must never deviate from the established and approved methods. A system must be used for anything other than that for which it was assigned.

Hydraulic fluid under pressure in a closed system presents many hazards. The pressurized fluid mixed with air is explosive. Coupling joints are under great stress when the system is pressurized, so personnel must be careful not to strike a line or fitting. Never tighten or loosen any pressurized fitting. All fittings must be carefully inspected for cleanliness and mechanical condition before mating. Sudden changes in system pressure often severely shock and stress system components. Valves, therefore, should not be opened or closed rapidly. Exceptions to these general rules are allowed when specifically authorized by approved procedures.

Hydraulic system gages should be continuously monitored. Do not rely completely on automatic safety devices, such as pressure relief valves. Operating and maintenance personnel must periodically check the condition of hydraulic systems to verify a safe working order. Pressure gages require special attention. Gages must be calibrated at specified intervals to assure the safe operation of the system.

Any high pressure system is dangerous and can cause serious injury or death. Personnel shall exercise great care when operating hydraulic systems. The probability and severity of accidents can be minimized by taking the following precautions.
1. All hydraulic systems must be operated in compliance with the safety regulations o the company.
2. Personnel shall be thoroughly trained and checked out on a hydraulic system before being authorized to operate the system.
3. If a hydraulic leak is discovered, repair the leak before continuing. Immediately report any leak to the supervisor.
4. Pressure must be bled off prior to performing corrective maintenance on a hydraulic system.
5. During operation, keep all parts of the body clear of any item that moves as a result of hydraulic pressure.

## Hydraulic Fluid Precautions.

Most hydraulic fluids are flammable and may cause skin irritation if prolonged contact occurs. Hydraulic fluid becomes a hazard if it is sprayed, heated to its flash point (200-225 F) soaked into clothing or rags, or subjected to conditions that cause rapid vaporization. Also, any spilled fluid can cause a slippery surface.

Hydraulic fluid shall be kept away from open flames and any spillage shall be immediately cleaned. If it is spilled on clothing, the clothes are to be removed and all contaminated portions of the skin shall be thoroughly washed with soap and water.

Safety.....ten safety commandments                                    A10-20
1. learn the safe way to do a job before starting.
2. think safety and act safety at all times.
3. obey safety rules and regulations....they are for your protection. Fire prevention/ exit drills/OSHA/MSDA sheets.
4. wear proper clothing and protection equipment.
5. conduct yourself properly at all times....horseplay is prohibited.
6. operate only the equipment authorized.
7. inspect tools and equipment for safe condition before starting work.
8. advice your superior promptly of any unsafe conditions or practice.
9. report any injury immediately to your superior.
10. support your safety program and take an active part in safety meetings.

tools and their use                                    A10-21
1. keep each tool in its proper storage place.
2. keep all tools in good condition.
3. keep all tool allowance complete.
4. use each tool only on the job for which it was designed.
5. Keep all tools within easy reach and where they cannot fall on the floor or into machinery.
6. never use damaged tools.

# Mathematics
A10-22
## Computing with the scientific calculator
### Casio; reference tables

1. Metrics and Prefixes
2. Standard Units of Measurement
3. Weights and Measures
4. Physical Constants
5. Conversion Factors
6. US, std gage sizes
7. Greek letters and Roman numerals
8. Number of days between same dates in different months.

## Statistical Quality assurance keywords

1. calculation of standard deviation- "s" calculated measure of the dispersion of a set of numerical values.

2. frequency chart- a table showing the value of a distribution with the tally of the number of times each value occurred. It normally is represented by a bar graph or histogram.

3. cell midpoint- the value used in a frequency chart to represent actual measurement value within the cell boundaries.

4. cell boundaries- the maximum and minimum values to be counted in a single cell.

5. mean- total of the measurement divided by the number of measurements and is represented a x bar, x; or the average.

6. median- middle score $\frac{n+1}{2}$, lower value of interval 1 [ $\frac{\text{number needed out of interval}}{\text{number in the interval}}$ (times width of interval).]

7. mode- most frequent score.....mode interval.

8. calculate the number of standard deviation between the mean and the upper or lower limits.   $z = \frac{x - \bar{x}}{S}$   or   $u = \frac{x - u}{\sigma}$

## 5. example

$$x = \frac{\text{sum. } x_i}{n},\qquad \frac{\text{sum. } fx_i}{n},\qquad n = \text{sum. } F$$

124

## group data

n = frequency column total......31          x = midpoint.......33

| class | f | x | f.x | f.x$^2$ |
|---|---|---|---|---|
| 29.5...36.5 | 2 | 33 | 66 | 2178 |
| 36.5...43.5 | 5 | 40 | 200 | 8000 |
| 43.5...50.5 | 8 | 47 | 376 | 17672 |
| 50.5...57.5 | 6 | 54 | 324 | 17496 |
| 57.5...64.5 | 4 | 61 | 244 | 14884 |
| 64.5...71.5 | 5 | 68 | 340 | 23120 |
| 71.5...78.5 | 1 | 75 | 75 | 5625 |
| | 31 | 378 | 1652 | 88975 |

$$s^2 = \frac{n(\text{sum } f.x^2) - (\text{sum } f.x)^2}{n(n-1)} \qquad s^2 = \frac{31(889750 - (1625)^2)}{(31)(30)}$$

$$s = 11.245$$

## ungroup data

$$s^2 = \frac{n(\text{sum } x^2) - (\text{sum } x^2)}{n(n-1)}$$

## math 6 percent principle

1. 6 days = $\frac{1}{10}$ of 60 days---- the interest is found by pointing off 3 places in the principle.     $1500 = $1.50

2. 60 days.... the interest is found by pointing off 2 places in the principle. $1500 = 15.00

3. 600 days = 10 times 60 days---- the interest if found by pointing off one place.                $1500 = $150.00

4. 6000 days.... The interest equals the principle. $1500 = $1500

1.  Read reference material A3-1, <u>The Complete Guide to Public Employment</u>. This book give examples on how to do a resume and type letters required during a job search.

Fill out an employment questionnaire for the employment ahead of time. This application questionnaire provides an opportunity to sell your qualification. Some tips for completing an application are as follow:

    1.  Prepare a personal data sheet.
    2.  Collect data that might be requested; dates, names, addresses, telephone numbers, etc......
    3.  Fill out the application neatly, check for errors, print clearly, and do not use abbreviations.
    4.  Follow direction and read the entire application before you complete it.
    5.  Be honest; however, provide only the information the employer is seeking or is necessary to sell your qualification.

2.  Target your qualification, have advance knowledge of the company before applying for the job or position. Some information resources available for this knowledge are
    1.  Million Dollar Directory Dun and Radstreet.
    2.  Standard of Poor's Register of Corporation, Directors and Executives.
    3.  Ward's Business Directory of Largest U.S. Companies.
    4.  Ward's Business of Major U.S. Private Companies.
    5.  MacMillan Directory of Leading Private Companies.
    6.  Corporate Report Fact Book.

3.  Use the Internet for job-search. Some Web sites that describe their business and list job opening are as follow:

    www.builder.com      www.hoovers.com      www.monster.com
      www.jobsource.com      www.collegeview.com

4.  Attend job fairs, check Employment Agencies, and expand your job search through Networking.

5.  Be prepared for interview. The purpose of an interview is to get acquainted and to learn about one another. Three common types of interviews are :
    1.  Telephone screening interview- Eliminate candidates based on criteria such as employment objectives, education or required skills.
    2.  In-person screening interview- Usually conducted by the human resource department. This screening selects the candidates to meet with the decision makers after a preliminary impression of the person's attitude, interest, and professional "style" for the job.
    3.  Selection interview- Conducted by the decision maker for evaluating qualification and to assess the "fit in" to the company management style.
    4.  Other types included: work sample, peer group, group, luncheon, stress and video conference interview

6. Be prepared to answer questions. Remember to keep your answers brief and to the point. Do not ramble on and on, keep the answers job related, and not personal.

### KEY INTERVIEWER QUESTIONS

1. What can you tell me about yourself? Do not provide personal information only give information that relates to school, training, and work experience.

2. Tell me some of your strength and weaknesses? This question is directed to Assess the "fit in" to the work environment of the company. Be honest and emphasize your strengths more than your weaknesses.

3. How did you hear about this job or position? Have something positive to say. This question will allow you to impress the interviewer. Show that you took the initiative to research the company and job positions.

4. Why should we hire you? Sum up the answers to question that you have answered, and point out that you have the attitude, interest, and professional style for the job.

7. Speak confidently and ask questions. Have questions ready to evaluate the job position, see if the job is right for you. If you ask the right questions, the interviewer is more likely to think you are interested in the position.

### KEY INTERVIEW QUESTIONS

1. What are the position requirements?

2. What would my workday consist of doing?

3. What would my work hours be?

4. What are some of my benefits for working for you?

5. What are my chances for advancement?

6. How do I fit? What is your management style?

7. What would be my position responsibility consists of?

8. Follow up after the interview. Meet all test exam dates required for the job.

1. Send a thank-you note. This lets the interviewer know that you are serious

2. Send a separate note to each person you interviewed with. You may be required to come back.

127

In the work place, you will be required to know the basic principles of Dimensional measurement and with certain basic concepts in the field of Physics.

Why do you need this theoretical knowledge? First of all, you can't very Well test, maintain, or repair equipment if you don't know how they work. Secondly, you can't really understand how your equipment works without training in the basic principles on which they work.

## DIMENSIONAL MEASUREMENT

Dimensional measurement is the foundation for mass production, interchangeability, and outsource procurement. The three fundamental dimensions-length, time, and either mass or force are sometime called ... Mechanical: Dimensions. Temperature the fourth fundamental dimension, is not a ....... Mechanical quality.

1. Scales- Used for linear measurement. The basic linear instrument is the ... Standard ruler.

2. Calipers- is an extension of the hook rule with a sliding jaw added. This Instrument can be used for either inside or outside measurements.

Micrometers- The principle of the micrometer is simply that of a screw Turning in a stationary nut. The parts to know are: frame, anvil, Barrel, thimble, screw, spindle ratchet, and spindle lock ring.

3. Gauges- Plug, Limit, Snap, Radius and Feeler...etc.

1. Volume- The amount of space with matter occupies.

2. Weight- The force of gravity exerted on an object.

3. Mass- A measure of the total quantity (variable) of matter in an object
      or body.

## Pressure and Weight

1. Pressure- The force acting against a given surface within a closed
      container.  Pressure is usually expressed in weight per unit area,
      when pressure is expressed in liquid terms, the liquid must be
      named.

2. Pressure gauges- classified according to where they are used, and
      according to their specific uses.

3. Density- the weight per unit volume of a substance.

4. Force- is anything that tends to produce, present, or modify that motion or
      the position of a body or substance.

## Torque and Temperature

1. Torque is a turning effort.  Torque is  developed even if no turning motion
resulted. On the other hand, work results ion the application of force moves
an object through a distance. Torque- expressed in weight- length.  Work-
expressed in length- weight.

2. Temperature- the quantities measure of the relative hotness or coldness of
      an object. Remember, all the temperature measuring
      instruments use some changing in material to indicate
      temperature. Two familiar temperature scales are the Celsius
      scales and the Fahrenheit scales.

## FLOW METER

The physical properties of fluids involved in flow metering are: pressure, specific weight or density, temperature, viscosity and velocity.

1. Flow may be measured either as Unit Volume Per Unit Time, Unit Weight Per Unit Time, or Unit Mass Per Unit Time.

2. A change in temperature of fluid affect both _pressure_ and _density._ An Increase in temperature causes an increase in pressure and a decrease in Density. A decrease of temperature causes a decrease in pressure and an Increase in density.

3. Viscosity is the internal resistance of a fluid which tends to prevent it form Flowing, for liquids, an increase in temperature decreases viscosity. For Gases, an increase in temperature increase viscosity.

## READING FLOW METER

1. Straight- reading read from left to right and all the number indicated by the small pointer above. When the next higher number is partly supposed, always read the lesser number, which is the number disappearing from sight.

2. Round- reading- Each division of any circle stands for one-tenth Of the whole number indicated by that circle. (Note: on some Meters then one cubic feet dial is for test only.

## MEASUREMENT VARIABLES

Almost any measurement variable may be either a controlled variable or a manipulated variable; it all depends upon the particular application.

1. Mass- quantity of variable
2. Force, Pressure, Torque- related variables
3. Rate- movement of variables include speed, velocity, acceleration, and flow.
4. Level- height of variable that is measured for liquid and solid only. Gases do not maintain a level but expand and fill whatever contains they are in.

Ref: A-I, Prescription Medicine/ Use / Pharmaceutical Address and PH# 1-573-996-7300.

## DIABETIES

Ref: A. (Amaryl), /Aventis Patient Assistance Program, P.O. Box 759 Somerville, NJ 08876
1-800-221-4025. Doctor complete section 1. Licensed Practitioner Section.

Ref: B. (Avandia), / Glaxosmithkine Foundation - /Access  To  Care, C/O Express Scripts/SDC
P.O. Box 2564 Maryland Heights, MO. 630430-0758.

## HEART/ ARTERIES

Ref: C. (Plavix),  /  C/O MHSA, Bristol-Myers Squibb PAF, P.O. Box 2118, Lakewood, NJ. 08701-9846
1-800-736-0003. /Doctor Complete Physician Information. Fax # 1-800-736-1611.

Ref: D. (Tiazac), Patient Assistance Program, Forest Pharmaceuticals, Inc. 13600 Shoreline Dr.
St. Louis, MO. 63045.  PH# 1-800-851-0758.

Ref: E. (Isorbil), Wyeth-Ayerst Laboratories, P. O. Box 13806, Philadelphia, PA. 19101.
Ph # 1-800-568-9938.  Doctor complete "Section I; Physician's Information.

## HIGH BLOOD PRESSURE

Ref: F. (Clonidine) Possible substitution: Catapres TTS patch. Boehringer Ingelhellm Pharmaceuticals,
Inc.  C/O Express Scripts Specialty Distr .Services. P.O. Box. 66555. St. Louis. MO. 63166-6555
Doctor completes "Physician Healthcare Professional" section 2. Application: 1-800-556-8317;
Medication question: 1-800-542-6257.

## WATER PILL

Ref: G. (Bumex), Possible substitution: Furosemide, and Zaroxolyn. Medeva Pharmaceuticals, Inc.
P.O. Box. 31766 Attn: Medeva Patient Assistance Program Customer Service. 1-800-258-4484.
Request Application. Fax # 1-973-562-2765.   www.rocheusa.com.  www.rxhope.com.

## CHOLESTEROL

Ref: H. (Lipitor), Parke-Davis, Connection To  Care. Ph # 1-800-707-8990. Doctor complete:
"Healthcare Practitioner Section". P.O.Box 66585. St. Louis, MO. 63166-6585.

## MINERIAL / REPLACEMENT

Ref: I. (Potassium chloride), Schering Laboratories, Patient Assistance Program. P.O. Box. 52122,
Phoenix, 85072. PH# 1=800-652-9485. Doctor complete "Physician's Role".

Use of Mensuration-Mensuration (indirect measurement) is of constant use in many trades, professions, and in many kinds of business. There are two kinds of measurement:
  1. Direct Measurement          2. Indirect Measurement.

Direct Measurement- Direct measurement consists in applying a unit to a magnitude of the same kind, to see how many times the unit is contained in it.

$$1 \text{ kg} = 1000g \qquad\qquad 1m = 1000 \text{ mm} = 100cm$$
$$1g = 1000mg \qquad\qquad 454g = 1 \text{ lb}$$
$$\text{liter} = 1000ml \qquad\qquad 2.54 = 1 \text{ cm}$$
$$1.09qt = 1 \text{ liter}$$

Equation and Formulas - An equation is the statement that two quantities are equal. A formula is a general rule expressed in symbols, usually in the form of an equation, stating relationship between quantities.

Ohm's Law    $I = E/R$ $\qquad\qquad E = I \times R \qquad\qquad R = E/R$

Power $\qquad\quad P = E \times I \qquad\qquad P = E^2 \times R \qquad P = I^2 \times R$

MENSURATION                    CONVERSION FACTORS

| To Convert | into | Multiply by | Conversely Multiply by |
|---|---|---|---|
| Acres | Square feet | $4.356 \times 10^4$ | $2.296 \times 10^{-5}$ |
| Acres | Square meters | 4047 | $2.471 \times 10^{-4}$ |
| Acres | Square miles | $1.5625 \times 10^{-3}$ | 640 |
| Amperes | Microamperes | $10 \times 10^6$ | $10^{-6}$ |
| Amperes | Micromicroamperes | $10 \times 10^{12}$ | $10^{-12}$ |
| Amperes | Milliamperes | $10^3$ | $10^{-3}$ |
| Amperes-hr | Coulombs | 3600 | $2.778 \times 10^{-4}$ |

Row 1 x Row 3 = Row 2          Row 2 x Row 4 = Row 1

132

| To Convert | into | Multiply by | Conversely Multiply by |
|---|---|---|---|
| Ampere-turns | Gilberts | 1.257 | 0.7958 |
| Ampere-turns per cm. | Ampere-turns per in. | 2.54 | 0.3937 |
| Angstrom units | inches | $3.937 \times 10^{-9}$ | $2.54 \times 10^{8}$ |
| Angstrom units | meters | $10^{-10}$ | $10^{10}$ |
| Bars | Atmospheres | $9.870 \times 10^{-7}$ | 1.0133 |
| Bars | Dynes per sq.cm. | $10 \times 10^{6}$ | $10 \times 10^{-6}$ |
| Bars | lbs per sq. in. | 14.504 | $6.8947 \times 10^{-2}$ |
| Btu | Ergs | $1.0548 \times 10^{10}$ | $9.468 \times 10^{-11}$ |
| Btu | Foot-pounds | 778.3 | $1.285 \times 10^{-3}$ |
| Btu | Joules | 1054.8 | $9.480 \times 10^{-6}$ |
| Btu | Kilogram-calories | 0.252 | 3.969 |
| Btu per hour | Horsepower- hrs | $3.929 \times 10^{-4}$ | 2545 |
| Bushels | Cubic feet | 1.2445 | 0.8036 |
| Calories, gram | Joules | 4.185 | 0.2389 |
| Centigrade | Celsius | 1 | 1 |
| Centigrade | Fahrenheit | (o C x 9/5 ) + 32=o F | (o F –32) x 5/9 = oC |
| Centigrade | Kelvin | o C + 273.1 = o K | o K-273.1 = oC |

Row 1 x Row 3 = Row 2          Row 2 x Row 4 = Row 1

| To Convert | into | Multiply by | Conversely Multiply by |
|---|---|---|---|
| Chains (surveyor's) | Feet | 66 | $1.515 \times 10^{-3}$ |
| Circular mils | Sq centimeters | $5.067 \times 10^{-6}$ | $1.973 \times 10^{5}$ |
| Circular mils | Square mils | 0.7854 | 1.273 |
| Cubic feet | Gallons(liq. U.S.) | 7.481 | 0.1337 |
| Cubic feet | Liters | 28.32 | $3.531 \times 10^{-2}$ |
| Cubic feet | Cubic centimeters | 16.39 | $6.102 \times 10^{-2}$ |
| Cubic inches | Cubic feet | $5.787 \times 10^{-4}$ | 1728 |
| Cubic inches | Cubic meters | $1.639 \times 10^{-5}$ | $6.102 \times 10^{4}$ |
| Cubic inches | Gallons(liq. U.S.) | $4.329 \times 10^{-3}$ | 231 |
| Cubic meters | Cubic feet | 35.31 | $2.832 \times 10^{-2}$ |
| Cubic meters | Cubic yards | 1.308 | 0.7646 |
| Cycles | Kilocycles | $10^{-3}$ | $10^{3}$ |
| Cycles | Megacycles | $10^{-6}$ | $10^{6}$ |
| Degrees(angle) | Mils | 17.45 | $5.73 \times 10^{-2}$ |
| Degrees(angle) | Radians | $1.745 \times 10^{-2}$ | 57.3 |
| Dynes | Pounds | $2.248 \times 10^{-6}$ | $4.448 \times 10^{5}$ |
| Ergs | Foot-pounds | $7.376 \times 10^{-8}$ | $1.356 \times 10^{7}$ |

Row 1 x Row 3 = Row 2      Row 2 x Row 4 = Row 1

| To Convert | into | Multiply by | Conversely Multiply by |
|---|---|---|---|
| Fahrenheit | Rankine | oF+459.58=oR | oR-459.58=oF |
| Faradays | Ampere-hours | 26.8 | $3.731 \times 10^{-2}$ |
| Farads | Microfarads | $10^{6}$ | $10^{-6}$ |
| Farads | Micromicrofarads | $10^{12}$ | $10^{-12}$ |
| Farads | Millifarads | $10^{3}$ | $10^{-3}$ |
| Fathoms | Feet | 6 | 0.16667 |
| Feet | Centimeters | 30.48 | $3.281 \times 10^{-2}$ |
| Feet | Meters | 0.3048 | 3.281 |
| Feet | Mils | $1.2 \times 10^{4}$ | $8.333 \times 10^{-5}$ |
| Foot-pounds | Gram-centimeters | $1.383 \times 10^{4}$ | $1.235 \times 10^{-5}$ |
| Foot-pounds | Horsepower-hours | $5.05 \times 10^{-7}$ | $1.98 \times 10^{6}$ |
| Foot-pounds | Kilogram-meters | 0.1383 | 7.233 |
| Foot-pounds | Ounce-inches | 192 | $5.208 \times 10^{-3}$ |
| Gallons(liq. U.S.) | Cubic meters | $3.785 \times 10^{-3}$ | 264.2 |
| Gallons(liq. U.S.) | Gallons(liq.Br.Imp) | 0.8327 | 1.201 |
| Gausses | Lines per sq.cm. | 1.0 | 1.0 |
| Gausses | Lines per sq. in. | 6.452 | 0.1555 |
| Gausses | Webers per sq. in. | $6.452 \times 10^{-8}$ | $1.55 \times 10^{7}$ |

Row 1 x Row 3 = Row 2      Row 2 x Row 4 = Row 1

| To Convert | into | Multiply by | Conversely Multiply by |
|---|---|---|---|
| Grams | Ounces(avdp.) | $3.527 \times 10^{-2}$ | 28.35 |
| Grams | Poundals | $7.093 \times 10^{-2}$ | 14.1 |
| Grams per cm. | Pounds per in. | $5.6 \times 10^{-2}$ | 178.6 |
| Grams per cu. cm | Pounds per cu. in. | $3.613 \times 10^{-2}$ | 27.68 |
| Henries | Microhenries | $10^{3}$ | $10^{-3}$ |
| Horsepower | Btu per minute | 42.418 | $2.357 \times 10^{-3}$ |
| Horsepower | Foot-lbs per minute | $3.3 \times 10^{4}$ | $3.03 \times 10^{-5}$ |
| Horsepower | Foot-lbs per second | 550 | $1.182- \times 10^{-3}$ |
| Horsepower | Horsepower(metric) | 1.014 | 0.9863 |
| Horsepower | Kilowatts | 0.746 | 1.341 |
| Inches | Centimeters | 2.54 | 0.3937 |
| Inches | Feet | $8.333 \times 10^{-3}$ | 12 |
| Inches | Meters | $2.54 \times 10^{-3}$ | 39.37 |
| Inches | Miles | $1.578 \times 10^{-5}$ | $6.336 \times 10^{4}$ |
| Inches | Mils | $10^{3}$ | $10^{-3}$ |
| Inches | Yards | $2.778 \times 10^{-3}$ | 36 |
| Joules | Foot-pounds | 0.7376 | 1.356 |
| Joules | Ergs | $10.^{7}$ | $10^{-7}$ |
| Joules | Watt-hours | $2.778 \times 10^{-4}$ | 3600 |

Row 1 x Row 3 = Row 2    Row 2 x Row 4 = Row 1

| To Convert | into | Multiply by | Conversely Multiply by |
|---|---|---|---|
| Kilograms | Tonnes | $10^{3}$ | $10^{-3}$ |
| Kilograms | Tons(long) | $9.842 \times 10^{-4}$ | 1016 |
| Kilograms | Tons(short) | $1.102 \times 10^{-3}$ | 907.2 |
| Kilograms | Pounds (avdp) | 2.205 | 0.4536 |
| Kilograms per sq. Meter | Pounds per sq.ft. | 0.2048 | 4.882 |
| Kilometers | Feet | 3281 | $3.408 \times 10^{-4}$ |
| Kilometers | Inches | $3.937 \times 10^{4}$ | $2.54 \times 10^{-5}$ |
| Kilometers | Light years | $1.0567 \times 10^{-13}$ | $9.4637 \times 10^{12}$ |
| Kilometers per hr. | Feet per minute | 54.68 | $1.829 \times 10^{-3}$ |
| Kilometers per hr | Knots | 0.5396 | 1.8532 |
| Kilowatt-hours | Btu | 3413 | $2.93 \times 10^{-4}$ |
| Kilowatt-hours | Foot-pounds | $2.655 \times 10^{6}$ | $3.766 \times 10^{-7}$ |
| Kilowatt-hours | Joules | $3.6\,10 \times 10^{6}$ | $2.778 \times 10^{-7}$ |
| Kilowatt-hours | Horsepower-hr. | 1.341 | 0.7457 |
| Kilowatt-hour | pounds water Evaporated from And at 212oF. | 3.53 | 0.284 |
| Kilowatt-hour | Watt-hours | $10^{3}$ | $10^{-3}$ |

Row 1 x Row 3 = Row 2          Row 1 x Row 3 = Row 2

| To convert | into | Multiply by | Conversely Multiply by |
|---|---|---|---|
| Knots | Feet per second | 1.1508 | 0.5925 |
| Knots | Meters per minute | 30.87 | 0.0324 |
| Knots | Miles per hour | 1.1508 | 0.867 |
| Lamberts | Candles per sq. cm. | 0.3183 | 3.142 |
| Lamberts | Candles per sq. in. | 2.054 | 0.4869 |
| Leagues | Miles | 3 | 0.33 |
| Links | Chains | 0.01 | 100 |
| Links(surveyor's) | Inches | 7.92 | 0.1263 |
| Liters | Bushels(dry U.S.) | $2.838 \times 10^{-2}$ | 35.24 |
| Liters | Cubic centimeters | $10^{-3}$ | $10^{3}$ |
| Liters | Cubic meters | $10^{-3}$ | $10^{3}$ |
| Liters | Cubic inches | 61.02 | $1.639 \times 10^{-3}$ |
| Liters | Gallons(liq.U.S.) | 0.2642 | 3.785 |
| Liters | Pints(liq. U.S.) | 2.113 | 0.4732 |
| $\text{Log}_{E} \text{N}$ | $\text{Log}_{10} \text{N}$ | 0.4343 | 2.303 |
| Lumens per sq. ft. | Foot-candles | 1 | 1 |
| Lux | Foot-candles | 0.0929 | 10.764 |
| Maxwells | Kilolines | $10^{-3}$ | $10^{3}$ |
| Maxwells | Megalines | $10^{6}$ | $10^{-6}$ |
| Maxwells | Webers | $10^{8}$ | $10^{-8}$ |

Row 1 x Row 3 = Row 2          Row 1 x Row 3 = Row 2

| To Convert | into | Multiply by | Conversely Multiply by |
|---|---|---|---|
| Meters | Centimeters | $10^2$ | $10^{-2}$ |
| Meters | Feet | 3.28 | $30.48 \times 10^{-2}$ |
| Meters | Inches | 39.37 | $2.54 \times 10^{-2}$ |
| Meters | Kilometers | $10^{-3}$ | $10^3$ |
| Meters | Miles | $6.314 \times 10^{-4}$ | 1609.35 |
| Meters | Yards | 1.094 | 0.9144 |
| Meters per minute | Feet per minute | 3.281 | 0.3048 |
| Meters per minute | Kilometers per hr. | 0.06 | 16.67 |
| Mhos | Micromhos | $10^6$ | $10^{-6}$ |
| Mhos | Millimhos | $10^3$ | $10^{-3}$ |
| Microfarads | Micromicrofarads | $10^6$ | $10^{-6}$ |
| Miles(nautical) | Feet | 6076.1 | $1.646 \times 10^{-4}$ |
| Miles(nautical) | Meters | 1852 | $5.4 \times 10^{-4}$ |
| Miles(statute) | Feet | 5280 | $1.894 \times 10^{-4}$ |
| Miles(statute) | Kilometers | 1.609 | 0.6214 |
| Miles(statute) | Light years | $1.691 \times 10^{-12}$ | $5.88 \times 10^{12}$ |
| Miles(statute) | Miles(nautical) | 0.869 | 1.1508 |
| Miles(statute) | Yards | 1760 | $5.6818 \times 10^{-4}$ |
| Miles per hour | Feet per minute | 88 | $1.136 \times 10^{-2}$ |
| Miles per hour | Feet per second | 1.467 | 0.6214 |

Row 1 x Row 3 = Row 2    Row 1 x Row 3 = Row 2

| To Convert | into | Multiply by | Conversely, Multiply by |
|---|---|---|---|
| Miles per hour | Kilometers per hour | 1.609 | 0.6214 |
| Miles per hour | Knots | 0.8684 | 1.152 |
| Milliamperes | Microamperes | $10^3$ | $10^{-3}$ |
| Millihenries | Microhenries | $10^3$ | $10^{-3}$ |
| Millimeters | Centimeters | 0.1 | 10 |
| Millimeters | Inches | $3.93 \times 10^{-2}$ | 25.4 |
| Millimeters | Microns | $10^3$ | $10^{-3}$ |
| Millivolts | Microvolts | $10^3$ | $10^{-3}$ |
| Mills | Minutes | 3.438 | 0.2909 |
| Minutes(angle) | Degrees | $1.666 \times 10^{-2}$ | 60 |
| Nepers | Decibels | 8.6886 | 0.1151 |
| Newtons | Dynes | $10^5$ | $10^{-5}$ |
| Newtons | Pounds(avdp.) | 0.2248 | 4.448 |
| Ohms | Milliohms | $10^3$ | $10^{-3}$ |
| Ohms | Micro-ohms | $10^6$ | $10^{-6}$ |
| Ohms | Micromicro-ohms | $10^{12}$ | $10^{-12}$ |
| Ohms | Megohms | $10^{-6}$ | $10^6$ |
| Ohms per foot | Ohms per meter | 0.3048 | 3.281 |
| Ounces(fluid) | Quarts | $3.125 \times 10^{-2}$ | 32 |
| Ounces(avdp.) | Pounds | $6.25 \times 10^{-2}$ | 16 |

Row 1 x Row 3 = Row 2      Row 2 x Row 4 = Row1

| To Convert | into | Multiply by | Conversely, Multiply by |
|---|---|---|---|
| Picofarad | Micromicrofarad | 1 | 1 |
| Pints | Quarts(liq.U.S.) | 0.50 | 2 |
| Pounds(force) | Newtons | 4.4482 | 0.2288 |
| Pounds carbon oxid. | Btu | 14,544 | $6.88 \times 10^{-5}$ |
| Pounds carbon oxid | Horsepower-hr. | 5.705 | 0.175 |
| Pounds carbon oxid | Kilowatt-hr. | 4.254 | 0.235 |
| Pounds of water(dist.) | Cubic feet | $1.603 \times 10^{-2}$ | 62.38 |
| Pounds of water(dist.) | Gallons | 0.1198 | 8.347 |
| Pounds per sq. in. | Dynes per sq.cm. | $6.8946 \times 10^{4}$ | $1.450 \, 10^{-5}$ |
| Poundals | Dynes | $1.383 \times 10^{4}$ | $7.233 \times 10^{-5}$ |
| Poundals | Pounds(avdp.) | $3.108 \times 10^{-2}$ | 32.17 |
| Quadrants | /Degrees | 90 | $11.111 \times 10^{-2}$ |
| Quadrants | / Radians | 1.5708 | 0.637 |
| Radians | Mils | $10^{3}$ | $10^{-3}$ |
| Radians | Minutes | $3.438 \times 10^{3}$ | $2.909 \times 10^{-4}$ |
| Radians | Seconds | $2.06265 \times 10^{5}$ | $4.848 \times 10^{-6}$ |
| Rods | Feet | 16.5 | $6.061 \times 10^{-2}$ |
| Rods | Miles | $3.125 \times 10^{-3}$ | 320 |
| Rods | Yards | 5.5 | 0.1818 |
| Rpm | Degrees per sec. | 6.0 | 0.1667 |

Row 1  x  Row 3  =  Row 2        Row 2  x  Row 4  =  Row 1

| To Convert | into | Multiply by | Conversely, Multiply by |
|---|---|---|---|
| Rpm | Radian per second | 0.1047 | 9.549 |
| Rpm | Rps | $1.667 \times 10^{-2}$ | 60 |
| Square feet | Acres | $2.296 \times 10^{-5}$ | 43.560 |
| Square feet | Square centimeters | 929.034 | $1.076 \times 10^{-3}$ |
| Square feet | Square inches | 144 | $6.944 \times 10^{-3}$ |
| Square feet | Square meters | $9.29 \times 10^{-2}$ | 10.764 |
| Square feet | Square miles | $3.587 \times 10^{-8}$ | $27.88 \times 10^{6}$ |
| Square feet | Square yard | $11.11 \times 10^{-2}$ | 9 |
| Square inches | Circular mils | $1.273 \times 10^{6}$ | $7.854 \times 10^{-7}$ |
| Square inches | Square centimeters | 6.452 | 0.155 |
| Square inches | Square mils | $10^{6}$ | $10^{-6}$ |
| Square inches | Square millimeters | 645.2 | $1.55 \times 10^{-3}$ |
| Square kilometers | Square miles | 0.3861 | 2.59 |
| Square meters | Square yards | 1.196 | 0.8361 |
| Square miles | Acres | 640 | $1.562 \times 10^{-3}$ |
| Square miles | Square yards | $3.098 \times 10^{6}$ | $3.228 \times 10^{-7}$ |
| Square millimeter | Circular mils | 1973 | $5.067 \times 1^{-4}$ |
| Square millimeter | Square centimeters | .01 | 100 |
| Square mils | Circular mils | 1.273 | 0.7854 |

Row 1 x Row 3 = Row 2        Row 2 x Row 4 = Row 1

| To Convert | into | Multilpy by | Conversely Multiply by |
|---|---|---|---|
| Tons (long) | Pounds (avdp.) | 2240 | $4.464 \times 10^{-4}$ |
| Tons (short) | Pounds | 2,000 | $5 \times 10^{-4}$ |
| Tonnes | Pounds | 2204.63 | $4.536 \times 10^{-4}$ |
| Varas | Feet | 2.7777 | 0.36 |
| Volts | Kilovolts | $10^{-3}$ | $10^{3}$ |
| Volts | Micro volts | $10^{6}$ | $10^{-6}$ |
| Volts | Mill volts | $10^{6}$ | $10^{-6}$ |
| Watts | Btu per hour | 3.413 | 0.293 |
| Watts | Btu per minute | $5.689 \times 10^{-2}$ | 17.58 |
| Watts | Ergs per second | $10^{7}$ | $10^{-7}$ |
| Watts | Foot-lbs per minute | 44.26 | $2.26 \times 10^{-2}$ |
| Watts | Foot-lbs per second | 0.7378 | 1.356 |
| Watts | Horsepower | $1.341 \times 10^{-3}$ | 746 |
| Watts | Kilogram-cal/min. | $1.433 \times 10^{-2}$ | 69.77 |
| Watts | Kilowatts | $10^{-3}$ | $10^{3}$ |
| Watts | Microwatts | $10^{6}$ | $10^{-6}$ |
| Watts | Mill watts | $10^{3}$ | $10^{-3}$ |

Row 1 x Row 3 = Row 2      Row 2 x Row 4 = Row1

143

| To Convert | into | Multiply by | Conversely, Multiply by |
|---|---|---|---|
| Watts-seconds | Joules | 1 | 1 |
| Webers | Maxwells | $10^{8}$ | $10^{-8}$ |
| Webers per sq meter | Gausses | $10^{4}$ | $10^{-4}$ |
| Yards | Feet | 3 | .3333 |
| Yards | Varas | 1.08 | 0.9259 |

Row 1 x Row 3 = Row 2 Row 2 x Row 4 = Row 1

Relationship: #1

If you are given Row 1 and need Row 2, multiply by Row 3 and convert units; Row 4 (conversely multiply by) tells you what number you must multiply by to convert your answer back to Row 1 to check your answer.

Relationship: #2

If you are given Row 2 and need Row 1, multiply by Row 4 and convert units; Row 3 (multiply by) tell you what number you must multiply by to convert your answer back to Row 2 to check you answer.

Relationship: #3

If you are given quantities of different units in Row 4 than you must convert the original quantity into one with a different convenient unit. Use Row 1 and Row 2 as your Ratio.

For example: One cubic feet contains 1728 cubic inches and one gallon contains 231 Cubic inches. One cubic feet contain how many gallons?

$$\frac{\#\text{ gallons}}{1\text{ cu. feet}} = \frac{1728\text{ cu. Inches}}{1\text{ cu. Feet}} \times \frac{1\text{ gallon}}{231\text{ cu. Inches}} = 7.481\ \frac{\text{gallons}}{\text{cu.feet}}$$

For example: If you are driving at 60 miles per hour, how many feet do you travel in 1 second?

$$\frac{\text{Feet}}{\text{Sec}} = 60\ \frac{\text{miles}}{\text{hr}} \times \frac{5280\text{ feet}}{1\text{ mile}} \times \frac{1\text{ hour}}{60\text{ min}} \times \frac{1\text{ minute}}{60\text{ sec}} = 88\ \frac{\text{feet}}{\text{sec}}$$

or 1.467 ft/sec @1 mile/hr.

For example : The speed of light is $3.00 \times 10^{10}$ cm/sec.

(a) How fast is this in miles/sec?

(b) How fast is this in miles/hr.?

Relationship: #3 (convert) cm / inches / feet / miles and second to hours

(a) $\dfrac{\text{miles}}{\text{Seconds}} = 3.00 \times 10^{10} \ \dfrac{\text{cm}}{\text{sec}} \times \dfrac{\text{inches}}{2.54 \text{ cm}} \times \dfrac{1\text{feet}}{12\text{in}.} \times \dfrac{1 \text{ mile}}{5280\text{ft}.} = 1.86 \times 10^{5}$ mi/sec

(b) $\dfrac{\text{miles}}{\text{Hour}} = 1.86 \times 10^{5} \ \dfrac{\text{miles}}{\text{sec}} \times \dfrac{60 \text{ sec}}{1 \text{ min}} \times \dfrac{60 \text{ min}.}{1 \text{ hour}} = 6.7 \times 10^{8}$ mi/hr

For example: (Conversion) Nautical miles and Statue miles.

If a statute mile is 5280 feet and a nautical mile is 6080 feet, by what number must a number of nautical miles be multiplied to convert it into status miles? By what number must a number of status miles be multiplied to convert it into nautical miles?

Nautical miles ( Row 2 ) x ( Row 4 ) = Row 1 (Statue miles).

Statue miles ( Row 1 ) x ( Row 3 ) = Row 2 (Nautical miles).

For example: Energy: Work per unit time ( Power multiplied by Time).

If the rate of electricity at a house is 3.37 cents per kilowatt-hour, and the monthly bill is $19.95, how many kilowatt-hours have been consumed.

Relationship: Power company's bills is for electrical energy not for power $W = P \times T$

Needed: Number of kilowatt hours consumed.
Given: Cost $19.95; Rate 3.37 cent / kilowatt-hour.

Kilowatt-hour $= \$19.95 \times \dfrac{100 \text{ cents}}{\$1} \times \dfrac{1 \text{ Kilowatt-hour}}{3.37 \text{ cents}} = 592$

## RATIOS

In math, chemistry, and science the solution to problems based on ratios, proportions, and variations involves no new principle. However, it is necessary first to become familiar with these topic rules, terms, and definitions in order to simplify solution to problems that would otherwise be more complicated.

### RATIO (Fractions)

A ratio is the relationship between two or more quantities. When a fraction is used to express a relationship the numerator and denominator take on individual significance.

It is essential to make clear which quantity is which; the first one named always goes on top (Antecedent) the numerator, and the second (Consequent) is the denominator of the fraction.

To reduce, increase, or simplify the terms of a ratio of two numbers, follow the rules that govern fractions.

### FRACTIONS RULES AND TERMS

1. Measurement Fractions- Result when we determine the smaller number from a larger number. EX: Out of an income of $2200, a man spends $400 for rent. What is the ratio of his rent to his income?  Solution: $400 : $2200 = 2/11 EX: If $2 .00 were spent for a rug at $3.00 per yard how many yards were brought? Solution: $2.00  :  $3.00 per yard = 2/3 yard.

2. Part Fraction- Result when we determine what number of equal sizes came from a larger number. Ex: If 4 equal lengths of pipe are to be cut from a 3- foot pipe, what is the size of each piece of pipe? Solution: 3-ft pipe : 4 pipes = 3/4 ft.

3. Division of fraction- Invert the divisor and multiply(Reciprocal).

   EX: $\frac{9}{10} / \frac{3}{5} = \frac{9}{10} \times \frac{5}{3} = 3 : 2$

   To find the reciprocal of a number, express the number as a fraction and then invert the fraction. When the numerator of a fraction is 1, the reciprocal is a whole number. EX:  The reciprocal of  $\frac{1}{1000}$  is   1000 ( Product is 1).

4. Lowest Common Denominator- Smallest of their common multipler.  EX: $\frac{5 a b}{5}$  $\frac{3 5}{3 5}$

   and $2 a b c$  is $10 a b c$.

5. Mixed Expression – Consist of one or more integral (Whole Number) term plus or minus one or more fractional term.EX: $1+ \frac{a + b}{a}; 12 + 3/8 = \frac{99}{*8}, X + \frac{X-3}{2} = \frac{3X-3}{2}$

- It is more convenient to use the improper fraction if further calculation are needed.

Complex Fraction- Fraction having one or more fraction in either or both of it terms.

6. Fraction(% Decimals) Common fraction are changed to percent by first expressing them as decimals. To change a decimal to percent multiply the decimal by 100 and annex the percent sign (%).

## RATIOS (TRIGONOMETRIC)

Trigonometry means "measurement by triangles." Trigonometry is a means of obtaining measurement of distance and angle indirectly; without use of scale drawing.

The angle is measured by means of a transit. This instrument contains one protractor by which the vertical angle are measured, and another by which horizontal angle are measured.

It is difficult to understand trigonometry problems without first learning the facts about angles, triangles, phthagorean theorem, and the relationship between the angles and the sides of a right triangle.

## ANGLES

1. Ray- Part of a line on one side of a point

2. Sides- Two lines which form an angle. The size of an angle refers to the amount of separation between its sides, and the unit of angular size is given in degrees.

3. Acute Angle- An angle smaller than a right angle, and less than 90 degrees.

4. Obtuse Angle- An angle larger than a right angle, and less than two right angles.

5. Complementary Angle- Two angles who sum is a right angle. (Each of the angles complement each other). EX: Three fifths of a certain angle equals three fourth of the complement of the angle. Solution: Let X = Angle.
Equation: $3/5 X = 3/4 (90-X)$; $12X = 15(90-X)$; $27X = 1350$; than $X = 50$ degrees.

6. Supplementary Angle- Two angles who sum is a straight angle or 180 degrees.

   EX: One fifth of the supplement of a certain angle exceeds four sevenths of the complement of the angle by 5 degrees. Find the angle. Solution: Let (180-X) be the Supplement angle and (90-X) be the Complement angle. Equation: $1/5 (180-X)-5 = 4/7 (90-X)$; $1260-7X-175 = 1800 -20X$; $13X = 715$; $X = 55$ degrees.

7. Angle of Elevation- An angle opposite the right angle that gives the hypotenuse its slop.

8. Angle of Depression- An angle formed when an imaginary line is drawn (tip of the slop or apex) parallel to one of the legs of the triangle; also equal to the angle of elevation.

9. Apex- Highest point of a triangle in a standard position.

147

## RIGHT TRIANGLES

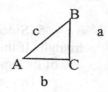

1. Triangle-Labeled using three capital letters, one at each vertex.
The sides are labeled using lowercase as follows: The side
opposite angle A(altitude), side opposite angle B(base); side
opposite angle C(hypotenuse).

2. Triangle Sides- The sides of the triangle are named in accordance with their
relationship to angle with Greek name of Theta   and its complementary angle (other
acute angle) with the Greek name of Alpha

| | | |
|---|---|---|
| Sine (Theta) = $\dfrac{a}{c}$ | Sine (Alpha) = $\dfrac{b}{c}$ | Secant (Theta) = $\dfrac{1}{\text{cosine}}$ |
| Cosine (Theta) = $\dfrac{b}{c}$ | Cosine (Alpha) = $\dfrac{a}{c}$ | Cosecant (Theta) = $\dfrac{1}{\text{Sine}}$ |
| Tangent (Theta) = $\dfrac{a}{b}$ | Tangent (Alpha) = $\dfrac{b}{a}$ | Cotangent (Theta) = $\dfrac{1}{\text{Tangent}}$ |

(a)  altitude  (b) base  (c) hypotenuse

3. Angle:Sides Ratio- The relationship between the angle and the sides of a right triangle
are expressed in terms of trigonometric ratio functions as follows: Table 1 gives the sine,
cosine, and tangent of angle from  0 degrees to  90 degrees. These ratios depend only on
the size of the angle, not on the actual length of the sides.

      For small angles the sine is small (near 0 ) and the cosine is large (near 1).
Therefore, sine and tangent increases as the angle increases; cosine decreases as the angle
increases.

4.  Triangle Perimeter- Sum of the length of its sides.  P = a + b + c.  EX: The perimeter
of a certain triangle is 49 feet. The second side is 5/4 of "1 less than the first side";  the
third size is  2/3  of "1 more than the first side". What are the sides of the triangle?
Solution: Find  X and substitute in the equation to find the other sides.
Equation:  X + 5/4 (X-1) + 2/3 (X + 1)  =  49 feet ; 12X + 15X –15 + 8X +8  =  588 ;
            35 X  =  595 ;  than  X =  17 ft;  therefore, the first side is 17ft, second side is
            20ft, and the third side is 12 ft.

5. Sum of the angle of a triangle is 180 degrees- Ex: If the three angles of a triangle have
a 1:2 :3 ratio; What is the size of each angle? Solution: Numerator is 180 degrees;
Denominator is the sum total of angles ratio of 6.  Equation:  180/6 = 30 degrees;
therefore, angle ratio is 30:60:90 which equals 180 degrees.

6   Area of triangle- Space bounded by its side  A =  1/2 ab.

## RIGHT TRIANGLE

7.  3 : 4 : 5 (Sided) Triangle- Any triangle with its sides in this ratio is a right triangle. If the hypotenuse is acting as the base, the triangle can be turned until one of its legs is the base.

    The use of a right triangle having its sides in the ration of 3 to 4 to 5 is often used in laying out the foundations of building. The procedure is as follow: ABC Triangle with C = 90 degrees.
    1.  A string is stretched forming line CB. The length of CB is 3 feet.
    2.  A second string is stretched, crossing line CB at C, directly above the point intended as the corner of the foundation. Point A on this line is 4 feet from C.
    3.  Attach a third string, 5 feet long, at B and A. When CB and CA are spread so that the BA is taut, angle ACB is a right triangle.

    EX: The perimeter of a ACB triangle is 48 feet, if one side is 12 feet and the longest side is 20 feet, how long is the other side? What is K the factor of proportionality? Solution: $3 K : 4 K : 5 K$; $P = a + b + c$ or $12 + b + 20 = 48$; $b = 48 - 32$ or $b = 16$ feet. Factor of proportionality (K) $= \dfrac{48}{3 + 4 + 5} = 4.$

    0     0     0

8.  30 : 60: 90 Triangle- The side opposite the 30 degree angle (shortest side) is equal to half the hypotenuse, or stated as a formula, $a = c / 2$. The side opposite the 60 degree angle is equal to half the hypotenuse times the square root of 3 which is (1.7321) see Table 2 ; or stated as a formula, $b = c / 2 \times 1.7321$.

    0     0     0

9.  45 : 45 : 90 Triangle- The side opposite the 45 degree angles are equal and each side equal to half the hypotenuse time square root of 2 which is (1.2599) see Table 2; or stated as a formula, $b = c / 2 \times 1.2599$. EX: In a certain isosceles triangle, each of the equal angle is 15 degrees more than one half the third angle. How large is each angle of the triangle? Find:X = Largest Angle, Y= Smallest Angle, and $X + 2 Y = 180$ degrees.    Solution: Find X and substitute into the equation. Equation: $1/2 (180-2Y) + 15 = Y$; $90 - Y + 15 = Y$; $Y = 52.5$ degrees. $X = 180 - 2 (52.5)$; therefore, the largest angle is 75 degrees and the two smallest angles are 52.5 degrees.  Note: Not all isosceles triangle are right triangles.

10. Similar Right Triangle-Two right triangles are similar if one of the acute angles of the first is equal to one of the acute angle of the second. This can be shown as $A = A'$ and $B = B'$ or $A' = X$ and $B' = 90 - X$. In addition, because the acute angle of both triangle are identical this makes the corresponding sides of both triangle proportional. Therefore, in solving for the unknown side of a similar triangle find the factor of proportionality (K) and multiply any side of the triangle by this factor will give the corresponding side of the second triangle. EX: The length of the side of one triangle are 8, 9, and 11 the length of the side of the second triangle corresponding to side 8 in the first triangle is 10. What is the K factor. $K = a' / a$ ; $b' / b$ ; $c' / c$ ( a' b' c' are unknown sides) $= 10 / 8 = 5/4$.

149

## RIGHT TRIANGLE

11. Pythagorean Theorem- Stated as a formula, $c^2 = a^2 + b^2$, where c is the hypotenuse a right triangle. (Use Table 2 for square of numbers 1 thru 134). Note: This theorem is only applicable to right triangles with two known sides. EX: Find the diagonals of rectangle whose side are 50 and 120.

Solution: $c^2 = (50)^2 + (120)^2$; $c^2 = 2500 + 14,400$; $c^2 = 16,900$; $c = $ square root of 16,900 is 130.

EX: The foot of a ladder whose length is 51 feet is placed 24 feet from a side of a building. How high on the side of the building does it reach: Find (a). Solution:

$c^2 = a^2 + b^2$; $a^2 = c^2 - b^2$; $a^2 = 51^2 - 24^2$; $a^2 = 2601-576$; $a = $ square root of 2025 which is 45 feet.

EX: A ladder whose foot stands 9 feet from a side of a building just reaches the top window 40 feet from the ground. How long is the ladder? Find (c).

Solution: $c^2 = a^2 + b^2$; $c^2 = (40)^2 + (9)^2$; $c^2 = 1600 + 81$; $c = $ square root of 1681 which is 41 feet.

$$aX^2 + bX = c$$

Ex: The altitude of a certain right triangle is 5 feet more than the base. The hypotenuse is 25 feet. What are its base and altitude? Let X = Altitude; Let X − 5 = Base.

Solution: $c^2 = X^2 + (X-5)^2$; $25^2 = X^2 + X^2 - 10X + 25$;

$$\frac{2X^2 - 10X - 600}{2} = X^2 - 5X - 300; \quad X = \frac{5 \pm \sqrt{25 - 4(-300)}}{2}; \frac{5 \pm \sqrt{1225}}{2};$$

$$\frac{5 + 35}{2} = 20; \quad X = 20 \text{ feet}; \quad X - 5 = 15 \text{ feet}.$$

12 $ax^2 + bx + c = 0$ QUADRATIC EQUATION $X = \dfrac{-b \pm \sqrt{b^2 - 4ac}}{2a}$

EX: The area of the main waiting room is 28,600 feet. The sum of its length and Width is 350 feet. What are its dimensions? Let X = Length; Let X − 350 = width.

Solution: $X(X - 350) = 28,600$

$$X = \frac{350 \pm \sqrt{350^2 - 4(28,600)}}{2a}; \quad X = \frac{350 \pm \sqrt{8100}}{2}$$

$X = \dfrac{350 + 90}{2}$; $X = \dfrac{440}{2}$; $X = 220$ feet.(Length); $350 - X = 130$ feet (Width).

## SPECIAL TRIANGLES

1. Scalene Triangle – No two of its sides equal and no two of its angles equal.

2. Isosceles Triangle- Has two sides equal in length, and two angle the same.

    EX: Solve the formula: $b^2 = a^2 + c^2$ ; Equation: $b = \pm \sqrt{a^2 + c^2}$

    EX: Solve the formula for ( c ); Equation: $c = \sqrt{b^2 - a^2}$

    EX: If the equal sides of an isosceles triangle are 25 inches long, and the altitude is 15 inches. Find the base.

    Solution: $b = \pm \sqrt{a^2 + c^2}$ ; $b = \sqrt{15^2 + 25^2}$   $b = 40$

3. Equilateral Triangle- Has all three sides equal in length and all three angles the Same. An equilateral triangle has three equal sizes of 12 feet each. What is the altitude?

    Equation: $\dfrac{Side \sqrt{3}}{2}$ ( see 30: 60 : 90 Triangle) or $a = \pm \sqrt{b^2 - c^2}$ ;

    $a = \pm \sqrt{6^2 - 12^2}$ ;   $a = \pm \sqrt{36 - 144}$ ;   $a = \sqrt{108} = 10.39$ inches.

4. Law of Sines –Any triangle, whether it's acute or obtuse, the follow is true:

    $$\frac{Side\ a\ (BC)}{Sine\ of\ angle\ A} = \frac{Side\ b\ (AC)}{Sine\ of\ angle\ B} = \frac{Side\ c\ (AB)}{Sine\ of\ angle\ C}$$

5. Oblique Triangle- Any triangle containing no right angle. Two types are acute and Obtuse. EX:

EX: If side is 20 units and angle A is 15 degrees and angle C is 85 degrees. Find the length of AB (side c)? See Table 1 for angle function values.

Solution: $\dfrac{20}{Sin\ 15\ degrees} = \dfrac{c}{sin\ 85\ degrees}$   $c = \dfrac{20\ sin\ 85\ degrees}{sin\ 15\ degrees}$

$C\ \dfrac{20\ (0.9962)}{0.2588} = 77$ units

TABLE:1     ANGLE : SIDE : RATIO:

1.  Finding side BC (a) altitude. EX: 145 feet from the foot of a high building the
    angle of elevation of the top is 39 degrees. How high is the building?
    Equation: Tan = a/b; Tan (.8098) = a / 145. Solution: .8098 X 145 = 117.42 ft(BC)

2.  To find the tangent of an angle not in the table. Find (X): Tangent 40 degrees and
    15 minutes? Note: 15/60 = ¼ degree.
    Solution: Tan 40 degrees  00 min. = .8391         Spread 1 degrees = .0302
              Tan 40 degrees  15 min. =    ?                 15 min.= .0075
              Tan 41 degrees  00 min. = .8693
    1/4  X  (.0302) =  .0075;  X = .8693 + .0075 = .8466

3.  Find side AC (b) base. EX: From the top of a hill known to be 150 ft. above the
    Plain, the angle of depression of a house is 22 degrees. How far away is the house
    from an imaginary point directly below the top of the hill? Equation: Tan = a / b;
    Tan(.4040)= 150 / b. Solution: .4040 X (b) = 150; b = 150 / .4040; AC (b) = 371.2

4.  To find the sine of an angle not in the table. Find (X): sine 27 degrees 25 minutes.
    Note: 25/60 = 5/12 degree.
    Solution:  Sin 27 degrees  00 min. = .4540         Spread 1 degrees = .0155
               Sin 27 degrees  25 min. =    ?                 25 min. = .0064
               Sin 28 degrees  00 min. = .4695
    5 / 12  X (.0155) = .0064;  X = .4540 + .0064 = .4604

5.  Solving problems by means of sines of angles. EX: If a telephone pole is 40 ft.
    long and the guy wire angle is set at 53 degrees and 15 minutes. How long is the
    guy wire? How far is the guy wire from the telephone pole? Find side AB(c) and
    side AC (b). Equation: Sin = a / c; Cos = b / c; Find (X) sin 53 degrees 15 minutes
    and cos 53 degrees 15 minutes.  Note: 15/60 = ¼ degree.
    Solution:  Sin 53 degrees  00 min. = .7986    Cos 53 degrees  00 min. = .6018
               Sin 53 degrees  15 min. =    ?      Cos 53 degrees  15 min. =    ?
               Sin 54 degrees  00 min. = .8090    Cos 54 degrees  00 min. = .5878
    ¼  X  .0104 = .0026;       X (sin) = .7986 +.0026 = .8012
    ¼  X  .0140 = .0035;       X (cos)= .6018 - .0035 = .5083
    Sin(.8012) = 40 / c ;  Solution: .8012  X  (c) = 40; c = 40 / ,8012;  AB (c) = 49.9 ft

6.  Solving problem by means of sine of angle; and find side AB ( c ) . EX: How long
    Must a guy wire be to reach from the top of a 25 ft. telephone pole to a point on
    the ground  20 ft. from the foot of the pole, and what angle will it make with the
    ground?
    Tan angle is 51 degrees and 20 minutes.  Side AB ( c) = 32ft.

In chemistry, so many chemical calculation require you to find the conversion factor and the mole ratio first before you can express the relationship between different units. Therefore, to change a quantity from one unit given to another, the original quality must be multiplied by a conversion factor of 1. That is the whole number can be considered to be the numerator of a fraction of which the denominator is 1.

EX: 1000ml = 1 liter; Conversion: 1000ml / 1 liter = 1 or 1 liter / 1000ml = 1.

Knowing what conversion factor to use is important, since most chemistry problems usually ask these question:

What is the ratio of mass (or weight) to volume?

What is the equation coefficient ratio?

How many moles?

What is the equation molecular weight?

What is the solution concentration unit?

It is important to recognize that all such calculation using the numerical Coefficient from a given balanced equation must be done in terms of "moles". Remember this, because the number of molecules in a mole is the same for all substance.

1 mole = $6 \times 10^{23}$ molecules or atoms. Mole- 1 mole of a substance weighs (w) grams, where w = molecular weight (Table of atomic weight). EX: $H_2O$ molecular weight is 18 g / mole.

Coefficient- A number written in front of another number and intended as a multiplier.     EX: $2H_2 + O_2 + 2H_2O$    Coefficient ratio: 2 : 1

2 mole $H_2$ / 1 mole $O_2$    Mole ratio: 2 : 1

What is the ratio of a compound of 10 sodium atoms (Na) 5 carbon atoms (C), and 15 oxygen atoms (O). State the formula.

Relationship: Divide by 5 (common factor).

10 (Na) : 5 ( C ) : 15 (O) = 2 (Na) : 1 ( C ) : 3 (O) ; $Na_2CO_3$ Note: subscript after the symbol tells the number of atom of that type.

Formula: $Na_2CO_3$    is a compound containing 2 atoms of sodium for every 1 atom of carbon for every 3 atoms of oxygen.

2. Show the balance equitation for the fermentation of sugar: $C_6H_{12}O_2$ to alcohol, $C_2H_6O$ ? What is the molecular weight of $CO_2$ ?

Equation: $C_6H_{12}O_6 = 2C_2H_6O + 2CO_2$

Molecular weight: 12g for C, 16g for each 2 O's = 44g.

3   If 72 g of sugar are used how many moles and how many (g) of alcohol are formed?
    Needed: moles of alcohol;     Given: 72 g of sugar;     Relationship: molecular weight
    of sugar is 180 g ; therefore, ( 1 mole of sugar = 180g ) ( 2 mole of alcohol = 46 g ).
    Note: 2 mole of alcohol are formed from 1 mole of sugar. (coefficient from the
    equation # 2
    Solution: moles alcohol = 72 g sugar  X   $\frac{1 \text{ mole}}{180 \text{ g sugar}}$   X  $\frac{2 \text{ mole alcohol}}{1 \text{ mole of sugar}}$ = 0.8 mole alcohol.

    grams alcohol = .08 mole X $\frac{46 \text{ g alcohol}}{1 \text{ mole}}$ = 37 grams.


4   Density – Important physical property of a substance that can be measured
    without chemically altering the substance. Density is defined as the ratio of mass
    (weight to volume). Expressed as: Density = $\frac{mass}{Vol}$   or  $D = \frac{M}{V}$; by rearranging
    we have  $V = \frac{M}{D}$

    Archimedes's principle: Volume = weight of liquid displaced (decrease in weight)
                                      density of liquid used: ml or cc


    EX: Sea water has a density of 1.025 g / ml. What is the weight of 1 liter of sea
        water? Needed: gram weight of 1 liter of sea water.  Given: a liter of sea
        water. Relationship: 1.025 g = 1 ml (conversion factor: 1000ml = 1 liter).
    Solution: g = 1 liter  X  $\frac{1.025 \text{ g}}{1 \text{ mil}}$  X  $\frac{1000 \text{ ml}}{1 \text{ liter}}$ = 1025 g

    Note: Since both weight and volume have units, density should always be
        Expressed in term of the unit used for measurement. EX: 1g/ml, 1 kg/l, etc.


5   Specific Gravity- The numerical value of specific gravity is the same as density.
    It tells us whether a liquid is more dense or less dense than water. EX: The
    specific gravity of the acid in car batteries tells whether the battery is fully
    charged or not; also used to determine the % of alcohol in beverages.
    Note: Specific gravity (has no unit). This property characteristic makes it different
        from density.
                    Specific Gravity = $\frac{\text{weight of a volume of substance}}{\text{weight of an equal volume of water}}$

    EX: A liter of mercury of mercury weighs 13.6 Kg. What is its density?
    Relationship:liter= 13.6 Kg or13.6 g/ml since 1 liter = 1000 ml and 1 Kg = 1000g.

    EX: If the density of a liquid is 0.8g/ml, what is the weight of 20 ml of the liquid?
    Needed: weight of 20 ml of liquid.   Given: 20 ml of the liquid.
    Relationship: Density 0.8g = 1ml.
    Solution: g = 20 ml  X  $\frac{0.8g}{1 \text{ ml}}$ = 16 g     Specific Gravity: 16

154

6. Primary Acid Standard.- Titrate (Example: first solution) of Oxalic acid dihydrate-

$$H_2C_2O_4 \cdot 2H_2O$$

Acid-Base Titration- A technique in which measured amount of acid and bases are
      bought together to neutralize each other.
Titration equiv pt.  N(acid)  X  Vol(acid)  =  N(base)  X  Vol(base).

Equivalence point indicator- Phenolphthalein indicator is colorless in acid but will turn
      Pink the moment you have the slightest excess of base.

Oxalic acid dihydrate- Molecular weight (126); Equiv = wt. (63), ½ of molecular wt.
      Because of its two acidic hydrogen ions per molecule.

7. Molarity-(M) The number of moles per liter of solution. Moles = M  X  Vol (in liters).
      Solute- dissolved substance used.   $M = \dfrac{\text{moles solute}}{\text{Liter solution}}$
      Solution- solvent used.
    Ex: How many moles of HCl are in 2 liter of 3 M HCl solution?
               Moles HCl = $\dfrac{\text{2 liters sol'n  X  3 moles HCl}}{\text{1 liter sol'n}}$ = 6 mole  HCl
        Concentration (normalities)
Normality-(N)  Normality of a solution is the number of equiv .per liter of solution.
                 $N = \dfrac{\text{equiv...solute (dissolved substance)}}{\text{liter solution (solvent)}}$
         +         -                             23
1 mole of H ions or of OH                  6.02 X 10     ions.
Equiv. = N  X  Vol (in liters). Equiv- Unit  devised to give a 1: 1 relationship.
Ex: If 2 moles are dissolved to make 4 liters of solution (sol'n). the concentration is
    2 moles / 4 liters (L)  = .5 M.  If .01  equiv. Is dissolved in 250 ml of sol'n the
    concentration is .01 equiv. 1.25L or .04 equiv. / L = .04 N.
    Solution:    $M = \dfrac{\text{2 mole solute}}{\text{4 liter solution}} = .5$    $N = \dfrac{.01 \text{ equiv. solute}}{250 \text{ ml} = .25 \text{ liter solution}} = .04$

8.  Concentration of Solution  (sol'n)- Per cent (or %) = g solute / 100g solution or
                                    g  solute / g solution X  100 %
    Ex: How many (g) of glucose are in 500g of 2 per cent glucose solution?
        Needed: g of glucose      Given: 500g of solution
      Relationship: 2g of glucose to every 100g of solution (2%).
    g = 500g sol'n  X  $\dfrac{\text{2g  glucose}}{\text{100g sol'n}}$ = 10g

8A. Dilute(reduced) Concentration of Sol'n-%(Wt./Vol)=g / solute / 100 ml solution.
When water is used as a dilute(density 1g = 1ml), it is common to use a wt.-vol %.
   Ex: You have a 2%(wt/vol) solution of NaCl, sodium chloride, ordinary table salt.
How many g of salt in 1 liter solution? Needed: g of salt.  Given: 1 liter sol'n.
How many ml of solution in 1 mole (58.5g / mole) ? Needed:  ml of sol'n 1 mole.
     Relationship:  2g of salt in every 100 ml of solution.

Solution:  g NaCl = 1000 ml sol'n X $\dfrac{\text{2g NaCl}}{\text{100 ml sol'n}}$ = 20g NaCl

Solution:  by rearranging % (wt / vol)  =  g solute / 100 ml solution.

ml = 1 mole NaCl  X $\dfrac{\text{58.5 g NaCl}}{\text{1 mole NaCl}}$ X $\dfrac{\text{100 ml sol'n}}{\text{2g NaCl}}$ = 2925 ml.

## FINDING THE PRECENTAGE

1. To find the percentage when base and rate are known: What number is 6% of 50?
.06 X 50 = 3; "of" has the same meaning as 1 / 4 of 15 = ? "of" means to multiply;
however, the rate must be changed from % to a decimal.

Fractional Percents-Part of 1%. Find 1% of the number and then find the fractional
part.  Ex:  1 / 4 % of 840 = ?          1 % of 840 = .01 X 840 = 8.40
      1 / 4 % of 840 = 8.40 X 1 /4 = 2.10

2. To find the rate when the base and percentage are known: 20 is what percent of 60 ?
60 base or multiplicand                      $\dfrac{20}{60} = \dfrac{1}{3}$ or 33 1/3 %
_? rate or multiplier
20 (percentage) or product
     Recall: That the product divided by one of its factor gives the other factor.

3. To find the base when the percentage and rate are known: The number 5 is 25% of
What number? Ex: 25% of ? = 5:  5 = 20 (base)
    ? (base)
 .25 (rate)  Percentage divided by rate equals base.
5.00 (percentage)

     Recall: We divide the product by its known factor to find the other factor.

## PROPORTION

In science many chemical and physical relations are expressed as proportions. A proportion is nothing more than an equation in which the members are ratios. In other words when two ratio are set equal to each other, a proportion is formed (4 numbers). Ex: a : b = c : d.

Since proportions rules are simplification rules of equation, having a knowledge of proportions rules often provides a quick method of solving word problems. This is because you can rearrange word problems as proportion operation (fraction) or mean proportional (no fraction).

## PROPORTION TERMS

1. Extremes- The first and last terms (a & d). Numerator of the first ratio and the Denominator of the second.

2. Means- The second and third terms (b & c). Denoninator of the first ratio and the Numerator of the second.

3. Factor of Proportionality- Common factor by which both terms of the ratio must be multiplied in order to show that the ratio are the same.

4. Proportion Operation- The product of the means equals the product of the extremes.
   Ex: bc = ad or ad = bc ;                    cb = da or bc = ad.

5. Means Proportional- Square root of means and extremes product. $\frac{A}{X} = \frac{X}{C}$;
   $X^2 = AC$ ; $X = +- \sqrt{AC}$ ; $8 = \frac{2}{32}$   $8 = \sqrt{2(32)}$   $8 = \sqrt{64}$

6. Inverse Proportion- The terms of the ratio that makes up the proportion are inter- change and the equation is still equal. Ex: a : c = b : d;  5/8 =10/16 or 5/10 =8/16

Note: Used in rates of speeds or ratio of doing work problems, because the more men we have, the less time is required. Therefore, you musst invert one of the ratios.

7. Alternation Proportion- Means are interchang and the equation is still equal.
   Ex:       a : c = b : d;          5/8 = 10/16 or 5/10 = 8/16

## PROPORTION WORD PROBLEMS

1. Solving problems by means of proportion that involves similar right triangle (see right triangle # 10; pp. 149).

2. If an automobile rums 36 mi on 2 gal. Of gas, how many miles will it run on 12 gal.?
   Solution: (ad = bc). X = miles on 12 gal.   Equation: 36 : X = 2 : 12;
   Equation: 2 : 12 = 36 : X; 2X = 36 X 12; X = 216 miles.

PROPORTATION PROBLEMS

3.  What number added to the terms of the fraction 5/8 and 2/3 makes the resulting
    fraction equal. Solution:  ad = bc.  X =  number added.
                    Equation:  5 + X : 8+ X = 2+ X : 3 + X
    5 + X (3 +X) = 8 + X (2 + X);  -2 X = 1,  X = - 1 /2 .

4.  A's age is twice B's age. If A's age 4 years from now be divided by B's age at that
    time, the quotient is 5/3. What are their ages? Solution:  ( d a  =  c b ).
                    Equation:  2 X = A's age,  X = B's age.
    3 (2 X + 4) = 5 (X + 4);  6 X + 12 = 5 X + 20;  X = 8 yrs.  2 X = 16 yrs.

5.  What number added to both terms of the fraction 5/8 changes that fraction into one
    whose value is 3 / 4 ? Solution: (d a = c b) X = number added.
                    Equation:  5 +X : 8 + X = 3 / 4
    20 + 4 X = 24 + 3 X;  X = 4.

6.  In a factory, there is one machine which can turn out a certain number of articles in 8
    hours, second which can do it in 16 hours, and a third in 220 hours. How long will it
    take all three machines working at the same time to fill the order for the number of
    articles. Solution: (LCD)  X = hrs together.
                    Equation:  X : 8 + X :  16 + X :  20
    20 X +10 X +8 X =160,   38 X = 160, X + 4.2 hours.

7.  The net profits in a stor which had sold $65,000 worth of goods were $4250. At the
    Same rate, what would be the profits from the sale of $85,000 worth of goods.
    Solution:  ( a d = b c )  X = Profit on sales of $85,000
                    Equation:  $4250 : $65,000 = X : $85,000.
    4250 (85,000) = 65,000 (X),   X = 5557.69.

8.  If a piece of city property 240 feet deep by 350 feet front cost $10,000 and is sold in
    lots  50 feet frontage at $2,000 each, what is the gain. Solution: ( a d : c b).
    X - Cost = Gain.    Equation:  50 : 2000 = 350 : X.
    50 X = 700,000 X = $14,000     $14,000 - $10,000 = $4,000 Gain.

9.  On a map having a scale of 1 in. to 50 mi., how many inches represent 540 mi?
    Solution: (b c = a d)  X = scale for 540 miles.
                    Equation:  1 : 50 = X : 540;
    50 X = 540,   X = 10.8 inches.

158

Variation is the name given to the study of the effects of changes among related quantities. Scientists when doing experiments are concerned with the change called related variables according some law of physic or math. The three types are direct, inverse and joint variation.

Direct Variation- Quantity can be expressed in terms of a second quantity multiplied by a constant. The constant is the ratio of the first quantity to the second quantity.

Ex: $P = 4s$   or   $A = s^2$   one variable and the constant P and A.

Variable-Letters used in an equation whose values are not fixed. Ex: $Y = 2X$ or $Y/X = 2$

$C = nc$. is the formula for the cost of (n) articles at the cost per article.

If (n) is constant, the total cost varies (directly) as (the cost per article). If ( c ) is constant then the total cost varies (directly) as (the number of the articles). If ( C ) is constant, the number of articles (n) varies (inversely) as (the cost per article); so that the number of articles decrease as the cost per article (increase).

Inverse Variation= The product of the two quantities is a constant or when the product of Any value of the one and the corresponding value of the other is constant.

Ex:  $A = LW$; A is a constant.   $L = A/W$;   $W = A/L$
Ex:  Boyle's law  (Pressure)(Volume) = Gas at a Constant Temperature.
Ex:  The intensity of light varies (inversely) as the (square) of the (distance) from the light. Select appropriate letters to represent these variables, and express this relation by a formula.
           Equation:   $I d^2 = K$, where I is the intensity, d is the distance,
                                K is a constant

Joint Variation - Quantity varies jointly as two or more other quantities. The constant is The ratio of the first quantity to the product of the other quantities. Ex: $A = L W$;

Also can be (two) variables with a constant understood. The formula for the area is an example of joint variation. If A is allow to vary, rather than being constant.

Ex:  $S = 1/2 C L$, is a formula in geometry. If S, C, and L are variables, then S Varies (jointly) as (C and L) . If (L) is constant, then (S) varies (directly) as ( C ). If (S) is constant, then ( C ) varies (inversely) as (L),  so when ( C ) increase , then (L) decreases.

The word "radical" is derived from the Latin word "radix," which means "root".

An expression such as $\sqrt{2}$   $\sqrt{5}$   or   $\sqrt{a+b}$   that exhibit's a radical sign, is referred to as a RADICAL. Radical are used to indicate root of a number.

The number under a radical sign is the RADICAN. The index of the root appears in he trough of the radical sign. The index tells what root of the radicand is intended, for example: cube, fourth power, etc.

The process of separating a radical into two radicals so that one radicand is a perfect power is called FACTORING.

The perfect power can than become the COEFFICIENT of the remaining radical after removing the radical sign.

In order to simplify radicals easily, it is convenient to know the square and cubes of hole numbers (see Table 2: Squares, Cubes, Square Roots, Cube Roots and Logs).

Every number has two square roots. They have equal absolute value but opposite signs. Of these two square roots, the positive one is call the principal square root. Thus,

$$\sqrt{9a^4 b^2} = \pm 3a^2 b$$

Rule- The square root of the product of two or more number equals the product of their square roots. Thus,

$$\sqrt{(4)(5)} \quad (2)(5) = 10 \quad \sqrt{(a)(b)} = \sqrt{a} \times \sqrt{b},$$

$$\sqrt{1764\ a^4} = \sqrt{4.441\ a^4} = \sqrt{(4)(9)(4)(9)\ a^4} = 42a^2$$

$$2 \times 3 \times 7 \times a^2$$

Find the principle square root of 80.

$$\sqrt{80} = \sqrt{(16)(5)} = 4 \times (\text{ Table 2 } \#5\ (2.2361) = 8.944$$

160

## EXPONENTS

### POSITIVE INTREGRAL EXPONENTS

1. Multiplication  $b^N \times b^M = b^{N+M}$  Power of a Fraction

2. Power of a Power  $(b^N)^M = b^{NM}$  $\left(\dfrac{a}{b}\right)^N = \dfrac{a^N}{b^N}$

3. Power of a Product  $(b\,c)^N = b^N c^N$  Zero Exponent  $b^0 = 1$

### FRACTIONAL EXPONENTS

$$b^{\frac{N(Power)}{D(Root)}} = \sqrt[D]{b^N} \qquad Ex: \; 32^{1/5} = \sqrt[5]{32} = 2$$

$$Ex: \; 4^{1/2} = \sqrt{4} = 2$$

$$Ex: \; 4^{-\frac{1}{2}} = \sqrt{4^{-1}} = 2^{-1} = 1/2$$

$$Ex: \; \sqrt{18X^3} = \sqrt{(9)(2)(X^2)(X)} = \sqrt{(9X^2)(2X)} = 3X\sqrt{2X}$$

### NEGATIVE EXPONENTS

Ex: $\dfrac{a^{-1}}{b} = \dfrac{b}{a}$  Note: Negative exponents has the effect of moving a fraction from top to bottom or (vice versa).

### DIVISION OF POWERS (EXPONENTS SUBTRACTION)

$$\frac{b^N}{b^N} = b^{M-N} \qquad OR \qquad \frac{1}{b^{N-M}}$$

## LOGARITHMS                                     A10-27.2

Logarithm represent a specialized use of exponents. By means of logarithms, computation with large masses of data can be greatly simplified. For example, many natural phenomena, such as rates of growth and decay, are most easily described in terms of logarithmic or exponential formulas.

## LOGARITHM TERMS

1. Raising a Power- Process of multiplication is replaced by addition, when using logarithms.

2. Extracting a Root- The process of division is replaced by subtraction, when using logarithms.

3. Exponential Form- $2^3 = 8$; $4^2 = 16$; $5^0 = 1$; $27^{2/3} = 9$; $b^X = N$.

4. Logarithmic Form- $\text{Log}_2 8 = 3$; $\text{Log}_4 16 = 2$; $\log_5 1 = 0$; $\text{Log}_{27} 9 = 2/3$

   $\text{Log}_{bn} = X$.

5. Natural Logarithm - Uses the base e which is an irrational number equal to 2.711828
   $\text{Log}_e 45$ or $\ln 45$

6. Common Logarithms- Logarithms with 10 as a base. Ex: $\text{Log} 100 = 2$ same a $\text{Log}_{10} 100 = 2$.

7. Natural Log to common Log conversion factor. (.4343).       Note: $1 = 10^0$

8. Common Log to natural Log conversion factor. (2.3026).

9. Fractional Logarithm- Usually written as a decimal.

10. Log of a Number- Expressing the number as a power of 10. Ex: $10^6 = 10^{.77815}$ ( Table 2).

11. Logarithms Positive Characteristic-The whole number is one less than the number of the digits to the left of the decimal point in the number. Ex: $\text{Log} 360 = 2.55630$.

12. Logarithms Negative Characteristic- Add one more than the number of zero between the decimal point and the first non-zero digit of the number.

13. Logarithms Negative Characteristic- Place a bar over characteristic. The number is one more than the number of zeros between the decimal point and the firs non-zero digit of the number.  Ex:
    $$\text{Log } 0.036 = \overline{2}.55630 \text{ (Table 2)}$$

14. Mantissa- Decimal part of l logarithm, and does not change when the decimal point Moves. Ex: Log. 45 and Log 450 has the same mantis.

In the business world the treatment of profit, loss, and discount, and other matters pertaining to money is based on percentage (refer to A10-27.1 pp. 156).

Retailers and merchants also use a secret code called "working keys". In some stores only the selling price is marked, while other stores may mark both the cost and selling price. For example, if a question arises from the customer about an item marked, the manager of the store can tell at once without referring to their books how much the item marked cost ant the selling price.

The marking key usually constructed of letters that corresponds to numbers 1 2 3 4 5 6 7 8 9 0. In addition, instead of using letter twice or three times, some special characters, are used a repeaters ( XY ). For example, let say the store uses "buy this one", as their marking key, and the item that normally sells for $ 50.00 is found to have a defect by a customer. The store manager can look on the tag marked (HEXY/TEXY), and know to sell that item at a reduced price of $ 40.00 without referring to the stores books.

Some terms and definitions used in doing business are as follow:
1.  List Price- Price the store hold themselves to all customers. Usually put high to avoid possible loss from unexpected changes.
2   Discounts- Deductions made from the list price.
3   Trade Discount- Discount made on account of the condition of the market, the size ot the order, the reliability and desirability of product.
4   Net Amount- Bill for goods after discount.
5   Gross Amount- Bill for goods
6   Single Discount- Discount computed as a certain rate per cent of the list price.
    Ex: Goods listed at $ 25.00 were sold at a discount of 25%. Find the selling price.
    Given: Selling Price ($25);    Given: Discount (25%).
    Solution: $25 –(.25 X $25) = Selling Price ($25 - $6.25) = $18.75.
6.  Wholesaler's Discount- Discount to retail dealer to enable a return on his investment.
7.  Margin – Selling price (retail price) minus cost (wholesale price). Ex: An article listed to sell retail at $20 was sold to the retail dealer at a discount of 25%. What rate increase (profit) did the retail dealer get?    Given:  Retail Price ($20)
    Solution: Retail Price $20 minus Wholesale Price  =  Margin  $5
            Return investment rate: Margin  /  Wholesale Price  = 33 1/3%.

Ex: A wholesaler wishes to sell an article at $15, to give the retailer (customer) a
    Reduction of 25% from the list price. What must he make the list price?
        Given:  $15 Retail Price        Given:  Discount 25%
        Solution: Retail Price ($15)  = 3 / 4 of the list price, List Price = 15 X 4 / 3 = $20.
Ex: A wholesaler wishes to sell an article for $12, but wishes to give his customer a
    Reduction of 40% from the list price. What must he make the list price?
        Given: $12 List Price = 60%; hence, $12  =  3 / 5 of the list price, which is $20.

## DEFINITIONS A10-28.1

1. Literal Number- A letter used to represent a number.
2. Absolute Value- Number without signs (+ or - ).
3. Term- A symbol or group of symbols separated from other symbols by a ( + or - ) sign.
4. Expression- One or more terms (Monomials- one term); (Binomials- two terms); (Polynomial-two or more terms); (Trinomial- three terms).
5. Like Terms- Terms containing the same variable and differ only in their coefficients. Like terms can be combined.
6. Unlike terms- Terms which do not have the same literal factors.
7. Ascending and Descending Powers- Exponents order from highest to lowest.
8. Parentheses, Brackets and Braces- Symbols of grouping which are to be treated as a single number expression. The number inside to be combined before using then in any other manner.
9. *Identity- Equation that is satisfied by all values of the literal numbers for which the two sides have any real meaning.*
10. Prime Number- An expression that has no factors except it self and 1. Ex: 1,2,3,5,7,11, etc.
11. Conditioned Equation- One that is true for only certain values of a variable (Literal Numbers).
12. Composite Number- All integers which are not prime. Ex: 4,6,8,9,10, etc.
13. First Degree Equation- One variable that is never multiplied by itself. The variable is involved in one or more operations of addition, subtraction, multiplication, and division.
14. Second Degree Equation- (Standard Form). $y = \underline{a} x^2 + \underline{b} x + \underline{c}$.

    1. The graph is a smooth parabola shaped curve pointing up if $a$ is positive. If $a$ is negative, the curve opens down.
    2. y- intercept is $c$ (the constant).
    3. Two x- intercept, $+$ & $-$ solution to problems.
    4. *x – intercept ( y is 0). In other words, you must factor equation for value of x when y = 0.*

15. *y – intercept-* The value of $y$ when $x = 0$ and the point where the line crosses the $y - axis$.

    Vertex- The low or high point on the curve.

    $$\frac{-b}{2a} \quad ; \quad \frac{4ac-b^2}{4a}$$

    Axis of Symmetry- Dash line center of vertex.
16. Abscissa- Starting point along the $x$ axis and perpendicular to $x$ axis.
17. *Ordinate-Starting point along the y axis and perpendicular to x axis.*
18. Cartesian Coordinate System- Rectangular (x & y) axis divided into (top right to left) quadrants of I &II, and (bottom left to right) quadrants of III & IV.
19. Coordinates- Made-up of both abscissa and ordinate locations along the $x$ & y axis. When giving the coordinates of a point, the abscissa is always given first.
20. Linear Equation- Applies to equation of the first degree, at the most two variables. Graft "curve" is a straight line. $\underline{a} x + \underline{b} y = \underline{c}$. (Standard Form) with $\underline{a}$ , $\underline{b}$ , and $\underline{c}$ being real numbers.
21. Inconsistent equation- No or false solution or if two linear equation the lines are parallel.
22. Arbitrary constants- Constants that be assigned different value for different problems. Usually *indicated by letters at the beginning of the alphabet.*
23. Dependent Equation- Infinitely many solution or identity, such as $0 = 0$.
24. Independent equation- Two equation having variables, but their solution are different.
25. Simultaneous Equations- Two independent equation which have only one common solutions.

164

## SOLVING AN EQUATION

1.  Both members of an equation may be divided by the same number without destroying the equality.
2.  The factors of a product may be rearranged in any order before finding the product.
3.  If any part of an expression are enclosed by parentheses (find the value inside first to clear the ( ).
4.  Do computation: Multiplication first, next do all the division, taking them in order from left to right.
          Then do the addition and subtractions, taking them in any order.

### INEQUALITY SIGN RULES

1.  Symbols "greater than" is $>$ ; "less than" is $<$ .
2.  Symbols "greater than or equal to" is $>$ ; "less than or equal to" is $<$ .
    Note: Reverse direction only whenever inequality is multiplied or divided by a negative number.
3.  Transposed- *Transferring a term from one side of the inequality to the other if and only if its sign is* changed as it opposes the inequality sign.
4.  Rewrite answer using < or < because it's clearer to visualize reading left to right, on the number line.
5.  Conditional inequality- True for only certain values of the variable.
6.  Absolute inequality- True for all values of the variable.

### POSITIVE & NEGATIVE NUMBER RULES

1.  The sign + and - are used to show opposite quantities between absolute value numbers.
2.  The sign must always be written before a negative numbers, the number is positive.
3.  Add + numbers and prefix the plus sign to the result.
4.  Add - *numbers and prefix the minus sign to the result.*
5.  Add + and - numbers, subtract the smallest value from the larger and prefix to the result the sign of the largest number.
6.  Adding a negative number is subtraction.
7.  Algebraic sum of two numbers will be smaller than one of them if on is negative.

### MULIPLICATION RULES

1.  Like signs the product is positive.   2.  Unlike signs the product is negative.

### PARENTHESIS RULES

1.  Parentheses preceded by a + sign; make no changes to terms within the parentheses.
2.  *Parentheses preceded by a - sign; make sign changes to terms within the parentheses.*
3.  Parentheses within other parentheses; combine terms within innermost parentheses. Then remove these parentheses first.
4.  Continue until all parentheses are removed and like terms are combined.

### PLACING TERMS INSIDE PARENTHESIS

1.  Do not change the signs of the terms within the parentheses if preceded by a plus sign.
2.  If terms are placed within parentheses preceded by a minus sign, their signs must be changed.

### DIVISION RULES

1.  The quotient of two numbers having like sign is positive.
2.  *The quotient of two numbers having unlike sign is negative.*

### EQUATION RULES

1.  When a term is transposed from one side of the equation and crosses the equal or inequality sign you Have to change the sign.
2.  Cancel term from both sides of the equation only if the term have (are preceded) the same sign.
Changing signs crossing the equal or inequality sign will not destroy the equality of the equation.

# APPENDIX A: REFERENCE TABLE

## UNIT OF MEASUREMENT
### STANDARD

### Distance ( Linear Measure)

| | |
|---|---|
| 12 in. = 1 ft. | 7.92 in. = 1 link (l) |
| 3 ft = 1yd. | 100(l). = 1 chain(ch) |
| 5.5 yd. = 1 rd. | 25(l) = 1 rod(rd.) |
| 320 rd. = 1 mi. | 4(rd) = 1chain |
| 5280 ft. = 1 mi. | 80chain = 1 mile |

### Nautical measure

6 ft = 1 fathom
120 fathom = 1 cable length
6080 feet = 1 nautical mi.
3 knots = 1 league

### Cubic ( Volume measure)

1728 cu in = 1 cu ft
27 cu ft = 1 cu yd
24.75 cu ft = 1 perch
128 cu ft = 1 cord

### Area ( Length Measure Square )

144 sq. in = 1 sq. ft
9 sq. in = 1 sq. yd
30.25 sq.yd = 1 sq. rd.
640 acres = 1 sq. mi.
16 sq. rd = 1 sq.chain
100 sq. ft = 1 sq.
30.25 sq. ft = 1 sq. r
36 sq. mi. = 1 township
10 sq. chains = 1 acre
160 sq.rd = 1 acre
43.560 sq. ft = 1 acre

### ( Circular Measure )

60 sec = 1 min
60 min = 1 degree
360 degrees = 1 circumference

## COMPARISON OF LIQUID AND DRY MEASURE

| | Gallon | QUART | PINT |
|---|---|---|---|
| Liquid | 231 cu in | 57.75 cu in | 28.875 cu in |
| Dry | 268.8 cu in | 62.2 cu in | 33.6 cu in |

## MEASURE OF CAPACITY

### Liquid Measure

2 cups = 1 pt.
2 pt. = 1 qt.
4 qt. = 1 gal.
1 gal = 4 qt = 8 pt. =16 cups
31.5 gal = 1 barrel

### Dry Measure

2 pt. = 1qt.
8 qt. = 1 pk
4 pk. = 1 bu.
1 bu = 4 pk= 32 qt=64pt

### APOTHECARIES' MEASURE

| | | |
|---|---|---|
| 60 minims | = 1 fluid drachm |
| 8 fluid drachms | = 1 fluid ounce |
| 16 fluid ounce | = 1 pint |
| 8 pints | = 1 gallon |

### APPROXIMATE MEASURE

1 bushel= 1.25 cu ft (1 heaped bushel= 1.6 cu ft
1 cu.ft = .625 heaped bushel  1cu ft = .8 bushel
1 ton coal = 35 cu ft.  1 ton timothy hay = 450 cu ft
1 ton clover hay = 550 cu ft

## MEASURE OF WEIGHT

### AVOIRDUPOIS WEIGHT

16 oz = 1 lb
100 lb = 1 hundredweight
2000 lb = 20 hundredweight = 1 ton

### LONG TON

28 lb = 1 quarter(qr.)
4qr. = 1 long hundredweight
20 long hundredweight = 1 long ton

# APPENDIX B: REFERENCE TABLE
## METRIC MEASURES

Metric System- is a decimal system because each unit is a decimal multiple of the next lower unit. In the measures of length, weight, and capacity, each unit is 10 time the next lower unit. In the measure of area, each unit is 100 times, and in the measure of volume, 1000 times the next lower unit.

The metric units of weight and capacity are derived from the meter as follow:

1 cc of water weighs 1 gram.     1 $dm^3$ of water weighs 1 kilogram

1 $dm^3$ = 1 liter.     1 $m^3$ of water = 1 tonneau = 2204.6 lb.

| Measure of Length | Measure of Area |
|---|---|
| 10 millimeters = 1 centimeter( cm) | 100 sq. millimeters (mm) = 1(sq. cm.)   $[cm.^2)$ |
| 10 centimeters = 1 decimeter(dm) | 100 sq. centimeters = 1(sq. dm)   = $dm^2$ |
| 10 decimeters = 1 meter(m) | 100 sq. decimeters = 1(sq. m.) |
| 10 meters     = 1 decameter(Dm) | 100 sq. meters = 1 (sq. Dm.) |
| 10 decameter  = 1 hectometer (Hm) | 100 sq. decameter = 1( sq. Hm) |
| 10 hectometers = 1 kilometer(Km) | 100 sq. hectometers = 1(sq. Km) |
| 10 kilometers  = 1 myriameter(Mm) | Hectare=100ares=10,000sq. M |
| 1 kilometer(km )= 1000meters = 6.6215 mile | Centare = 1 sq.meter |
| 1 meter(m)         =   100 centimeters | |
| 1 centimeter(cm) =    10 millimeters(mm) | |

1 nanometer(nm) = 1 x $10^{-9}$

1 picometer(pm) = 1 x $10^{-12}$

1 Angstrom(A) = 1 x $10^{-10}$      1 inch = 2.54 centimeter

| Measure of Weight | | Measure of capacity | |
|---|---|---|---|
| 10 milligrams(mg)  = | 1 centigram(cg) | 10 milliliter(ml)  = | 1 centiliter(cl) |
| 10centigrams       = | 1 decigram(dg.) | 10 centiliters    = | 1 deciliter(dl) |
| 10 decigrams       = | 1 gram(g) | 10 deciliters     = | 1 liter(l) |
| 10 grams           = | 1 decagram(Dg) | 10 liters         = | 1 decaliter(Dl) |
| 10 decagrams       = | 1 hectogram(Hg) | 10decaliters      = | 1 hectoliter(Hl) |
| 10 hectograms      = | 1 kilogram(Kg) | 10 hectoliters    = | 1 kiloliter(Kl) |
| 10 kilograms       = | 1 microgram(Mg.) | | |

## CUBIC MEASURE

1000 cu($mm^3$) = 1 cu($cm^3$) or (cc)      1000 cu centimeters = 1 cu decimeter($dm^3$)

1000 cu decimeters  = 1 cubic meter ($m^3$)

## APPENDIX B: REFERENCE TABLE
### Conversions To Metric Measures

|  | Symbol | When You Know | Multiply By | To Find | Symbol |
|---|---|---|---|---|---|
| | In | inches | 2.54 | centimeters | cm |
| | Ft | feet | 30.48 | centimeters | cm |
| LENGTH | Yd | yards | 0.9 | meters | m |
| | Mi | miles | 1.6 | kilometers | km |
| | In sq | square inches | 0.5 | sq centimeters | cm sq |
| | Ft sq | square feet | 0.09 | square meters | m sq |
| AREA | Yd sq | square yards | 0.8 | square meters | m sq |
| | Mi sq | square miles | 2.6 | sq kilometers | km sq |
| | | Acres | 0.4 | hectares | ha |
| | Oz | ounces | 28 | grams | g |
| MASS | Lb | pounds | 0.45 | kilograms | kg |
| (Weight) | | Short tons (2000 lb) | 0.9 | tonnes | t |
| | Tsp | teaspoons | 5 | milliliters | ml |
| | Tbsp | tablespoons | 15 | milliliters | ml |
| | Fl oz | fluid ounces | 30 | milliliters | ml |
| | C | cups | 0.24 | liters | l |
| VOLUME | Pt | pints | 0.47 | liters | l |
| | Qt | quarts | 0.95 | liters | l |
| | Gal | gallons | 3.8 | liters | l |
| | Ft cu | cubic feet | 0.03 | cubic meters | m cu |
| | Yd cu | cubic yards | 0.76 | cubic meters | m cu |

| TEMPERATURE | $C=5/9 (F-32)$ | | | $F=9/5C+32$ | |
|---|---|---|---|---|---|
| | Fahrenheit | | | Celsius | |

### Conversions From Metric Measures

|  | Symbol | When You Know | Multiply By | To Find | Symbol |
|---|---|---|---|---|---|
| | mm | millimeters | 0.04 | inches | in |
| | Cm | centimeters | 0.4 | inches | in |
| LEGNTH | M | meters | 3.3 | feet | ft |
| | M | meters | 1.1 | yards | yd |
| | Km | kilometers | 0.6 | miles | mi |
| | Cm sq | square centimeters | 0.16 | square inches | in sq |
| | In sq | square meters | 1.2 | square yards | yd sq |
| AREA | Km sq | square kilometers | 0.4 | square miles | mi sq |
| | Ha | hectares (10,000m sq) | 2.5 | acres | |
| | G | grams | 0.035 | ounces | oz |
| MASS | Kg | kilograms | 2.2 | pounds | lb |
| (Weight) | T | tonnes (1000 kg) | 1.1 | short tons | |
| | Ml | milliliters | 0.03 | fluid ounces | fl oz |
| | L | liters | 2.1 | pints | pt |
| | L | liters | 1.06 | quarts | qt |
| VOLUME | L | liters | 0.26 | gallons | gal |
| | M cu | cubic meters | 35 | cubic feet | ft cu |
| | M cu | cubic meters | 1.3 | cubic yards | yd cu |

## METRIC PREFIXES AND POWER OF 10

| | | | |
|---|---|---|---|
| DEKA- OR DECA | $10^1 = 10$ | HECTO- | $10^2 = 100$ |
| KILO- | $10^3 = 1000$ | MEGA- | $10^6 = 1,000,000$ |
| DECI- | $10^{-1} = 0.1$ (or 1/10) | CEMTI- | $10^{-2} = 0.01$ (or 1/100) |
| MILLI- | $10^{-3} = 0.001$ (or 1/1000) | MICRO- | $10^{-6} = 0.000001$ (or 1/1,000,000) |

| LENGTH | AREA | VOLUME |
|---|---|---|
| 1 in = 2.540 cm | 1 in sq = 6.452 cm sq | 1 in cu = 16.387 cm cu. |
| 1 ft = 0.3048 m | 1 ft sq = 929 cm sq | 1 ft cu = 0.0283 m cu. |
| 1 yd = 0.9144 m | 1 yd sq = 0.8361 m sq | 1 yd cu = 0.7646 m cu. |
| 1 mi = 1.6093 km | 1 mi sq = 2.59 km sq | 231 in cu = 3.7853 liters |

1 cu ft of fresh water = 62.5 pounds

## WEIGHT          METRIC UNITS IN U.S. UNITS

| | | |
|---|---|---|
| 1 grain = 0.0648 gram | 1 meter = 39.37 inches | 1 yard = .9144 meter |
| 1 ounce = 23.3495 grams | 1 sq meter = 1.196 sq yd | 1 sq yard = .8361 sq meter |
| 1 pound = 453.592 grams | 1 hectare = 2.471 acres | 1 acre = 40.47 ares = .4047 hectare |
| 1 pound = 0.4536 kilograms | 1 bushel = .3524 hectorliter | 1 hectoliter = 2.8377 bushel |

1 liter = .908 dry quart = 1.0567 liquid quart

1 grain = .0648 gram          1 gram = 15.432 grains

1 pound = .4536 kilogram          1 kilogram = 2.2046 pounds

## MISCELLANEOUS MEASURES

| PAPER | TROY WEIGHT | METRIC/STANDARD |
|---|---|---|
| 24 sheets = 1 quire | 24 grains = 1 pennyweight | 1 gram = 15.4324 grains |
| 20 quires = 1 ream | 20 pennyweight = 1 ounce | 1 gram = 0.03527 ounces |
| 2 reams = 1 bundle | 12 ounces = 1 pound | 1 gram = 0.002205 pound |
| 5 bundles = 1 bale | | 1 kilogram = 2.2046 pounds |

# WEIGHTS & MEASURES & FORMULAS

## TABLES OF METRIC WEIGHTS AND MEASURES
### Linear Measure

| | | |
|---|---|---|
| 10 millimeters (mm) | = 1 centimeter (cm) | |
| 10 cm | = 1 decimeter (dm) | = 100 mm |
| 10 dm | = 1 meter (m) | = 1,000 mm |
| 10 m | = 1 dekameter (dam) | |
| 10 dam | = 1 hectometer (hm) | = 100 m |
| 10 hm | = 1 kilometer (km) | = 1,000 m |

### Area Measure

| | | |
|---|---|---|
| 100 sq. mm. (mm2) | = 1 sq. cm. (cm²) | |
| 10,000 cm² | = 1 square meter (m²) | =1,000,000 mm² |
| 100 m² | = 1 are (a) | |
| 100 a | = 1 hectare (ha) | =10,000 m² |
| 100 ha | = 1 sq. km (km²) | =1,000,000 m² |

### Fluid Volume Measure

| | | |
|---|---|---|
| 10 milliliters (ml) | = 1 centiliter (cl) | |
| 10 cl | = 1 deciliter (dl) | = 100 ml |
| 10 dl | = 1 liter(L) | = 1,000 ml |
| 10 L | = 1 dekaliter (dal) | |
| 10 dal | = 1 hectoliter (hl) | = 100 L |
| 10 hl | = 1 kiloliter (kl) | = 1,000L |

### Cubic Measure

| | | |
|---|---|---|
| 1,000 cubic mm. (mm³) | = 1 cubic cm. (cm³) | |
| 1,000 cm³ | = 1 cubic dm. (dm³) | = 1,000,000 cm³ |
| | | = 1,000,000,000 mm³ |

### Weight

| | | |
|---|---|---|
| 10 milligrams (mg) | = 1 centigram (cg) | |
| 10 cg | = 1 decigram (dg) | = 100 mg |
| 10 dg | = 1 gram (g) | = 1,000 mg |
| 10 g | = 1 dekagram (dag) | |
| 10 dag | = 1 hectogram (hg) | = 100 g |
| 10 hg | = 1 kilogram (kg) | = 1,000 g |
| 1,000 kg | = 1 metric ton (t) | |

## MEASURES OF ELECTRICITY AND TERMINOLOGY

**Watt**— the unit of power (electrical, mechanical, thermal, etc.) Electrical power is given by the product of the voltage and the current.

**Joule**— what energy is sold by. However in common practice the billing of electrical energy is expressed in terms of the **kilowatt-hour**, which is 3,600,000 joules or 3.6 megajoules.

**Horsepower**— a non-metric unit sometimes used in mechanics. It is equal to 746 watts.

**Ohm**— the unit of electrical resistance and represents the physical property of a conductor that offers a resistance to flow of electricity, permitting just 1 ampere to flow at 1 volt of pressure.

**Ampere**— a unit of electric current that is equivalent to the steady current produced by one volt applied across a resistance of one ohm.

## MEASURES OF FORCE AND PRESSURE

**Dyne** = force needed to accelerate a 1-gram mass 1 centimeter per second squared = 0.000072 poundal

**Poundal** = force needed to accelerate a 1-pound mass 1foot per second squared = 13,825.5 dynes = 0.138255 newtons

**Newton** = force needed to accelerate a 1 kilogram mass 1 meter per second squared

**Pascal** (pressure) = 1 newton per meter squared = 0.020885 pound per foot squared

**Atmosphere** (air pressure at sea level) = 2,116.102 pound per foot squared = 14.6952 pound per inch squared = 1.0332 kilograms per centimeter squared = 101.323 newtons per meter squared

## TABLE OF U.S. CUSTOMARY WEIGHTS AND MEASURES
### Linear Measure

| | | | |
|---|---|---|---|
| 12 inches (in) | = 1 foot (ft) | | |
| 3 ft | = 1 yard (yd) | | |
| 5½ yd | = 1 rod (rd), pole, or perch (16½ ft) | | |
| 40 rd | = 1 furlong (fur) | = 220 yd | = 660 ft |
| 8 fur | = 1 statute mile (mi) | = 1,760 yd | = 5,280 ft |
| 3 mi | = 1 league | = 5,280 yd | = 15,840 ft |
| 6076.11549 ft. | = 1 International Nautical Mile | | |

### Liquid Measure

When necessary to distinguish the liquid pint or quart form the dry pint or quart, the word liquid or the abbreviation liq should be used in combination with the name or abbreviation of the liquid.

| | | |
|---|---|---|
| 4 gills | = 1 pints (pt) | = 28.875 in³ |
| 2 pt | = 1 quart (qt) | = 57.75 in³ |
| 4 qt | = 1 gallon (gal) | = 231 in³ = 8 pt = 32 gills |

### Area Measure

Squares and cubes of units are sometimes abbreviated by using superscripts. For example, ft² means square foot, and ft³ means cubic foot.

| | | |
|---|---|---|
| 144 in² | = 1 square foot (ft²) | |
| 9 ft² | = 1 square yard (yd²) | = 1,296 in² |
| 30¼yd² | = 1 square rod (rd²) | = 272¼ ft² |
| 160 rd² | = 1 acre | = 4,840 yd² = 43,560 ft² |
| 640 acres | = 1 square mile (mi²) | |
| 1 mi² | = 1 section (of land) | |
| 6 mi² | = 1 township | = 36 sections = 36 mi² |

### Cubic Measure

| | |
|---|---|
| 1 cubic foot (ft³) | = 1,728 cubic inches (in³) |
| 27 ft³ | = 1 cubic yard (yd³) |

### Troy Weight

| | | |
|---|---|---|
| 24 grains | = 1 pennyweight (dwt) | |
| 20 dwt | = 1 ounce troy (oz t) | = 480 grains |
| 12 oz t | = 1 pound troy (lb t) | = 240 dwt = 5,760 grains |

### Dry Measure

When necessary to distinguish the dry pint or quart from the liquid pint or quart, the word dry is used in combination with the name or abbreviation of the dry unit.

| | | |
|---|---|---|
| 2 pints (pt) | = 1 quart (qt) | = 67.2006 in³ |
| 8 qt | = 1 pech (pk) | = 537.605 in³ = 16 pt |
| 4 pk | = 1 bushel (bu) | = 2,150.42 in³ = 32 qt |

### Avoirdupois Weight

When necessary to distinguish the avoirdupois ounce or pound from the troy ounce or pound, the word avoirdupois or the abbreviation avdp is used in combination with the name or abbreviation of the avoirdupois unit. The grain is the same in avoirdupois and troy weight.

| | | |
|---|---|---|
| 27¹¹/₃₂ grains | = 1 dram (dr) | |
| 16 dr | = 1 ounce (oz) | = 437½ grains |
| 16 oz | = 1 pound (lb) | = 256 dr = 7,000 grains |
| 100 lb | = 1 hundredweight (cwt) | |
| 20 cwt | = 1 ton | = 2,000 lb |

(In gross or long measure, the following values are recognized).

| | | |
|---|---|---|
| 112 lb | = 1 gross or long hundredweight | |
| 20 gross or long hundredweight | = 1 gross or long ton | = 2,240 lb |

# APPENDIX D:
# ELEMENTS, ATOMIC WEIGHTS & DISCOVERERS

| Element | SYM | # | WT | Element | SYM | # | WT |
|---|---|---|---|---|---|---|---|
| Actinium | Ac | 89 | 277 | Molybdenum | Mo | 42 | 95.94 |
| Aluminum | Al | 13 | 26.9815 | Neodymium | Nd | 60 | 144.24 |
| Americium | Am | 95 | 243 | Neon | Ne | 10 | 20.183 |
| Antimony | Sb | 51 | 121.75 | Neptunium | Np | 93 | 237 |
| Argon | Ar | 18 | 39.948 | Nickel | Ni | 28 | 58.71 |
| Arsenic | As | 33 | 74.9216 | Nielsbohrium | Ns | 107 | 262 |
| Astatine | At | 85 | 210 | Niobium | Nb | 41 | 92.906 |
| Barium | Ba | 56 | 137.34 | Nitrogen | N | 7 | 14.0067 |
| Berkelium | Bk | 97 | 249 | Nobelium | No | 102 | 259 |
| Berylium | Be | 4 | 9.0122 | Osmium | Os | 76 | 190.2 |
| Bismuth | Bi | 83 | 208.980 | Oxygen | O | 8 | 15.9994 |
| Boron | B | 5 | 10.811 | Palladium | Pd | 46 | 106.4 |
| Bromine | Br | 35 | 79.904 | Phospbonus | P | 15 | 30.9738 |
| Cadmium | Cd | 48 | 122.40 | Platinum | Pt | 78 | 195.09 |
| Calcium | Ca | 20 | 40.08 | Plutonium | Pu | 94 | 242 |
| Californium | Ci | 98 | 251 | Polonium | Po | 84 | 210 |
| Carbon | C | 6 | 12.0115 | Potassium | K | 19 | 39.102 |
| Cerium | Ce | 58 | 140.12 | Praseodymium | Pr | 59 | 140.907 |
| Cesium | Cs | 55 | 132.905 | Promethium | Pm | 61 | 147 |
| Chlorine | Cl | 17 | 35.453 | Protactinium | Pa | 91 | 231 |
| Chromium | Cr | 24 | 51.996 | Radium | Ra | 88 | 226 |
| Cobalt | Co | 27 | 58.9332 | Radon | Rn | 86 | 222 |
| Copper | Cr | 29 | 63.546 | Rhenium | Re | 75 | 186.2 |
| Curium | Cm | 96 | 247 | Rhodium | Rh | 45 | 102.905 |
| Dysprosium | Dy | 66 | 162.50 | Rubidium | Rb | 37 | 85.47 |
| Einsteinium | Es | 99 | 245 | Ruthenium | Ru | 44 | 101.07 |
| Erbium | Er | 68 | 167.26 | Rutherfordium | Rf | 104 | 261 |
| Europium | Eu | 63 | 151.96 | Samarium | Sm | 62 | 150.35 |
| Femium | Fm | 100 | 257 | Scandium | Sc | 21 | 44.956 |
| Fluorine | F | 9 | 18.9984 | Seaborgium | Sg | 106 | 266 |
| Francium | Fr | 87 | 223 | Selenium | Se | 34 | 78.96 |
| Gadolinium | Gd | 64 | 157.25 | Silicon | Si | 14 | 28.086 |
| Gallium | Ga | 31 | 69.72 | Silver | Ag | 47 | 107.868 |
| Gemanium | Ge | 32 | 72.59 | Sodium | Na | 11 | 22.9898 |
| Gold | Au | 79 | 196.967 | Strontium | Sr | 38 | 87.62 |
| Hafnium | Hf | 72 | 178.49 | Sulfur | S | 16 | 32.064 |
| Hahnium | Ha | 105 | 262 | Tantalum | Ta | 73 | 180.948 |
| Hassium | Hs | 108 | 265 | Technetium | Tc | 43 | 99 |
| Helium | He | 2 | 4.0026 | Tellurium | Te | 52 | 127.60 |
| Holmium | Ho | 67 | 164.930 | Terbium | Tb | 65 | 158.924 |
| Hydrogen | H | 1 | 1.00797 | Thalium | Ti | 81 | 204.37 |
| Indium | In | 49 | 114.82 | Thorium | Th | 90 | 232.038 |
| Iodine | I | 53 | 126.9044 | Thulium | Tm | 69 | 168.934 |
| Indium | Ir | 77 | 192.2 | Tin | Sn | 50 | 118.69 |
| Iron | Fe | 26 | 55.847 | Titanium | Ti | 22 | 47.90 |

# ELEMENTS, ATOMIC WEIGHTS & DISCOVERERS

| | | | | | | | |
|---|---|---|---|---|---|---|---|
| Krypton | Kr | 36 | 83.80 | Tungsten | W | 74 | 183.85 |
| Lanthanum | La | 57 | 138.91 | Uranium | U | 92 | 238.03 |
| Lawrencium | Lr | 103 | 262 | Vanadium | V | 23 | 50.942 |
| Lead | Pb | 82 | 207.19 | Xenon | Xe | 54 | 131.30 |
| Lithium | Li | 3 | 6.939 | Ytterbium | Yb | 70 | 173.04 |
| Lutetium | Lu | 71 | 174.97 | Yttrium | Y | 39 | 88.905 |
| Magnesium | Mg | 12 | 24.312 | Zinc | Zn | 30 | 65.37 |
| Maganese | Mn | 25 | 54.9380 | Zirconium | Zr | 40 | 91.22 |
| Mercury | Hg | 80 | 200.59 | | | | |

# UNITED STATES FACTS

## ALASKA

Largest State-656,424 sq. mi.
Aleutian Island- Easternmost point
Barrow , Alaska- Northernmost City
Amchitka Island-Easternmost Settlement
Semisopochnoi Island-Easternmost point
Atka Alaska- Westernmost City
Wrangell, St. Elias- Largest national park.
Mt. Mckinley- Highest mountain.

## RHODE ISLAND

Smallest State- 1,545 sq. mi.

## HAWAII

Kalawo-Smallest County
Hilo- Southernmost City
Naalehs-Southernmost Settlement
Ka Lae- Southernmost point.
Mt. Waialeale, Hawaii- Rainiest spot.

## CALIFORNIA

San Bernardino County- Largest County
Calpatria- Lowest Settlement
Death Valley- Lowest point.
Mt. Whitney- Highest Mountain.

## U.S. STATISTICS

Longest river- Mississippi- Missouri
Deepest lake- Crater Lake, Oregon.
Deepest gorge- Hells Canyon, Snake River,
          Oregon-Idaho.
Tallest building- Sears Tower, Chicago,Ill.
          1,454 ft.
Tallest Structure- TV tower, Blanchard ND.
          2,063 ft.
Highest bridge- Royal Gorge, Colorado.
          1,053 ft. above water.

Highest waterfall- Yosemite Falls
Largest gorge- Grand Canyon,Colorado
          River, Arizona.

Largest building- Boeing 747 Plant,
          47 acres.          Everett, Washington
Longest bridge span- 4,260 ft.
          Verrazano-Narrowe, NY.
Deepest well- Washita county OK.
          31,441 ft.

# MATHEMATICAL FORMULAS & CONVERSIONS

## COMMON FRACTIONS CONVERTED TO DECIMALS

| | | | | | |
|---|---|---|---|---|---|
| 1/64 | .015625 | 11/32 | .34375 | 43/64 | .671875 |
| 1/32 | .03125 | 23/64 | .359375 | 11/16 | .6875 |
| 3/64 | .046875 | 3/8 | .375 | 45/64 | .703125 |
| 1/16 | .0625 | 25/64 | .390625 | 23/32 | .71875 |
| 5/64 | .078125 | 13/32 | .40625 | 47/64 | .734375 |
| 3/32 | .09375 | 27/64 | .421875 | 3/4 | .75 |
| 7/64 | .1009375 | 7/16 | .4375 | 25/32 | .78125 |
| 1/8 | .125 | 29/64 | .453125 | 51/64 | .796875 |
| 9/64 | .140625 | 15/32 | .46875 | 13/16 | .8125 |
| 5/32 | .15625 | 31/64 | .484375 | 53/64 | .828125 |
| 11/64 | .171875 | 1/2 | .5 | 27/32 | .84375 |
| 3/16 | .1875 | 33/64 | .515625 | 55/64 | .859375 |
| 13/64 | .203125 | 17/32 | .53125 | 7/8 | .875 |
| 7/32 | .21875 | 35/64 | .546875 | 57/64 | .890625 |
| 15/64 | .234375 | 9/16 | .5625 | 29/32 | .90625 |
| 1/4 | .25 | 37/64 | .578125 | 59/64 | .921875 |
| 17/64 | .265625 | 19/32 | .59375 | 15/16 | .9375 |
| 9/32 | .28125 | 39/64 | .609375 | 61/64 | .953125 |
| 19/64 | .296875 | 5/8 | .625 | 31/32 | .96875 |
| 5/16 | .3125 | 41/64 | .640625 | 63/64 | .984375 |
| 21/64 | .328125 | 21/32 | .65625 | 1 | 1 |

## MATHEMATICAL FORMULAS

To find the circumference of a Circle – Multiply 2 Pi (6.2832) by the radius.

To find the area of a Circle- Multiply the square of the diameter by .7854

Rectangle- Multiply the length of the base by the height.

Sphere(surface)- Multiply the square of the radius by 3.1416 and multiply by 4

Square- Square the length of one side.

Trapezoid- Add the two parallel side, multiply by the height and divide by 2.

Triangle- Multiply the base by the height and divide by 2.

To find the volume of a the following:

Cone- Multiply the square of the radius ob the base by 3.1416, multiply by the Height , and divide by 3.

Cube- Cube the length of one edge.

Cylinder- Multiply the square of the radius of the base by 3.1416, and multiply by the height

Pyramid- Multiply the area of the base by the height and divide by 3.

Rectangular Prism- Multiply the length by the width by the height.

Sphere- Multiply the cube of the radius by 3.1416 multiply by 4, and divide by 3.

Quadratic Equation – An equation of the second degree.

$$X = \frac{-b \pm \sqrt{b^2 - 4ac}}{2a}$$

Coefficient – Any factor of a product.

| | | | |
|---|---|---|---|
| Absence | Caterpillar | Deteriorate | Fluorescent |
| Abnormal | Catastrophe | Deterrent | Foreigner |
| Academic | Century | Diarrhea | Forfeit |
| Accelerate | Census | Die, dying, died | Fortunately |
| Accompany | Character | Difference | Friend |
| Achievement | Chief | Dilemma | Frontier |
| Acquaintance | Circuit | Diploma | |
| Acquire | Coercion | Disappear | Galloped |
| Address | Colloquial | Disappoint | Gauge |
| Aerial | Colonel | Discipline | Goddess |
| Aggressor | Commission | Disillusioned | Government |
| Agreeable | Committee | Disobeyed | Governor |
| A lot | Comparison | Dissolve | Grammar |
| Altitude | Competent | | Guarantee |
| Altogether | Completely | Economical | |
| Amateur | Conceive | Ecstasy | Heaven |
| Analogous | Condemn | Eerie | Height |
| Analysis | Conjure | Efficient | Hero, Heroes |
| Answer | Conscience | Electrician | Hindrance |
| Apparatus | Conscious | Elegant | Horizontal |
| Apparently | Consensus | Embarrass | Humorous |
| Appearance | Consequential | Emperor | Humor |
| | Consistent | Enormous | Hungrily |
| Appropriate | Conspiracy | Enthusiasm | Hygiene |
| Argument | Corroborate | Especially | Hypothesis |
| Arraignment | Counterfeit | Essential | |
| Article | Courteous | Exaggerate | Identical |
| Assassinate | Criticism | Exceed | Illegibly |
| Associate | Cruelty | Excellent | Immediately |
| Attachment | Curiosity | Except | In between |
| Awkward | Curricular | Excitement | Infinite |
| | Curiosity | Exercise | Innocence |
| Bachelor | Curricular | Exhibition | Installment |
| Balloon | | Exhibition | Instantaneous |
| Basically | Deceit | Exhilarating | Insurrection |
| Beautiful | Decision | Existence | Intellectual |
| Beginning | Defensive | Experience | Intelligence |
| Believe | Deficient | Extravagant | Intention |
| Beneficial | Definite | Extremely | Interested |
| Burglar | Democracy | | Irrelevant |
| Business | Descendant | Faculty | Irresistible |
| | Descent | Familiar | Isosceles |
| Calendar | Description | Feasible | |
| Campaign | Despair | February | Jealous |
| Caricature | Desperately | Feminine | Jeopardy |
| Carriage | Detached | Fiery | Jewelry |

# EASILY MISSPELLED WORDS

| | | | |
|---|---|---|---|
| Maintain | Poisonous | Reference | Aluminum |
| Marriage | Possession | Referring | Bacteria |
| Marvelous | Precede | Refrigerator | Confidence |
| Medicine | Precipitate | Religious | Despicable |
| Messenger | Preferred | Repetition | Efficiency |
| Metaphor | Prejudice | Reservoir | Fundamental |
| Miniature | Preparation | Restaurant | Geography |
| Misspell | Presence | Rhyme | Hemisphere |
| | Primitive | Rhythm | Jurrisdiction |
| Miraculous | Principle(base) | Rouge | Knowledge |
| Miscellaneous | Privilege | | Lieutenant |
| Murmured | Probably | Sacrilegious | Maneuver |
| Murmuring | Procedure | Silhouette | Naturalization |
| Mystifying | Proceed | Simultaneous | Obituary |
| | Professor | Sincerely | Participate |
| Naïve | Propeller | Souvenir | Qualification |
| Necessary | Psychology | Statistics | Rendezvous |
| Negotiate | Publicly | Symmetry | Syphilis |
| Neighbor | Punctuation | | Thesaurus |
| Noticeable | Pursue | Technical | University |
| Nuisance | | Technique | Valedictorian |
| | Quality | Temperature | Waiver |
| Occur(red) | Quantity | Temporary | Xylen |
| Occurrence | Quietly | Tendency | Yeoman |
| Opportunity | | Tobacco | Zoology |
| | Really | Tomorrow | |
| Ordinarily | Receipt | Twelfth | |
| Originally | Receive | Tyranny | |
| Overrule | Recommend | | |
| Paralyzed | Referee | Undoubted | |

Source: <u>Writing Skills Handbook,</u> by Bazerman/Wiener, Houghton Mifflin Co. @ 1993
3 rd Edition. One Deacon St. Boston, Ma. ISBN: 0+-395-61455-4

## TABLE 1
## VALUE OF TRIGONOMETRIC RATIO

| ANGLE | SIN | COS | TAN | ANGLE | SIN | C 0S | TAN |
|-------|------|------|------|-------|------|------|---------|
| 1 | .0175 | .9998 | .0175 | 46 | .7193 | .6947 | 1.0355 |
| 2 | .0349 | .9994 | .0349 | 47 | .7314 | .6820 | 1.0724 |
| 3 | .0523 | .9986 | .0524 | 48 | .7431 | .6691 | 1.1106 |
| 4 | .0698 | .9976 | .0699 | 49 | .7547 | .6561 | 1.1504 |
| 5 | .0872 | .9962 | .0875 | 50 | .7660 | .6428 | 1.1918 |
| 6 | .1045 | .9945 | .1051 | 51 | .7771 | .6293 | 1.2349 |
| 7 | .1219 | .9925 | .1228 | 52 | .7880 | .6157 | 1.2799 |
| 8 | .1392 | .9903 | .1405 | 53 | .7986 | .6018 | 1.3270 |
| 9 | .1564 | .9877 | .1584 | 54 | .8090 | .5878 | 1.3764 |
| 10 | .1736 | .9848 | .1763 | 55 | .8192 | .5736 | 1.4281 |
| 11 | .1908 | .9816 | .1944 | 56 | .8290 | .5592 | 1.4826 |
| 12 | .2079 | .9781 | .2126 | 57 | .8387 | .5446 | 1.5399 |
| 13 | .2250 | .9744 | .2309 | 58 | .8480 | .5299 | 1.6003 |
| 14 | .2419 | .9703 | .2493 | 59 | .8572 | .5150 | 1.6643 |
| 15 | .2588 | .9659 | .2679 | 60 | .8660 | .5000 | 1.7321 |
| 16 | .2756 | .9613 | .2867 | 61 | .8746 | .4848 | 1.8040 |
| 17 | .2924 | .9563 | .3057 | 62 | .8829 | .4695 | 1.8040 |
| 18 | .3090 | .9511 | .3249 | 63 | .8910 | .4540 | 1.9026 |
| 19 | .3256 | .9455 | .3443 | 64 | .8988 | .4384 | 2.0503 |
| 20. | .3420 | .9397 | .3640 | 65 | .7063 | .4226 | 2.1445 |
| 21 | .3584 | .9336 | .3839 | 66 | .9135 | .4067 | 2.2460 |
| 22 | .3746 | .9272 | .4040 | 67 | .9205 | .3907 | 2.3559 |
| 23 | .3907 | .9205 | .4245 | 68 | .9272 | .3746 | 2.4751 |
| 24 | .4067 | .9135 | .4452 | 69 | .9336 | .3584 | 2.6051 |
| 25 | .4226 | .9063 | .4663 | 70 | .9397 | .3420 | 2.7475 |
| 26 | .4384 | .8988 | .4877 | 71 | .9455 | .3256 | 2.9042 |
| 27 | .4540 | .8910 | .5095 | 72 | .9511 | .3090 | 3.0777 |
| 28 | .4695 | .8829 | .5317 | 73 | .9563 | .2924 | 3.2709 |
| 29 | .4848 | .8746 | .5543 | 74 | .9613 | .2756 | 3.4874 |
| 30 | .5000 | .8660 | .5774 | 75 | .9659 | .2588 | 3.7321 |
| 31 | .5150 | .8572 | .6009 | 76 | .9703 | .2419 | 4.0108 |
| 32 | .5299 | .8480 | .6249 | 77 | .9744 | .2250 | 4.3315 |
| 33 | .5446 | .8387 | .6494 | 78 | .9781 | .2079 | 4.7046 |
| 34 | .5592 | .8290 | .6745 | 79 | .9816 | .1908 | 5.1446 |
| 35 | .5736 | .8192 | .7002 | 80 | .9848 | .1736 | 5.6713 |
| 36 | .5878 | .8090 | .7265 | 81 | .9877 | .1564 | 6.3138 |
| 37 | .6018 | .7986 | .7536 | 82 | .9903 | .1392 | 7.1154 |
| 38 | .6157 | .7880 | .7813 | 83 | .9925 | .1219 | 8.1443 |
| 39 | .6293 | .7771 | .8098 | 84 | .9945 | .1045 | 9.5144 |
| 40 | .6428 | .7660 | .8391 | 85 | .9962 | .0872 | 11.4300 |
| 41 | .6561 | .7547 | .8693 | 86 | .9976 | .0698 | 14.3010 |
| 42 | .6691 | .7431 | .9004 | 87 | .9986 | .0523 | 19.0810 |
| 43 | .6820 | .7314 | .9325 | 88 | .9994 | .0349 | 28.6360 |
| 44 | .6947 | .7193 | .9657 | 89 | .9998 | .0175 | 57.2900 |

## TABLE 1.1
## VALUE OF TRIGONOMETRIC RATIO

| ANGLE | COT | SEC | CSC | ANGLE | COT | SEC | CSC |
|---|---|---|---|---|---|---|---|
| 1 | 57.29 | 1.000 | 57.30 | 46 | .9657 | 1.440 | 1.390 |
| 2 | 28.64 | 1.001 | 28.65 | 47 | .9325 | 1.466 | 1.367 |
| 3 | 19.08 | 1.001 | 19.11 | 48 | .9004 | 1.494 | 1.346 |
| 4 | 14.30 | 1.002 | 14.34 | 49 | .8693 | 1.534 | 1.325 |
| 5 | 11.43 | 1.004 | 11.47 | 50 | .8391 | 1.556 | 1.305 |
| 6 | 9.514 | 1.006 | 9.567 | 51 | .8098 | 1.589 | 1.287 |
| 7 | 8.144 | 1.008 | 8.206 | 52 | .7813 | 1.624 | 1.269 |
| 8 | 7.115 | 1.010 | 7.185 | 53 | .7536 | 1.662 | 1.252 |
| 9 | 6.314 | 1.012 | 6.392 | 54 | .7265 | 1.701 | 1.236 |
| 10 | 5.671 | 1.015 | 5.759 | 55 | .7002 | 1.743 | 1.221 |
| 11 | 5.145 | 1.019 | 5.241 | 56 | .6745 | 1.788 | 1.206 |
| 12 | 4.705 | 1.022 | 4.810 | 57 | .6494 | 1.836 | 1.192 |
| 13 | 4.331 | 1.026 | 4.445 | 58 | .6249 | 1.887 | 1.179 |
| 14 | 4.011 | 1.031 | 4.134 | 59 | .6009 | 1.942 | 1.167 |
| 15 | 3.732 | 1.035 | 3.864 | 60 | .5774 | 2.000 | 1.155 |
| 16 | 3.487 | 1.040 | 3.628 | 61 | .5543 | 2.063 | 1.143 |
| 17 | 3.271 | 1.046 | 3.420 | 62 | .5317 | 2.130 | 1.133 |
| 18 | 3.078 | 1.051 | 3.236 | 63 | .5095 | 2.203 | 1.122 |
| 19 | 2.904 | 1.058 | 3.072 | 64 | .4879 | 2.281 | 1.113 |
| 20 | 2.747 | 1.064 | 2.924 | 65 | .4663 | 2.366 | 1.103 |
| 21 | 2.605 | 1.071 | 2.790 | 66 | .4452 | 2.459 | 1.095 |
| 22 | 2.475 | 1.079 | 2.669 | 67 | .4245 | 2.559 | 1.086 |
| 23 | 2.356 | 1.086 | 2.559 | 68 | .4040 | 2.669 | 1.079 |
| 24 | 2.246 | 1.095 | 2.459 | 69 | .3839 | 2.790 | 1.071 |
| 25 | 2.145 | 1.103 | 2.366 | 70 | .3640 | 2.924 | 1.064 |
| 26 | 2.050 | 1.113 | 2.281 | 71 | .3443 | 3.072 | 1.058 |
| 27 | 1.963 | 1.122 | 2.203 | 72 | .3249 | 3.236 | 1.051 |
| 28 | 1.881 | 1.133 | 2.130 | 73 | .3057 | 3.420 | 1.046 |
| 29 | 1.804 | 1.143 | 2.063 | 74 | .2867 | 3.628 | 1.040 |
| 30 | 1.732 | 1.155 | 2.000 | 75 | .2679 | 3.864 | 1.035 |
| 31 | 1.664 | 1.167 | 1.942 | 76 | .2493 | 4.134 | 1.031 |
| 32 | 1.600 | 1.179 | 1.887 | 77 | .2309 | 4.445 | 1.026 |
| 33 | 1.540 | 1.192 | 1.836 | 78 | .2126 | 4.810 | 1.022 |
| 34 | 1.483 | 1.206 | 1.788 | 79 | .1944 | 5.241 | 1.019 |
| 35 | 1.428 | 1.221 | 1.743 | 80 | .1763 | 5.759 | 1.015 |
| 36 | 1.376 | 1.236 | 1.701 | 81 | .1584 | 6.392 | 1.012 |
| 37 | 1.327 | 1.252 | 1.662 | 82 | .1405 | 7.185 | 1.010 |
| 38 | 1.280 | 1.269 | 1.624 | 83 | .1228 | 8.206 | 1.008 |
| 39 | 1.235 | 1.287 | 1.589 | 84 | .1051 | 9.567 | 1.006 |
| 40 | 1.192 | 1.305 | 1.556 | 85 | .0875 | 11.470 | 1.004 |
| 41 | 1.150 | 1.325 | 1.524 | 86 | .0699 | 14.340 | 1.002 |
| 42 | 1.111 | 1.346 | 1.494 | 87 | .0524 | 19.110 | 1.001 |
| 43 | 1.072 | 1.367 | 1.466 | 88 | .0349 | 28.650 | 1.001 |
| 44 | 1.036 | 1.390 | 1.440 | 89 | .0175 | 57.30 | 1.000 |
| 45 | 1.000 | 1.414 | 1.414 | 90 | .0000 | | 1.000 |

## TABLE 1.2
### VALUE OF TRIGONOMETRIC (CIRCULAR) RADIANS

| Radians | SIN | COS | TAN | Radians | SIN | COS | TAN |
|---|---|---|---|---|---|---|---|
| .00 | .0000 | 1.0000 | .0000 | .15 | .1494 | .9888 | .1511 |
| .01 | .0100 | 1.0000 | .0100 | .16 | .1593 | .9872 | .1614 |
| .02 | .0200 | .9998 | .0200 | .17 | .1692 | .9856 | .1717 |
| .03 | .0300 | .9996 | .0300 | .18 | .1790 | .9838 | .1820 |
| .04 | .0400 | .9992 | .0400 | .19 | .1889 | .9820 | .1923 |
| .05 | .0500 | .9988 | .0500 | .20 | .1987 | .9801 | .2027 |
| .06 | .0600 | .9982 | .0601 | .21 | .2085 | .9780 | .2131 |
| .07 | .0699 | .9976 | .0701 | .22 | .2182 | .9759 | .2236 |
| .08 | .0799 | .9968 | .0802 | .23 | .2280 | .9737 | .2341 |
| .09 | .0899 | .9960 | .0902 | .24 | .2377 | .9713 | .2447 |
| .10 | .0998 | .9950 | .1003 | .25 | .2474 | .9689 | .2553 |
| .11 | .1098 | .9940 | .1104 | .26 | .2571 | .9664 | .2660 |
| .12 | .1197 | .9928 | .1206 | .27 | .2667 | .9638 | .2768 |
| .13 | .1296 | .9916 | .1307 | .28 | .2764 | .9611 | .2876 |
| .14 | .1395 | .9902 | .1409 | .29 | .2860 | .9582 | .2984 |
| | | | | | | | |
| .30 | .2955 | .9553 | .3093 | .45 | .4350 | .9004 | .4831 |
| .31 | .3051 | .9523 | .3203 | .46 | .4439 | .8961 | .4954 |
| .32 | .3146 | .9492 | .3314 | .47 | .4529 | .8916 | .5080 |
| .33 | .3240 | .9460 | .3425 | .48 | .4618 | .8870 | .5206 |
| .34 | .3335 | .9428 | .3537 | .49 | .4706 | .8823 | .5334 |
| .35 | .3429 | .9394 | .3650 | .50 | .4794 | .8776 | .5463 |
| .36 | .3523 | .9359 | .3764 | .51 | .4882 | .8727 | .5594 |
| .37 | .3616 | .9323 | .3879 | .52 | .4969 | .8678 | .5726 |
| .38 | .3709 | .9287 | .3994 | .53 | .5055 | .8628 | .5859 |
| .40 | .3894 | .9211 | .4228 | .54 | .5141 | .8577 | .5994 |
| .41 | .3986 | .9171 | .4346 | .55 | .5227 | .8525 | .6131 |
| .42 | .4078 | .9131 | .4466 | .56 | .5312 | .8473 | .6269 |
| .43 | .4169 | .9090 | .4586 | .57 | .5396 | .8419 | .6410 |
| .44 | .4259 | .9048 | .4708 | .58 | .5480 | .8365 | .6552 |
| | | | | | | | |
| .59 | .5564 | .8309 | .6696 | .71 | .6518 | .7584 | .8595 |
| .60 | .5646 | .8253 | .0841 | .72 | .6594 | .7518 | .8771 |
| .61 | .5729 | .8196 | .6989 | .73 | .6669 | .7452 | .8949 |
| .62 | .5810 | .8139 | .7139 | .75 | .6816 | .7317 | .9316 |
| .63 | .5891 | .8080 | .7291 | .76 | .6889 | .7248 | .9505 |
| .64 | .5972 | .8021 | .7445 | .77 | .6961 | .7179 | .9697 |
| .65 | .6052 | .7961 | .7602 | .78 | .7033 | .7109 | .9893 |
| .66 | .6131 | .7900 | .7761 | .79 | .7104 | .7038 | 1.009 |
| .67 | .6210 | .7838 | .7923 | .80 | .7174 | .6967 | 1.030 |
| 68 | .6288 | .7776 | .8087 | .81 | .7243 | .6895 | 1.050 |
| .69 | .6365 | .7712 | .8253 | .82 | .7311 | .6822 | 1.072 |
| .70 | .6442 | .7648 | .8423 | .83 | .7379 | .6749 | 1.093 |

## TABLE 1.2
### VALUE OF TRIGONOMETRIC (CIRCULAR) RADIANS

| Radians | SIN | COS | TAN | Radians | SIN | COS | TAN |
|---------|-----|-----|-----|---------|-----|-----|-----|
| 84 | .7446 | .6675 | 1.116 | 94 | .8076 | .5898 | 1.369 |
| 85 | .7513 | .6600 | 1.138 | 95 | .8134 | .5817 | 1.398 |
| 86 | .7578 | .6524 | 1.162 | 96 | .8192 | .5735 | 1.428 |
| 87 | .7643 | .6448 | 1.185 | 97 | .8249 | .5653 | 1.459 |
| 88 | .7707 | .6372 | 1.210 | 98 | .8305 | .5570 | 1.491 |
| 89 | .7771 | .6294 | 1.235 | 99 | .8360 | .5487 | 1.524 |
| | | | | | | | |
| 1.00 | .8415 | .5403 | 1.557 | 1.14 | .9086 | .4176 | 2.176 |
| 1.01 | .8468 | .5319 | 1.592 | 1.15 | .9128 | .4085 | 2.234 |
| 1.02 | .8521 | .5234 | 1.628 | 1.16 | .9168 | .3993 | 2.296 |
| 1.03 | .8573 | .5148 | 1.665 | 1.17 | .9208 | .3902 | 2.360 |
| 1.04 | .8624 | .5062 | 1.704 | 1.18 | .9246 | .3809 | 2.427 |
| 1.05 | .8674 | .4976 | 1.743 | 1.19 | .9284 | .3717 | 2.498 |
| 1.06 | .8724 | .4889 | 1.784 | 1.20 | .9320 | .3624 | 2.572 |
| 1.07 | .8772 | .4801 | 1.827 | 1.21 | .9356 | .3530 | 2.650 |
| 1.08 | .8820 | .4713 | 1.871 | 1.22 | .9391 | .3436 | 2.733 |
| 1.09 | .8866 | .4625 | 1.917 | 1.23 | .9425 | .3342 | 2.820 |
| 1.10 | .8912 | .4536 | 1.965 | 1.24 | .9458 | .3248 | 2.912 |
| 1.11 | .8957 | .4447 | 2.014 | 1.25 | .9490 | .3153 | 3.010 |
| 1.12 | .9001 | .4357 | 2.066 | 1.26 | .9521 | .3058 | 3.113 |
| 1.13 | .9044 | .4267 | 2.120 | 1.27 | .9551 | .2963 | 3.224 |
| | | | | | | | |
| 1.28 | .9580 | .2867 | 3.341 | 1.42 | .9887 | .1502 | 6.581 |
| 1.29 | .9608 | .2771 | 3.467 | 1.43 | .9901 | .1403 | 7.055 |
| 1.30 | .9636 | .2675 | 3.602 | 1.44 | .9915 | .1304 | 7.602 |
| 1.31 | .9662 | .2579 | 3.747 | 1.45 | .9927 | .1205 | 8.238 |
| 1.32 | .9687 | .2482 | 3.903 | 1.46 | .9939 | .1106 | 8.989 |
| 1.33 | .9711 | .2385 | 4.072 | 1.47 | .9949 | .1006 | 9.887 |
| 1.34 | .9735 | .2288 | 4.256 | 1.48 | .9959 | .0907 | 10.980 |
| 1.35 | .9757 | .2190 | 4.455 | 1.49 | .9967 | .0807 | 12.350 |
| 1.36 | .9779 | .2092 | 4.673 | 1.50 | .9975 | .0707 | 14.100 |
| 1.37 | .9799 | .1995 | 4.913 | 1.51 | .9982 | .0608 | 16.430 |
| 1.38 | .9819 | .1896 | 5.177 | 1.52 | .9987 | .0508 | 19.670 |
| 1.39 | .9817 | .1798 | 5.471 | 1.53 | .9992 | .0408 | 24.500 |
| 1.40 | .9854 | .1700 | 5.798 | 1.54 | .9995 | .0308 | 32.460 |
| 1.41 | .9871 | .1601 | 6.165 | 1.55 | .9998 | .0208 | 48.080 |
| | | | | | | | |
| 1.56 | .9999 | .0108 | 92.620 | 1.57( ½ Pi ) | 1 .000 | .0008 | 1256 |

# TABLE 2

## SQUARES, CUBES, SQUARE ROOTS, CUBE ROOTS, AND LOGARITHMS

| NO | SQUARE | CUBE | SQUARE ROOT | CUBE ROOT | LOGARITHMS |
|---|---|---|---|---|---|
| 1 | 1 | 1 | 1.0000 | 1.0000 | 0.00000 |
| 2 | 4 | 8 | 1.4142 | 1.4422 | 0.47712 |
| 3 | 9 | 27 | 1.7321 | 1.4422 | 0.47712 |
| 4 | 16 | 64 | 2.0000 | 1.5874 | 0.60206 |
| 5 | 25 | 125 | 2.2361 | 1.7100 | 0.69897 |
| 6 | 36 | 216 | 2.4495 | 1.8171 | 0.77815 |
| 7 | 49 | 343 | 2.6458 | 1.9129 | 0.84510 |
| 8 | 64 | 512 | 2.8284 | 2.0000 | 0.90308 |
| 9 | 81 | 729 | 3.0000 | 2.0801 | 0.95424 |
| | | | | | |
| 10 | 100 | 1000 | 3.1623 | 2.1544 | 1.00000 |
| 11 | 121 | 1331 | 3.3166 | 2.2240 | 1.04139 |
| 12 | 144 | 1728 | 3.4641 | 2.2894 | 1.07918 |
| 13 | 169 | 2197 | 3.6056 | 2.3513 | 1.11394 |
| 14 | 196 | 2744 | 3.7417 | 2.4101 | 1.14613 |
| 15 | 225 | 3375 | 3.8730 | 2.4662 | 1.17609 |
| 16 | 256 | 4096 | 4.0000 | 2.5198 | 1.20412 |
| 17 | 289 | 4913 | 4.1231 | 2.5713 | 1.23045 |
| 18 | 324 | 5832 | 4.2426 | 2.6207 | 1.25527 |
| 19 | 361 | 6859 | 4.3589 | 2.6684 | 1.27875 |
| | | | | | |
| 20 | 400 | 8000 | 4.4721 | 2.7144 | 1.30103 |
| 21 | 441 | 9261 | 4.5826 | 2.7589 | 1.32222 |
| 22 | 484 | 10648 | 4.6904 | 2.8020 | 1.34242 |
| 23 | 529 | 12167 | 4.7958 | 2.8439 | 1.36173 |
| 24 | 576 | 13824 | 4.8990 | 2.8845 | 1.38021 |
| 25 | 625 | 15625 | 5.0000 | 2.9240 | 1.39794 |
| 26 | 676 | 17576 | 5.0900 | 2.9625 | 1.41497 |
| 27 | 729 | 19683 | 5.1962 | 3.0000 | 1.43136 |
| 28 | 784 | 21952 | 5.2915 | 3.0366 | 1.44716 |
| 29 | 841 | 24389 | 5.3852 | 3.0723 | 1.46240 |
| | | | | | |
| 30 | 900 | 27000 | 5.4772 | 3.1072 | 1.47712 |
| 31 | 961 | 29791 | 5.5678 | 3.1414 | 1.49136 |
| 32 | 1024 | 32768 | 5.6569 | 3.1748 | 1.50515 |
| 33 | 1089 | 35937 | 5.7446 | 3.2075 | 1.51851 |
| 34 | 1156 | 39304 | 5.8310 | 3.2396 | 1.53148 |
| 35 | 1225 | 42875 | 5.9161 | 3.2711 | 1.54407 |
| 36 | 1296 | 46656 | 6.0000 | 3.3019 | 1.55630 |
| 37 | 1369 | 50653 | 6.0828 | 3.3322 | 1.56820 |
| 38 | 1444 | 54872 | 6.1644 | 3.3620 | 1.57978 |
| 39 | 1521 | 59316 | 6.2450 | 3.3912 | 1.59106 |

## TABLE 2
### SQUARES, CUBES, SQUARE ROOTS, CUBE ROOTS, AND LOGARITHMS

| NO | SQUARE | CUBE | SQUARE ROOT | CUBE ROOT | LOGARITHM |
|---|---|---|---|---|---|
| 40 | 1600 | 64000 | 6.3246 | 3.4200 | 1.60206 |
| 41 | 1681 | 68921 | 6.4031 | 3.4482 | 1.61278 |
| 42 | 1764 | 74088 | 6.4807 | 3.4760 | 1.62325 |
| 43 | 1869 | 79507 | 6.5574 | 3.5034 | 1.63347 |
| 44 | 1936 | 85184 | 6.6332 | 3.5303 | 1.64345 |
| 45 | 2025 | 91125 | 6.7082 | 3.5569 | 1.65321 |
| 46 | 2116 | 97336 | 6.7823 | 3.5830 | 1.66273 |
| 47 | 2209 | 103823 | 6.8557 | 3.6088 | 1.67210 |
| 48 | 2304 | 110592 | 6.9282 | 3.6342 | 1.68124 |
| 49 | 2401 | 117649 | 7.0000 | 3.6593 | 1.69020 |
| 50 | 2500 | 125000 | 7.0711 | 3.6840 | 1.69897 |
| 51 | 2601 | 132651 | 7.1414 | 3.7084 | 1.70757 |
| 52 | 2704 | 140608 | 7.2111 | 3.7325 | 1.71600 |
| 53 | 2809 | 148877 | 7.2801 | 3.7563 | 1.72428 |
| 54 | 2916 | 157464 | 7.3485 | 3.7798 | 1.73239 |
| 55 | 3025 | 166375 | 7.4162 | 3.8030 | 1.74036 |
| 56 | 3136 | 175616 | 7.4833 | 3.8259 | 1.74819 |
| 57 | 3249 | 185193 | 7.5498 | 3.8485 | 1.75587 |
| 58 | 3364 | 195112 | 7.6158 | 3.8709 | 1.76343 |
| 59 | 3481 | 205379 | 7.6811 | 3.8930 | 1.77085 |
| 60 | 3600 | 216000 | 7.7460 | 3.9149 | 1.77815 |
| 61 | 3721 | 226981 | 7.8102 | 3.9365 | 1.78533 |
| 62 | 3844 | 238328 | 7.8740 | 3.9579 | 1.79239 |
| 63 | 3969 | 250047 | 7.9373 | 3.9791 | 1.79934 |
| 64 | 4096 | 262144 | 8.0000 | 4.0000 | 1.80618 |
| 65 | 4225 | 274625 | 8.0623 | 4.0207 | 1.81291 |
| 66 | 4356 | 287496 | 8.1240 | 4.0412 | 1.81954 |
| 67 | 4489 | 300763 | 8.1854 | 4.0615 | 1.82607 |
| 68 | 4624 | 314432 | 8.2462 | 4.0817 | 1.83251 |
| 69 | 4761 | 3228509 | 8.3066 | 4.1016 | 1.83885 |
| 70 | 4900 | 343000 | 8.3666 | 4.1213 | 1.84510 |
| 71 | 5041 | 357911 | 8.4261 | 4.1408 | 1.85126 |
| 72 | 5184 | 373248 | 8.4853 | 4.1608 | 1.85733 |
| 73 | 5329 | 389017 | 8.5440 | 4.1793 | 1.86332 |
| 74 | 5476 | 405224 | 8.6023 | 4.1983 | 1.86923 |
| 75 | 5625 | 421875 | 8.6603 | 4.2172 | 1.87506 |
| 76 | 5776 | 438976 | 8.7178 | 4.2358 | 1.88081 |
| 77 | 5929 | 456533 | 8.7750 | 4.2543 | 1.88649 |
| 78 | 6084 | 474552 | 8.8318 | 4.2727 | 1.89209 |
| 79 | .6241 | 493039 | 8.8882 | 4.2908 | 1.89763 |
| 80 | 6400 | 512000 | 8.9443 | 4.3089 | 1.90309 |
| 81 | 6561 | 531441 | 9.0000 | 4.3267 | 1.90849 |
| 82 | 6724 | 551368 | 9.0554 | 4.3445 | 1.91381 |
| 83 | 6889 | 571787 | 9.1104 | 4.3621 | 1.91908 |

## TABLE 2
## SQUARES, CUBES, SQUARE ROOTS, CUBE ROOTS, AND LOGARITHMS

| NO | SQUARE | CUBE | SQUARE ROOT | CUBE ROOT | LOGARITHM |
|---|---|---|---|---|---|
| 84 | 7056 | 592704 | 9.1652 | 4.3795 | 1.92428 |
| 85 | 7225 | 614125 | 9.2195 | 4.3968 | 1.92942 |
| 86 | 7396 | 636056 | 9.2736 | 4.4140 | 1.93450 |
| 87 | 7225 | 658503 | 9.3274 | 4.4310 | 1.93952 |
| 88 | 7744 | 681472 | 9.3808 | 4.4480 | 1.94448 |
| 89 | 7921 | 704969 | 9.4340 | 4.4647 | 1.94939 |
| | | | | | |
| 90 | 8100 | 729000 | 9.4868 | 4.4814 | 1.95424 |
| 91 | 8281 | 753571 | 9.5394 | 4.4979 | 1.95904 |
| 92 | 8464 | 778688 | 9.5917 | 4.5144 | 1.96379 |
| 93 | 8649 | 804357 | 9.6437 | 4.5307 | 1.96848 |
| 94 | 8836 | 830584 | 9.6954 | 4.5468 | 1.97313 |
| 95 | 9025 | 857375 | 9.7468 | 4.5629 | 1.97772 |
| 96 | 9216 | 884736 | 9.7980 | 4.5789 | 1.98227 |
| 97 | 9409 | 912673 | 9.8489 | 4.5947 | 1.98677 |
| 98 | 9604 | 941192 | 9.8995 | 4.6104 | 1.99123 |
| 99 | 9801 | 970299 | 9.9499 | 4.6261 | 1.99564 |
| | | | | | |
| 100 | 10000 | 1,000,000 | 10.0000 | 4.6416 | 2.00000 |
| 101 | 10201 | 1,030,301 | 10.0499 | 4.6570 | 2.00432 |
| 102 | 10404 | 1,061,208 | 10.0995 | 4.6723 | 2.00860 |
| 103 | 10609 | 1,092,727 | 10.1489 | 4.6875 | 2.01284 |
| 104 | 10816 | 1,124,864 | 10.1980 | 4.7027 | 2.01703 |
| 105 | 11025 | 1,157,625 | 10.2470 | 4.7177 | 2.02119 |
| 106 | 11236 | 1,191,016 | 10.2956 | 4.7326 | 2.02531 |
| 107 | 11449 | 1,225,043 | 10.3441 | 4.7475 | 2.02938 |
| 108 | 11664 | 1,259,712 | 10.3923 | 4.7622 | 2.03342 |
| 109 | 11881 | 1,295,029 | 10.4403 | 4.7769 | 2.03743 |
| | | | | | |
| 110 | 12100 | 1,331,000 | 10.4881 | 4.7914 | 2.04139 |
| 111 | 12321 | 1,367,631 | 10.5357 | 4.8059 | 2.04532 |
| 112 | 12544 | 1,404,928 | 10.5830 | 4.8203 | 2.04922 |
| 113 | 12769 | 1,442,897 | 10.6301 | 4.8346 | 2.05308 |
| 114 | 12996 | 1,481,544 | 10.6771 | 4.8488 | 2.05690 |
| 115 | 13225 | 1,520,875 | 10.7238 | 4.8629 | 2.06070 |
| 116 | 13456 | 1,560,896 | 10.7703 | 4.8770 | 2.06446 |
| 117 | 13689 | 1,601,613 | 10.8167 | 4.8910 | 2.06819 |
| 118 | 13924 | 1,643,032 | 10.8628 | 4.9049 | 2.07188 |
| 119 | 14161 | 1,685,159 | 10.9087 | 4.9187 | 2.07555 |
| | | | | | |
| 120 | 14400 | 1,728,800 | 10.9545 | 4.9324 | 2.07918 |
| 121 | 14641 | 1,771,561 | 11.0000 | 4.9461 | 2.08279 |
| 122 | 14884 | 1,815,848 | 11.0454 | 4.9597 | 2.08636 |
| 123 | 15129 | 1,860,867 | 11.0905 | 4.9732 | 2.08991 |
| 125 | 15625 | 1,953,125 | 11.1803 | 5.0000 | 2.09691 |
| 126 | 15876 | 2,000,376 | 11.2250 | 5.0133 | 2.10037 |
| 127 | 16129 | 2,048,383 | 11.2694 | 5.0265 | 2.10380 |

TRIGONOMETRIC EQUATIONS

The simplest type of trigonometric equation is that which a function of an angle is equal to a constant. Solving right triangle problems (A10-27.1 pp. 147-152) show some simple trigonometric equations.

When a trigonometric equation is not of the simplest type, the procedure is to derive two or more simple equations that yield all the solution of the given equation. Algebraic operation, trigonometric identities and functions, are some of the tools used for solving trigonometric equation that are expressed as:  Angle in degree measure.............. Angle in radian measure........................ .........................Real numbers...........

## ALGEBRAIC OPERATION- TRANSPOSITION OF TERMS

$$\text{If } A = \frac{B}{C} ; \quad \text{Then } B = AC ; \quad C = \frac{B}{A} \quad \text{If } \frac{A}{B} = \frac{C}{D}, \quad A = \frac{BC}{D}, \quad B = \frac{AD}{C}$$

$$D = \frac{BC}{A}$$

$$\text{If } A = \frac{1}{D\sqrt{BC}}, \quad \text{Then } A^2 = \frac{1}{D^2 BC}, \quad B = \frac{1}{D^2 A C}, \quad C = \frac{1}{D^2 A B}, \quad D = \frac{1}{A\sqrt{BC}}$$

$$\text{If } A = \sqrt{B^2 + C^2}, \quad \text{Then } A^2 = B^2 + C^2, \quad B = \sqrt{A^2 - C^2}, \quad C = \sqrt{A^2 - B^2}$$

## TRIGONOMETRIC FUNDAMENTAL IDENTITIES

When working with trigonometric fundamental identities, it may be observed that if the sine, cosine, and tangent of an angle are known, the other three functions can be had immediately from the reciprocal relations. In addition, the product of each pair of reciprocals is unity of 1. For example: $\sin\theta\cos\theta = 1$, $\cos\theta\sec\theta = 1$, $\tan\theta\cot\theta = 1$

Remember, a combination of algebraic operation and substitutions from the fundamental identities is needed to simplify a given expression. Listed below are eight relations of the trigonometric functions that should be memorized, because an identity should be recognizable when it is solved for any function occurring in it. For example, the identity:

$$\sin^2\theta + \cos^2\theta = 1 \text{ when solved for } \sin\theta, \text{ becomes } \sin\theta = \pm\sqrt{1 - \cos^2\theta}$$

$$\sin\theta = \frac{1}{\csc\theta} \quad \text{or} \quad \csc\theta = \frac{1}{\sin\theta} ; \quad \cos\theta = \frac{1}{\sec\theta} \quad \text{or} \quad \sec\theta = \frac{1}{\cos\theta}$$

$$\tan\theta = \frac{1}{\cot\theta} \quad \text{or} \quad \cot\theta = \frac{1}{\tan\theta}, \quad \tan\theta = \frac{\sin\theta}{\cos\theta} \quad \cot\theta = \frac{\cos\theta}{\sin\theta}$$

$$\sin^2\theta + \cos^2\theta = 1, \quad 1 + \tan^2\theta = \sec^2\theta, \quad 1 + \cot^2\theta = \csc^2\theta$$

## TRIGONOMETRIC FUNCTION

Trigonometric functions are ratios whose domains or range are determined by the measure of the angle. For example, if $\theta$ is an angle of measure of 60 degrees, we write $\sin\theta = 60$ degrees. Listed below are equations used to define the trigonometric function.

Listed are equation used to define the trigonometric function ratio. In addition, it is helpful to become familiar with terms and definitions used in these equations.

1.  x (abscissa);  y (ordinate)- (See Algebra definitions A10-28.1 pp.164)
2.  Distance (d)- To find the distance (d) between two points, add the square of the difference of the abscissas (x) to the square of the difference of the ordinates (y) and take the positive square root of the sum.
3.  r (range)- Distance point on the coordinate plane from the origin (O).

$$d = \sqrt{(x_2 - x_1)^2 + (y_2 - y_1)^2} \qquad r = \sqrt{(x - 0)^2 + (y - 0)^2}$$

$$\sin\theta = \frac{ordinate}{distance} = \frac{y}{r} \qquad\qquad \text{cosecant}\,\theta = \frac{distance}{ordinate} = \frac{r}{y}$$

$$\text{cosine}\,\theta = \frac{abscissa}{distance} = \frac{x}{r} \qquad\qquad \text{secant}\,\theta = \frac{distance}{abscissa} = \frac{r}{x}$$

$$\text{tangent}\,\theta = \frac{ordinate}{abscissa} = \frac{y}{x} \qquad\qquad \text{cotangent}\,\theta = \frac{abscissa}{ordinate} = \frac{x}{y}$$

### SIGNS OF THE FUNCTIONS BY QUADRANTAL ANGLE

In the rectangular coordinate system there are equal quadrants (90 degree) that are numbered I to IV. Each quadrant angle are expressible as functions of angles between 0 degrees and 90 degrees. With this in mind, when you look at quadrant I to IV signs visualize an angle as positive (rotation is towards the terminal side or counterclockwise) or an angle is negative (rotation is towards the initial side or clockwise) with the x-axis as the reference plane.

When you look at the three graphs, changing the sign of an angle does not change the angle value of its cosine and secant; however, changing the sign of an angle reverses the sign of the sine and cosecant, and the tangent and cotangent. ( note: angle signs are bracketed). In addition, shown below in tabular form for value of 0 degrees, 90 degrees, 180 degrees, 270 degrees.

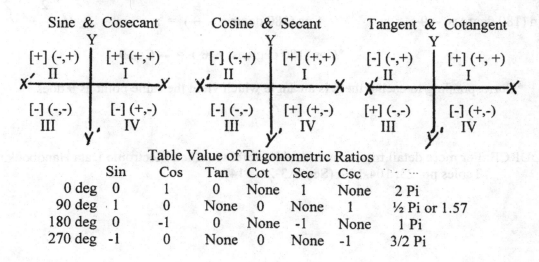

### Table Value of Trigonometric Ratios

|         | Sin | Cos | Tan  | Cot  | Sec  | Csc  |             |
|---------|-----|-----|------|------|------|------|-------------|
| 0 deg   | 0   | 1   | 0    | None | 1    | None | 2 Pi        |
| 90 deg  | 1   | 0   | None | 0    | None | 1    | ½ Pi or 1.57 |
| 180 deg | 0   | -1  | 0    | None | -1   | None | 1 Pi        |
| 270 deg | -1  | 0   | None | 0    | None | -1   | 3/2 Pi      |

Refer to signs of the functions by quadrant angle three graphs you need to remember that the distance (r) appearing in the definition of the trigonometric functions is stated as positive. This is why the signs of the value of the functions depend on the signs of x and y.

Note: x and y coordinate points are shown in parentheses ( ).
Signs of the trigonometric functions for the quadrants are bracketed [ ].

The ratio y/x and x/y are positive if x and y have like signs and negative if x and y have unlike signs ( ) ; the Tan θ and Cot θ signs [ ] are positive if θ is in quadrant I or quadrant III and negative if θ is in quadrant II or quadrant IV. Accordingly, Sin θ and Csc θ and Cos θ and Sec θ signs [ ] trigonometric values of the functions depends on the signs of x and y.

## POLAR COORDINATE SYSTEM (r, θ)

Coordinates of a point (pair of numbers) on a graph are its distance from a fixed point and a direction from a fixed line. The angle θ gives the direction from a horizontal line and, r gives the distance from a point of the line.

## RECTANGULAR COORDINATE SYSTEM (x, y)

Coordinates of a point (pair of numbers) on a graph are located by its directed distance (distance of the point from the coordinate axes) from two perpendicular lines.

## COORDINATE SYSTEM TRANSFORMATION

$$\text{Sin } \theta = \frac{y}{r} \qquad\qquad \text{Cos } \theta = \frac{x}{r} \qquad\qquad \text{Tan } \theta = \frac{y}{x}$$

$$y = r \text{ Sin } \theta \qquad\qquad x = r \text{ Cos } \theta \qquad\qquad \theta = \text{Tan}^{-1} \frac{y}{x}$$

$$\text{Sin } (180 \text{ degrees } - \theta) = y \qquad \text{Cos } (180 \text{ degrees } - \theta) = x \qquad r = \pm \sqrt{x^2 + y^2}$$

$$*\text{Cos } (180 \text{ degrees } + \theta) = -\text{Cos } \theta$$

*Corresponding to each θ there is an angle which yield the same point as θ does.

SOURCE: For more detail trigonometric tables refer to Allied Electronic Data Handbook. Tables pp. 23, 104-109. (See: A3-24 # 14).

# TABLE NOTES: 4          TRIGONOMETIC (CIRCULAR) FUNCTION

Trigonometric circular function unit of measure called the radian system is derived from the ratio of the circumference of a circle to its diameter by the Greek letter Pi, whose value is approximately 3.1416

The formula for the circumference of a circle is $C = 2 Pi r$ means the length of one radius (1/2 diameter ) can be measured off along the circumference 2 Pi (6.2832) times without overlapping.

In the use of the radian system the word "radian" is frequently omitted. Thus 2 Pi is 360 degrees, and Pi is 180 degrees. In addition, 2 Pi is called the period of the function of an angle for (sine, cosine, secant and cosecant), and Pi is for (tangent and cotangent).

Listed below in tabular form is the graph of a sine curve of trigonometric function of an angle sine (Table 1), in integral multiples of Pi / 6 or 30 degrees.

Note: That the variation of the sine function recur in intervals of 2 Pi.

| Deg | 0 | $\frac{Pi}{6}$ | $\frac{Pi}{3}$ | $\frac{Pi}{2}$ | $\frac{2 Pi}{3}$ | $\frac{5 Pi}{6}$ | Pi | $\frac{7 Pi}{6}$ | $\frac{4 Pi}{3}$ | $\frac{3 Pi}{2}$ | $\frac{5 Pi}{3}$ | $\frac{11 Pi}{6}$ | 2 Pi |
|------|---|------|------|------|------|------|----|------|------|------|------|------|------|
| Sine | 0 | .5 | .87 | 1 | .87 | .50 | 0 | -.50 | -.87 | -1 | -.87 | -.50 | 0 |

The radian unit of measure is defined ( $S = r\theta$ ) among the quantities S (arc ) r (radius) and )$\theta$ (radian measured Table 1.2). This means that the radius and arc are measured of the same linear unit when there equal, the angle measured equals 1 radian.

This is the heart of the radian system. Some radian constants are as follow.

1 radian = $\frac{180 \text{ degrees}}{Pi (3.1416)}$ = 57.296 degrees or 57 degrees and 17.7 minutes.

2 Pi radian = 360 degrees

1 Pi radian = 180 degrees

1 degree = $\frac{Pi (3.1416)}{(180 \text{ degrees})}$ radian = .017453

.1 degree = 6 minutes          .2 degree = 12 minutes          .3 degree = 18 minutes
.4 degree = 24 minutes          .5 degree = 30 minutes          .6 degree = 36 minutes
.7 degree = 42 minutes          .8 degree = 48 minutes          .9 degree = 54 minutes

Ex: Express .296 degree in terms of minutes measured.

minutes = .296 X $\frac{60 \text{ minutes}}{1 \text{ degree}}$ = 17.76 minutes

A central angle of 45 degrees intercepts and arc of 5 feet. Find the radius of the circle.

Solution; ( $S = r\theta$ ) = .7852 ( r = S ) change 45 degrees to radians measured
45 (.01745) = .8752 radian.          $\frac{5 \text{ ft ( S )}}{.7852 (\theta)}$ = 6.36 ft

Note: When the radius and size of arc measured are of equal unit
S = $\theta$ ( radius is chosen as the unit length)

## TABLE NOTES: 5    LOGARITHMS (Characteristic and Mantissa)

When a logarithm is expressed as an integer plus a decimal (between 0 and 1), the integer is called the characteristic and the decimal (Table 2) is called the mantissa.
Refer to Logarithms term A10-27.2 pp.162.
Note: Exponent form is an integral power of 10 called scientific notation. In this notation a number is expressed as a product. The first factor has the significant digits with a decimal point just after the first digit, and the second factor is an integral power of 10.

### LOGARITHMS TO DIFFERENT BASES (pp.162 # 7 & # 8)

$$\text{Log}_{10}\ N = .4343\ \text{Log}_{e}\ N \qquad\qquad \text{Log}_{e}\ N = 2.3026\ \text{Log}_{10}\ N$$

### ANTILOG

Finding the antilog of a number is the reverse of finding the logarithm. That is, if Log N = X, then N = antilog X. The procedure for finding the antilog is to first locate the mantissa in the log tables and determine its corresponding number. Secondly, place the decimal as indicated by the characteristic. Ex: Find the antilog of 8.8407-10

Solution: 8.8407-10 = 0.0693 or scientific notation: $6.93\ X\ 10^{-2}$

### LOGARITHM OPERATIONS

Logarithm operations are expressed by the follow formulas.

The logarithm of a product is equal to the sum of the logarithm of the factor.
$$\text{Log}\ (\ a\ X\ b\ ) = \text{Log}\ a + \text{Log}\ b$$

The logarithm of a quotient is equal to the logarithm of the dividend minus the logarithm of the divisor.     $$\text{Log}\ (\ \frac{a}{b}\ ) = \text{Log}\ a - \text{Log}\ b$$

The logarithm of a power of a number is equal to the exponent times the logarithm of the number.
$$\text{Log}\ (\ a^{b}\ ) = b\ \text{Log}\ a$$

The logarithm roots.     $$\text{Log}\ \sqrt[b]{a} = \frac{\text{Log}\ a}{b} \qquad \text{Ex: Find}\ \sqrt[3]{343}$$

Ex: Log of 343 = 2.5353 divided by 3 = .8451, the antilog of .8451 is 7.

SOURCE :For more detail tables on Powers, Roots, Reciprocals, and Logarithms refer to Allied Electronics Data Handbook. Tables pp. 92-103. (See: A3-24 #14).

Printed in the United States
By Bookmasters